Vox Feminae

Studies in
Medieval Woman's Songs

John F. Plummer, editor

Studies in Medieval Culture, XV
MEDIEVAL INSTITUTE PUBLICATIONS
Western Michigan University, Kalamazoo, Michigan—1981

Library of Congress Cataloging in Publication Data

Vox feminae : studies in medieval woman's songs.

    (Studies in medieval culture ; 15)
    Bibliography: p.
    Contents: Woman's song in medieval Latin /
Anne Howland Schotter—Voice and audience: the
emotional world of the cantigas de amigo /
Kathleen Ashley—The woman's song in medieval
German poetry / William E. Jackson—[etc.]
    1. Poetry, Medieval—History and criticism—
Addresses, essays, lectures. 2. Lyric poetry—
History and criticism—Addresses, essays, lectures.
3. Women in literature—Addresses, essays, lectures.
I. Plummer, John F. (John Francis), 1944–
II. Series.
CB351.S83 vol. 15   [PN691] 809.1'9352042
ISBN 0-918720-12-5 (pbk.)

Library of Congress Catalog Number   81-3981
                             AACR2

Cover and book design by FAIRFAX, Clair Dunn, designer

By "woman's song" (*Frauenlied, cantiga de amigo, chanson de femme*) is traditionally meant simply a love lyric whose speaker is female. The distinction between female and male is made, then, not on the level of performer or of composer, but of character, the speaking voice. As will be seen, most of these lyrics are anonymous; many were written by male poets. "Woman's song" thus does not imply a contrast between songs written by women and those written by men. *Frauenlieder* and *chanson de femme* first found currency as generic terms in studies of two kinds of lyrics: anonymous female-voiced songs (which were felt to be popular or quasi-popular in origin), and songs in the female voice written by known male court poets (which were seen as something like imitations of earlier, popular, female-voiced songs). The terms have not normally been used, however, nor are they used in these essays, to speak of the songs of aristocratic women poets like Christine de Pisan, the Countess of Dia, or Marie de Clèves. It is the artistic *use* of the female voice (as role, *persona*, or rhetorical stance) in particular lyrical traditions or by particular poets, that is at issue here. The study of medieval woman's song is primarily the study of the image of a voice.

As is suggested by the essays collected here, woman's songs are to be found in all parts and periods of medieval Europe. The songs these papers study were composed in Latin, Portuguese, English, Irish, German, and French, and date from at least as early as the tenth century up through the fifteenth. Broad as this range may seem, the possibilities were even broader. To deal adequately with most of the texts and most of the issues, critical and historical, pertaining to medieval woman's songs would have required not a volume but a small library. The aim here was not to "cover" the field but to approach some specific areas in which work seemed most appropriate. In several cases the essays supply literary criticism in areas which have hitherto known mostly literary history. Others map or re-map a part of the field previously not well charted. The Introduction is an attempt to provide a context for the essays themselves, touching briefly on some of the more important periods and genres of woman's song which are *not* specifically treated in any of the essays, and outlining some of the historical and critical treatments which form the growing body of research in this field. It is hoped that the combination of these essays and the cumulative bibliography which follows them will offer an introduction and guide to those who are not familiar with woman's song, and a stimulation to those who are.

With the exception of that of Mary Beth Winn, these essays were originally presented, in shorter form, at the Thirteenth or Fourteenth International Congresses on Medieval Studies sponsored by the Medieval Institute of Western Michigan University in 1977–78. My thanks are due to Professor Otto Gründler, Director of the Medieval Institute, for providing an opportunity for us to exchange ideas; to Professor Clifford Davidson for suggesting the possibility of publication; and to Dr. Thomas H. Seiler, Managing Editor of Medieval Institute Publications, and his assistant, Dr. Elise Jorgens, for their help in preparing the manuscript for publication.

John F. Plummer
Nashville, March 1980

Contents

Introduction 5
   John F. Plummer

Woman's Song in Medieval Latin 19
   Anne Howland Schotter

Voice and Audience: The Emotional World
of the *cantigas de amigo* 35
   Kathleen Ashley

The Woman's Song in Medieval German Poetry 47
   William E. Jackson

The Woman's Songs of Hartmann von Aue 95
   Hubert Heinen

Woman's Songs in Irish, 800–1500 111
   Ruth P.M. Lehmann

The Woman's Song in Middle English
and its European Backgrounds 135
   John F. Plummer

The "Other" Voice: Woman's Song, its Satire
and its Transcendence in Late Medieval British Literature 155
   Maureen Fries

Poems by "The Lady" in *La Chasse et
le départ d'Amours (1509)* 179
    Mary Beth Winn

Bibliography 199

Notes on Contributors 222

Abbreviations

Used in Notes
and Bibliography

ABäG	Amsterdamer Beiträge zur Älteren Germanistik
ADA	Anzeiger für Deutsches Altertum und Deutsche Literatur
AKG	Archiv für Kulturgeschichte
AnM	Annuale Medievale
BAWS	Bayerische Akademie der Wissenschaften, Philosophische– Historische Klasse, Sitzungsberichte
BdF	Boletim de Filologia
BGDSL	Beiträge zur Geschichte der Deutschen Sprache und Literatur (Tübingen)
BHR	Bibliothèque d'Humanisme et Renaissance
BHS	Bulletin of Hispanic Studies
BRAE	Boletín de la Real Academia Española
CA	Cuadernos Americanos
CCM	Cahiers de Civilisation Médiévale (Xe–XIIe Siècles)
ChauR	Chaucer Review
CI	Cuadernos del Idioma

CL	Comparative Literature
CN	Cultura Neolatina
CollG	Colloquia Germanica, Internationale Zeitschrift für Germanische Sprach- und Literaturwissenschaft
CS	Cahiers du Sud
DAEM	Deutsches Archiv für Erforschung des Mittelalters
DBGÜ	Deutsche Beiträge zur Geistigen Überlieferung
DU	Der Deutschunterricht: Beiträge zu zeiner Praxis und Wissenschaftlichen Grundlegung
DVLG	Deutsche Vierteljahrschrift für Literaturwissenschaft und Geistesgeschichte
EC	Étude Celtique
EETS	Early English Text Society
ELH	Journal of English Literary History
ELN	English Language Notes
ES	English Studies: A Journal of English Language and Literature
GAG	Göppinger Arbeiten zur Germanistik
GL&L	German Life and Letters
GQ	German Quarterly
GR	Germanic Review
GRM	Germanisch–Romanische Monatsschrift, Neue Folge
HR	Hispanic Review
HumB	Humanitas: Rivista di Cultura (Brescia, Italy)
JEGP	Journal of English and Germanic Philology
JS	Journal des Savants
KRQ	Kentucky Romance Quarterly
LiLi	Zeitschrift für Literaturwissenschaft und Linguistik
MÆ	Medium Ævum
MLN	Modern Language Notes
MLQ	Modern Language Quarterly
MLR	Modern Language Review
MS	Medieval Studies (Toronto)
Neophil	Neophilologus (Groningen, Netherlands)
NM	Neuphilologische Mitteilungun: Bulletin de la Société Néophilologique
N&Q	Notes and Queries
NRFH	Nueva Revista de Filología Hispánica (Mexico City)
OGS	Oxford German Studies
OL	Orbis Litterarum: International Review of Literary Studies
PLL	Papers on Language and Literature: A Journal for Scholars and Critics of Language and Literature
PMLA	Publications of the Modern Language Association of America

2

PQ	Philological Quarterly
PSuQ	Philologische Studien und Quellen
RF	Romanische Forschungen
RFE	Revista de Filología Española
RHM	Revista Hispánica Moderna: Columbia University Hispanic Studies
RJ	Romanistisches Jahrbuch
RLC	Revue de Littérature Comparée
RomN	Romance Notes
RPh	Romance Philology
SATF	Société des Anciens Textes Francais
TLL	Travaux de Linguistique et de Littérature Publiés par le Centre de Philologie et de Littératures Romanes de l'Université de Strasbourg
UES	Unisa English Studies: Journal of the Department of English
WW	Wirkendes Wort: Deutsche Sprache in Forschung und Lehre
YCGL	Yearbook of Comparative and General Literature
ZCP	Zeitschrift für Celtische Philologie
ZDA	Zeitschrift für Deutsches Altertum und Deutsche Literatur
ZDP	Zeitschrift für Deutsche Philologie (Berlin, W. Ger.)
ZRP	Zeitschrift für Romanische Philologie

Introduction

Eterna doncella enamorada, eterno grito,
repetido siempre et siempre nuevo!

Dámaso Alonso

Dès l'instant qu'elles ont été écrites,
sinon composées, les chansons-de-toiles
ont tiré leur séduction de leur archaïsme
réel ou afectée. Elles sont née vieilles.

Michel Zink

The remarks cited here may serve to illustrate two important critical
interests in medieval woman's songs. The first bespeaks a romantic
fascination (I do not use "romantic" pejoratively) with "a primitive
world of women dancing and chanting stanzas of love"[1]—a fascination which is primarily literary-historical. The second suggests an
interest in the songs for the light they may shed on medieval lyrical
aesthetics, an aesthetics which, recent research suggests, may have
been particularly formal and self-conscious. Both kinds of interest
may be satisfied in the study of medieval woman's song.

Many woman's songs are very old, and much of the scholarly
attention they have received has been called forth by this alterity,
proven of some, suspected of many others. But as important as the
age of the songs are the implications of that age. Because many of
the songs are older than much of the courtly (e.g., troubadour)
poetry, it has been suspected, and argued with both learning and
fervor, that such female-voiced song is the source of the courtly
poetry. Closely related but not identical with this argument is one
which sees woman's songs as the only remnants of precourtly
popular song, perhaps a popular tradition whose roots stretch back
intact into the late classical period, or whose roots may in fact lie
deeper, and wider, than that. From another perspective the earliest
woman's songs may be only imitations of popular song, though
nonetheless important indicators of its nature.

The interest in the age of woman's songs, though it has led up
some blind alleys, is not unjustified. A capitulary of Charlemagne

from 789 strictly forbidding nuns to compose or send *winneleodas*—friend songs, or *cantigas de amigo* ("uuinileodas scribere vel mittere")—is taken generally as good evidence that educated women were then composing not merely amatory letters but songs.[2] Unfortunately, none of the offending compositions has survived. Following the same line of reasoning—that it is pointless to condemn what is never done—the complaints of churchmen against the "lewd songs of dancing women" which can be heard from the sixth century onward [3] may serve to demonstrate that woman's song began very early, if indeed there was ever a period when it did not exist. According to Theodor Frings, the artful, male-voiced courtly poetry of love from France and Germany in the twelfth and thirteenth centuries grew out of a fertile, female-voiced, universal folk poetry.[4] Without denying the possible influence of Arabic poetry, the formative role of the social and cultural milieu of Provence, or the importance of Latin poetry and liturgy, Frings pointed to the universal woman's songs "from Portugal to China" as the source of courtly poetry. Songs from China, Russia, Serbia, Egypt, Greece, Sweden, and Norway, among others, were adduced in this argument, and in Walther von der Vogelweide's *Frauenlied* "Under der linden" Frings sought to demonstrate an "unbroken ascent" from the folk foundation of a May Dance to the peak of Minnesinger art.[5] The theory of the popular origins of troubadour lyric did not, of course, originate with Frings. Gaston Paris' articles of 1891–92, reviewing and extrapolating from Jeanroy's landmark *Origines de la poésie lyrique en France* of 1889, had offered the argument that medieval love songs go back to pagan May dances.[6] Nineteenth-century scholars as a whole, in fact, subscribed to some form or other of the theory of popular origins. The appeal of a theory of primitive lyricism (more sincere, more pure, more serious, than courtly songs, but which had been swept away by them) for romantic scholarship is evident, and its connections to romantic theories of folk poetry are carefully traced in a recent volume by Frenk Alatorre.[7]

Leo Spitzer defended both the neo-romanticism of Frings and the romanticism of nineteenth-century scholarship against the charge of "inventing" a dancing, singing medieval folk out of a need to believe in the popular genius: "Could [romantic scholars] not, in spite of or perhaps because of their specific motivations, have discovered an actually existing historical feature of medieval poetry?"[8] Frings' argument was buttressed significantly, in Spitzer's view, by the first extensive publication during the late 1940's of the *jarchas*, brief, female-voiced lyrical pieces in a Romance dialect from eleventh-century Spain. These Mozarabic verses form the final lines of Arabic and Hebrew *muwashshahs*, a poetic form composed generally of five strophes. The *jarchas*, of which sixty-one have now been published,[9] are the oldest known secular poems in a Romance vernacular. Their early date, and their resemblance in tone and statement to other woman's songs, led Spitzer to conclude that Frings had been correct in suspecting that woman's songs lay at the base of all medieval love poetry. "The content of these very simple 11th–13th century Mozarabic stanzas is strictly that of the German and Romance *Frauenlieder*," and "it is the *villancico*, not the *zéjel* [a learned Arabic poetic form], that forms the nucleus of popular Spanish (or Romance) poetry, and therefore the explanation of troubadour poetry must start with these simplest popular forms attested by the *jarchas* much earlier than the first Provençal poems."[10]

There are actually several conclusions here, and I would like to separate them, because Spitzer's formulation can lead us through the complex of arguments which has grown up around this topic. First, there is the assertion of affinities between the early *jarchas* and later woman's songs, second, the idea that the woman's songs are popular, and third, that they are the source of troubadour and other courtly poetry about love. The resemblances between the *jarchas* and the Gallego-Portuguese *cantigas de amigo*[11] include actual shared turns of phrase, the use of the word "friend" (*habib=amigo*) for the lover, the frequent appearance of the girl's mother as auditor, and the often impassioned, "un-courtly," sometimes woeful, sometimes joyful speech of the young girl. Ramon Menéndez Pidal found enough similarities to conclude that "the primitive Andalusian songs, the [Portuguese] *cantigas de amigo* and the Castillian *villancicos* appear clearly as three branches of one trunk, with roots in the soil of the peninsula."[12] The similarities within the peninsular tradition once accepted, there has been some debate over whether the extant lyrics reflect, as Menéndez Pidal argued, a parallel growth from a common Iberian stock (which might reach back before the Arabic invasion), or whether either Portuguese or Andalusian lyricism is the primary stock, with the other (or others, counting the later *villancicos*) a subsidiary branch. The *muwashshah* as a genre was introduced in Spain around 900, and Peter Dronke, among others, has suggested that, especially bearing in mind the early complaints of the Church councils, popular Romance songs must antedate even the first *muwashshahs*.[13] It must be added, however, that the early date of the *muwashshah* does not prove an equally early date for *jarchas* in Romance dialect; *jarchas* were also composed in colloquial Arabic. But the further back in time such woman's songs appear to recede, the greater the likelihood, perhaps, that the tradition was indigenous in Romanized Europe as a whole. Pierre Le Gentil felt that "originally, one poetic tradition was implanted [throughout Romania] at a time when Romania still formed a relatively homogeneous entity."[14] Such an idea is reinforced by the similarities between *jarchas, cantigas de amigo*, and the *refrains* of French poetry and the Italian *strambotti*.[15] The image of a pan-Romanic lyric tradition is attractive, and in a thoughtful and carefully reasoned article P. F. Ganz has suggested that such a tradition could be conceived of in terms wide enough to envelop the songs which may lie behind the earliest German *Frauenklage*.[16]

Whether one would choose to follow Spitzer and Frings in the belief in a global tradition of primitive *Frauenlieder* is a slightly different question. Dronke has offered, in this regard, a lyric by Sappho which, in a pinch, could easily pass for a *cantiga de amigo*,[17] but one wonders whether, having included everything in one group, one would not choose to begin afresh with some distinctions. Clearly there are close affinities—thematic, formal, and no doubt historic—between the *jarchas, cantigas de amigo*, and *refrains*. An alternative (though I do not offer it as preferable) to Ganz's hypothesis of a pan-European popular woman's song tradition might be to see the early *Frauenlieder* of Germany as stemming from a *winneleodas* tradition separate from the Romance tradition. One might also ask whether, given that the extant Iberian, French, and German woman's songs are almost without exception the work of sophisticated court poets, the historical fact that wants further study is the flourishing in courtly circles all over Europe during the late twelfth and early- to mid-thirteenth centuries of female-voiced poetry which is "something like" popular song. It may be, in other words, that our preoccupation with looking behind some of these lyrics has prevented our looking at them and at the people who wrote and enjoyed them. In any case, there is clearly historical work which can still be done.

Turning to the idea that woman's songs are the font of medieval courtly poetry about love, Frings and Spitzer here run into the very heavy traffic of the claims made by proponents of sources ranging from Arabic poetry to Latin liturgical music, from the structure of Provençal society to Catharist thought. The subject is far too broad even to survey here,[18] and its pursuit would shed little light on the Woman's songs *per se*. But students of the woman's songs must be grateful to those who have studied them for what they might tell us of the origins of courtly poetry and to those whose analyses have sought to demonstrate the dependence or independence of one poetic tradition or another.[19] Without the often acrimonious debate such studies have produced, the early woman's songs might have rested in relative obscurity. Today, however, there is considerably less interest in "explanations" of the sources of troubadour poetry than when Spitzer wrote, and Peter Dronke's demonstration that the sentiments of the troubadours were not in fact new, and that "researches into European courtly poetry should . . . be concerned with the variety of sophisticated and learned *development* of *courtois* themes, not with seeking specific origins for the themes themselves,"[20] has been widely accepted.

The third implication of Spitzer's claims, that the woman's songs are popular, merits further exploration. It is certainly true that there existed woman's songs prior to the twelfth century, prior even to the earlier *jarchas*, about which we know almost nothing, and (or nevertheless?) scholarship is almost unanimous in asserting that this song was popular. The relationships between what has vanished and what we have as texts today and between both early and late woman's songs and male-voiced courtly lyric remain problematic. Spitzer's inclusion of the Portuguese *cantigas de amigo* in the body of popular woman's song involved him from the outset in serious difficulty. Because these lyrics were written by court poets, including them would deprive the term "popular" of any useful meaning. The same objection holds for the inclusion of many of the German *Frauenlieder*, written by known *Minnesinger* associated with German courts. Though Jeanroy believed that the French *refrains* were remnants of an earlier popular tradition, he felt that many of those which have come down to us "are very modern, and as little popular as possible,"[21] and Gaston Paris declined to see even the *refrains* as true representatives of early popular verse.[22] Aurelio Roncaglia has claimed that the *jarchas* were also learned, not popular, productions, and his claim is based on Biblical and Classical echoes which he finds in them.[23] Popular song as conceived of by the romantics—a communal production of a generalized shared consciousness—has in any case been cast into serious doubt. For Frenk Alatorre, the *jarchas* (or rather the tradition which lies behind them) are the product of a "popular school" of poets, an observation based on the striking coherence of "themes, psychological modalities, and modes of expression"[24] found in them. The "popular school" of poets implies a much greater sense of poetic self-consciousness and consciousness of a particular tradition than does the image of the spontaneous creativity of a May dance.

The debate can become sterile, especially when pursued on an abstract level. As Peter Dronke has warned, "'Popular' and 'courtly'—the words are common currency wherever lyrics are discussed. The faces of these coins have almost been worn away, they are so much used." Dronke's solution is to accept the definition of popular poetry as "composed not by a people but for it."[25] This formulation allows us to avoid theories of communal or spontaneous composition, and shifts the emphasis from composer to audience. It does not, however, settle the problem entirely; the *jarchas* are parts of, citations within, the learned artistry of the *muwashshahs*, whose audience must have been happy with a macaronic, highly cultivated form of song. Everything about the *muwashshah* bespeaks sophistication, a sophistication which Le Gentil labeled *folklorisme*,[26] the use by sophisticated poets of the "simpler" Romance lyric within their own. Roncaglia spoke of this same process, "of transposing (with the effect of giving atmosphere, of *recherché* sentiment, of irony and all these things together) the more ingenuous expressions of 'popular' culture into an otherwise quite self-conscious climate."[27] J. B. Trend felt that the *jarchas* were "not folk-poems, but artistic, *culto* poems, inspired by folk poems."[28] Whether the *jarchas* as we find them are popular, or imitations of popular song, or something else which we have not yet found the proper term for, their relationship to the refined *muwashshah* is quite complex, and it is precisely the complexity of this relationship between the woman's song and "refined" poetry which will reward further study.[29]

A complex relationship of a similar sort obtains, as Le Gentil observed, between other male and female voices in Iberia and France: "The Arabs make the *jarcha* the end-point of their compositions; the Galacians use parallelism, the Castillians gloss using the strophe-with-turn in the *estribillo* and the *villancico*; the French do likewise, with greater variety, in the *rondeau*, the *virelai*, and the *ballette*. . . ."[30] The French *refrains*, to which the *jarchas* and *cantigas de amigo* have so often been compared, appear in a great variety of texts, chiefly of the twelfth and thirteenth centuries—*rondeaux*, *chansons*, *motets*, *virelais*, romances, stories, didactic prose texts, and in the margins of manuscripts.[31] *Refrains* often serve as refrains in the modern sense—a repeated unit of one or more lines at the end of successive stanzas, similar to the burden of a carol—but the two terms are not synonymous. The *refrain* is used at the beginning, the middle, and at the end of the single-strophed *rondeau*, and it may occur a single time in a multi-strophed song. An example of the use of a *refrain* in a *rondeau* is as follows:

> *Vous arez la druerie,*
> *amis, de moi,*
> *ce que mes mariz n'a mie.*
> Vos l'avez bien deservie
> en bone foi.
> *Vos. . . . .*
> Mesdissant sont en agait

et main et soir
por nos faire vilonie.
Vous. . . . .[32]

(*You will have the pleasure,*
Friend, of me,
That my husband never will.
You have well deserved it
In good faith.
You will have. . . . .
Slanderers are on their guard
Both day and night
To work us harm.
You will have. . . . .)

Boogard gives, as an example of the many uses of the *refrain*, the case of number 1375 of his collection, "*Ne vos repentez mie de loiaument amer.*" This text is found in a *rondeau*, in the sixth strophe of a song by Pierre de Corbie, at the end of the seventh strophe of a song by Colart le Boutellier, in a series of *refrains* at the end of the third strophe of a song by Baude de la Kakerie, at the end of the fifth strophe of a religious lyric, and is cited in the *Court de Paradis* and in one of the *Miracles* of Gautier de Coinci.[33] Clearly the *refrains* were conceived of as independent units that might be "cited" in a great variety of contexts. It was these many citations—Boogard prints over 1800 *refrains*—which Jeanroy mined in his efforts to reconstruct the original lyricism of France, "the song placed in the mouth of a young girl." But asking whether the *refrains* he had before him might be the remnants of popular song itself, he concluded that "it is possible that we might find, out of the whole, a few such [popular songs], but it is probable also that there is a crowd of others which were made in imitation of them, and may barely resemble them at all."[34]

Again, then, one is faced with woman's songs which seem to have some connection, tenuous or direct, with precourtly lyricism, but which have been preserved, or imitated, by more conscious craftsmen. If Le Gentil saw this phenomenon as folkloristic and Trend as something more *raffiné* and condescending, Pierre Bec would prefer to scrap wholesale the diachronic approach to woman's song versus aristocratic song. Admitting that the tradition of the woman's song is older than the texts in which we tend to find it, Bec feels nevertheless that a strictly chronological division between woman's song and man's song is both historically overly simple and critically misleading. The distinction between popular and aristocratic, woman's song and man's song offered by Jeanroy and Paris "rests on a line of cleavage which is almost entirely chronological (not registral), and too systematic. As if . . . the traditionalizing lyric [*lyrique traditionalisante*], in its themes and forms, had not survived the wave of courtliness, especially in the north, thereby proving that the traditionalizing lyric is contemporary with the courtly."[35] One important feature of Bec's formulations, which should be of considerable value to future work in this area, is the subtle though important shift from the use of "popular versus aristocratic" to "popularizing versus aristocraticizing" lyrics, and from "traditional" to "traditionalizing." All of this is more than a bit awkward in English, of course, but it allows Bec and his reader to avoid falling into the trap of seeing the combination of the woman's song with courtly forms (as in the *motet*) as a combination of ancient and modern or of courtly and popular, and to avoid, in examining a *chanson de mal mariée* of the thirteenth or fourteenth century, the temptation to see it as a miraculous survival of a primitive form. Rather the male- and female-voiced songs were produced simultaneously, sometimes even in one lyric (an example of what Bec called registral interference), with aesthetic effects which have yet to be adequately explored.

The female voice in French lyrics is usually, like that of the young girl in the Iberian songs, direct in expression, active in feeling joy and pain, and frequently sensuous. Thus the voice is often in tonal opposition to the male voice in the *chanson courtoise*. A similar opposition is found in the contrasting image of the male in the *chanson* who suffers from the distance (usually emotional rather than spatial) of the woman, versus the woman of the *chanson de femme* who suffers the torments of the distance (usually spatial) of the man, her *ami (=amigo, habib)*. Such remarks must not be construed as implying that the relation between woman's song and *chanson courtoise* in French is simple or monolithic. The great variety of types of French woman's song, associated with certain themes or dramatic situations—*chanson de mal mariée, chanson de nonne, aube, chanson de toile, chanson d'ami*—and their appearance in such a variety of forms—*rondeaux, virelai, ballette, refrains, chanson*—insured a richness of possibilities.

The *chanson de toile* may serve as a single example of this richness. This is a narrative lyrical genre, whose setting is typically a high window at which a well-born lady and her young daughter sit at their sewing. Within this context we hear the young girl speak or sing, and we also, at the end of each stanza, hear a *refrain*, which may or may not fit exactly the narrative in progress. Here the archaizing quality of the woman's voice comes to the fore; the meter of the *chansons de toile* is usually the decasyllabic line of the *chanson de geste*, and assonance is used in preference to rhyme. The setting, of course, resembles that of the fairy-tale. A number of the extant pieces are cited in romances, notably *Guillaume de Dole* by Jean Renart, dated about 1228, which mentions three. The first of these is introduced as being sung by one of the characters, an older woman, who apologizes in advance for singing such an old-fashioned song. She has been asked to sing by her son, who has, accompanied by a visitor, interrupted the needlework in which she had been engaged with her young and beautiful daughter. This is the earliest known *chanson de toile*, and Jean may have either invented the type to suit the narrative moment in *Guillaume de Dole* or written this scene into the romance in order to use the song. In either case, the interplay of allusion, and sought-after effect of atmosphere, was an apparent success, since two other writers followed within a few years with romances endowed with *chansons de toile*, and the bulk of all the examples of the type appear to have been written within the space of some twenty years.[36]

The relationship between the tradition of woman's song discussed so far and two Old English poems in the female voice is less than clear, though one is included by Dronke in a chapter on the *cantigas de amigo*[37] and both were labeled *Frauenlieder* by Malone.[38] "Wulf and Eadwacer" and "The Wife's Lament" are both contained in the tenth-century Exeter Book. "Wulf and Eadwacer" appears to be the words of a woman who speaks of her lover, Wulf, from whom she is separated by both distance and a family feud. "The Wife's Lament" also speaks of separation, here between husband and wife, with the wife lamenting her husband's absence and her own exile to a solitary cave.

Dronke might be overly sanguine in suggesting that "'Wulf and Eadwacer' may give us some impression of what [*winneleodas*] were like,"[39] but certainly the poem is closer in age than any other Germanic woman's song to those poems which provoked the Carolingian proscription. Clifford Davidson has argued that both the Old English poems and some Latin woman's songs found in a manuscript from Canterbury and dated in the mid-eleventh century (the Cambridge Songs) bespeak the real possibility that a "cultural milieu of women, distinct from the men's warrior world as represented in the heroic poetry of the age, was sufficiently separate to generate popular patterns of cultural expression" which could have included woman's songs.[40] But both "Wulf and Eadwacer" and "The Wife's Lament" have proven terribly resistant to explication. It has been argued on at least two recent occasions that "The Wife's Lament" is not a woman's song at all; Rudolph Bambas saw the poem as a thane's lament for his lord, and Martin Stevens also argued for a male speaker.[41] Alain Renoir, who has outlined the Germanic literary tradition of "separation and suffering women" against which he feels the poem should be understood, has also noted that scholars disagree over even such fundamentals as how many characters are in the poem, and that "in recent years various interpretations have respectively construed the speaker as a dead woman, a live man, a sorceress-elect, a mistreated wife, a minor heathen deity, and an allegorical voice yearning for the union of Christ and the Church."[42] Renoir has also pointed out that the two Old English woman's songs "stand like parallel pieces immediately before and after Riddles I–LIX in the Exeter Book," that "Wulf and Eadwacer" was for some time believed to be the first in the series of riddles, and that "The Wife's Lament" opens with the word "Ic," a rarity in Old English poems except for two groups—the Psalms and the riddles themselves.[43] Riddling has also been discussed by P. J. Frankis, who suggested cross-textual punning between "Wulf and Eadwacer" and "Deor," another Exeter Book poem of lament, spoken by a man.[44]

One despairs of drawing a tidy conclusion from these contradictory pieces of evidence, but it does seem likely that "Wulf and Eadwacer" and "The Wife's Lament" are both caught up in complications which call our attention to contexts—the heroic tradition, the riddles, the architecture of the Exeter Book—larger than themselves. It is not impossible that they are simply woman's songs, but, as I hope even this most cursory of glances at medieval female-voiced lyrics has suggested, we have no woman's songs which are "simply" that.

Research in the woman's song must continue to move along several lines. We are faced with such abiding historical problems as the dating of some texts, and the firm establishment of others. We would like to know more about the social contexts in which the songs were produced, and the role played by the songs in those contexts. There remains work to be done on the relations between and among the different language groups, and the relations between male and female voices within specific language groups and within individual poems. Phenomenological and structuralist studies of individual lyrics, collections, and entire traditions should prove especially fruitful. In short, every issue important to medieval lyricism as a whole is raised in the study of woman's song, and it is likely that further research in this field will prove crucial in our understanding of the history and esthetics of song.

The essays that follow require little introduction. There are some cross-references among them, but each is written as an independent contribution to a specific field.

Anne Schotter's essay on the Latin songs deals with the voices of the Latin tradition, and the ways in which the audience's response to the songs was manipulated by their authors' use of other Latin poetry and of Biblical, classical, and medieval resources. Kathleen

Ashley's investigation of the Portuguese *cantigas de amigo* works towards a phenomenology of the genre, an approach which supplies much-needed insights into the specificity of these lyrics which have in the past largely been seen as monolithic, especially by scholars for whom the *cantigas* have been primarily evidence in larger questions of origins and international traditions.

In the German tradition, William Jackson's and Hubert Heinen's essays offer both a survey and specific textual criticism. Jackson's masterful survey of the history of scholarship on the *Frauenlieder* and of the *Frauenlieder* themselves, poet by poet, is a comprehensive and detailed introduction to the field, while Heinen's close reading of Hartmann von Aue's *Frauenlieder* and a *Wechsel* which is perhaps his demonstrates the versatility of the form in the hands of a master poet.

Ruth Lehmann's essay on the Old Irish poems breaks new ground in a variety of ways. She calls our attention to a group of poems which will be unfamiliar to most readers and, in the process, introduces the very concept of "woman's song" to Old Irish studies.

My essay and that of Maureen Fries are complementary in the sense that they divide Middle English poetry between them. I deal with independent lyrics, chiefly carols, while Fries deals primarily with lyrics "embedded" in the works of Chaucer and the Scottish poets. I point to the traditional and generic qualities of the woman's voice in the Middle English lyrics, and Fries demonstrates the breadth of tonalities in female voices to be found in the late medieval British tradition.

Mary Beth Winn's essay, finally, describes in detail the manipulation of the woman's voice and its relationship to the male-voiced poems found in a specific volume of French poetry printed in 1509.

 *Notes*

[1]Leo Spitzer, "The Mozarabic Lyric and Theodor Frings' Theories," *CL*, 4 (1952), 21.

[2]See Ibid., p. 15, note 19 for another understanding of the word *uuinileodas.*

[3]See Gustav Gröber, "Zur Volkskunde aus Concilienschlüssen und Capitularien," *Festschrift K. Weinhold* (Leipzig, 1893); F.M. Warren, "The Romance Lyric from the Standpoint of Antecedent Latin Documents," *PMLA*, 19 (1911), 280–314; and in this volume, Plummer, "The Middle English Woman's Song," note 10.

[4]Theodore Frings, *Minnesinger und Troubadours*, Deutsche Akademie der Wissenschaften zu Berlin, Vorträge und Schriften, 34 (Berlin:

Akademie, 1949); "Frauenstrophe und Frauenlied in der frühen deutschen Lyrik," in *Gestaltung Umgestaltung: Festschrift H. A. Korff,* ed. Joachim Müller (Leipzig: Koehler & Amelang, 1957), pp. 13–28; *Die Anfänge der europäischen Liebesdichtung im 11. und 12. Jahrhundert, BAWS,* 1960, Heft 2 (Munich: Bayerischen Akademie, 1960); and "Altspanische Mädchenlieder aus des Minnesangs Frühling," *BGDSL,* 73 (1951), 176–96.

[5]Frings, *Minnesinger und Troubadours,* p. 19.

[6]Paris, "Les Origines de la poésie lyrique en France," *JS,* 1891, pp. 674–88, 729–42; 1892, pp. 155–67, 407–30; Alfred Jeanroy, *Les Origines de la poésie lyrique en France au moyen âge* (Paris, 1889).

[7]Margit Frenk Alatorre, *Las Jarchas mozarabes y los comienzos de la lyrica romanica* (Guanajuato: Colegio de México, 1975).

[8]Spitzer, p. 4.

[9]The exact number is a matter of dispute since some *jarchas* are almost entirely in Arabic and should perhaps not be considered as Romance pieces. See Frenk Alatorre, p. 105.

[10]Spitzer, pp. 8, 14.

[11]For editions, studies, and manuscript information, see the relevant section of the cumulative bibliography.

[12]"Cantos románicos andalusíes continuadores de una lírica latina vulgar," *BRAE,* 31 (1951), 230.

[13]*The Medieval Lyric* (London: Hutchinson, 1968), p. 90.

[14]"La strophe zadjalesque, les khardjas et le problème des origines du lyrisme roman," *Romania,* 84 (1963), 222.

[15]Frenk Alatorre, *Las Jarchas,* pp. 162–66; Aurelio Roncaglia, "Di una tradizione lirica pretrovadoresca in lingua volgare," *CN,* 11 (1951), 213–49; Frenk Alatorre, "Jarŷas mozárabes y estribillos franceses," *NRFH,* 6 (1952), 281–84.

[16]"The 'Cancionerillo mozárabe' and the Origin of the Middle High German 'Frauenlied,'" *MLR,* 48 (1953), 301–09.

[17]*Medieval Latin and the Rise of European Love Lyric,* 2nd ed. (Oxford: Clarendon Press, 1968), I, 8.

[18]Convenient surveys are Frenk Alatorre's *Las Jarchas,* and Gerald Gillespie, "Origins of Romance Lyrics: A Review of Research," *YCGL,* 16 (1967), 16–32.

[19]For example, Dámaso Alonso, "Cancioncillas *de amigo* mozárabes," *RFE,* 33 (1949), 297–349, believes that the mozarabic tradition developed first; Jole Scudieri Ruggieri, "Riflessioni su *kharge* e *cantigas d'amigo,*" *CN,* 22 (1962), 5–35, held that the Portuguese lyrics were earlier; and M. Rodrigues Lapa, *Licões de literatura portuguesa: època medieval,* 6th ed. (Coimbra, 1966), argued for a parallel development.

[20]*Medieval Latin,* I, p. xvii.

[21]*Origines,* p. xx.

[22]*JS,* 1891, p. 613.

[23]Roncaglia, see n. 15 above.

[24]*Las Jarchas,* p. 135.

[25] *Medieval Latin*, I, p. 1.

[26] Le Gentil, 215.

[27] Roncaglia, 231.

[28] "The Oldest Spanish Poetry," in *Hispanic Studies in Honour of I. Gonzalez Llubera*, ed. Frank Pierce (Oxford: Dolphin, 1959), p. 427.

[29] See Klaus Heger. *Die bisher veröffentlichten Ḫarǧas und ihre Deutungen*, Beihefte, ZRP, 101 (Tübingen: Niemeyer, 1969), 44 ff., and the valuable full-length study of the problem by Linda Fish Compton, *Andalusian Lyrical Poetry and Old Spanish Love Songs: The Muwashshah and its Kharja* (New York: New York Univ. Press, 1976).

[30] Le Gentil, 222–23.

[31] Nico H. J. Van Den Boogaard, *Rondeaux et refrains* (Paris: Klincksieck, 1969), pp. 14–15.

[32] Boogaard, no. 171.

[33] Boogaard, pp. 16–17.

[34] *Origines*, 115.

[35] Pierre Bec, *La Lyrique française au moyen-âge* (Paris: Picard, 1977), I, p. 59.

[36] For an excellent consideration of the implications, aesthetic and historical, of the interpenetration of the "archaic" and contemporary, the "popular" and "sophisticated," see Michel Zink, *Belle: Essai sur les chansons de toiles* (n.p.: Champion, 1978); see also, for the various kinds of *chanson de femme*, Bec, I, pp. 57–141.

[37] *Medieval Lyric*, pp. 91–92.

[38] Kemp Malone, "Two English *Frauenlieder*," *CL*, 14 (1962), 106–17.

[39] *Medieval Lyric*, p. 91.

[40] "Erotic 'Woman's Songs' in Anglo-Saxon England," *Neophil*, 59 (1975), 451–62.

[41] Bambas, "Another View of the Old English 'Wife's Lament,'" *JEGP*, 62 (1963), 303–09; Stevens, "The Narrator of 'The Wife's Lament,'" *NM*, 69 (1968), 72–90.

[42] "A Reading Context for *The Wife's Lament*," in *Anglo-Saxon Poetry: Essays in Appreciation*, ed. Dolores W. Frese and Lewis E. Nicholson (Notre Dame: Notre Dame Univ. Press, 1975), p. 236.

[43] "A Reading of the *Wife's Lament*," *ES*, 58 (1977), 15–16, 8–10.

[44] "*Deor* and *Wulf and Eadwacer*: Some Conjectures," *MÆ* 31 (1962), 161–75. This suggestion has been extensively pursued by James Anderson in "*Deor* and *Wulf and Eadwacer*: Exposing a Familiar Heroic Theme in Two Adjacent Poems of the Exeter Book," paper read at the Fourteenth Congress on Medieval Studies, Western Michigan University, May, 1979. See also Anderson's dissertation (Kansas, 1978), "Strange, Sad Voices: The Portraits of Germanic Women in the Old English Exeter Book," in which he argues that the two poems are elaborate riddles built on elegiac and heroic themes.

Anne Howland Schotter

Woman's Song
in Medieval Latin

Within the corpus of Latin love lyrics written between the eleventh
and the thirteenth centuries is a small group of woman's songs—
lyrics in the female voice—which deserve the scrutiny that their
vernacular counterparts are beginning to receive.[1] Although there
has been some speculation as to the possibility of female authorship,
we may assume that these poems were written by men[2] and, hence,
constitute a projection of women's erotic experience. The lyrics all
agree in presenting this experience as unhappy, because of either
frustration or desolation at abandonment: they differ in the
response they invite to this unhappiness. One tradition invites sympathy, using the Latin language to incorporate echoes of those few
earlier Latin works which had given imaginative voice to women in
love. A second tradition, however, invites scorn, in a way very like
the cynical Latin goliardic poetry which treats women merely as
objects of men's pleasure. Such woman's songs use Latin—a language which was no one's "mother" tongue and was seldom taught
to women—to express antifeminism with impunity; for the medieval
Latin love lyric was written not only by men but for men, to be
performed before a male clerical audience, and this audience exerted
far less pressure to idealize love than did the sexually mixed audience of the vernacular lyric.[3]

19

Latin woman's song should be seen in relation to the corpus of the medieval Latin love lyric, which, taken as a whole, expresses some attitudes distinctly different from those expressed in vernacular lyrics. The overwhelming majority of these lyrics are "man's songs"—lyrics in the male voice. Although the received opinion is that they are totally sensual, having almost nothing to do with "courtly love," Peter Dronke has argued that some of the ones in less well-known manuscripts such as the Ripoll collection express courtly sentiments reminiscent of those in the male-voiced lyrics of the troubadours and Minnesinger.[4] The disagreement on this subject suggests that the Latin love lyric actually contains two traditions, idealistic and cynical, to one or the other of which woman's song as well as man's song can be assigned. Though it would be tempting to call the former "Solomonic" and the latter "Ovidian," the Song of Songs and the works of Ovid are too complex to be characterized simply. Nonetheless, the fact remains that both sources are important for our understanding of the two traditions.[5]

The influence of the Song of Songs on the idealistic tradition of woman's song is evident in a number of ways. Because it is in the form of a dialogue between Bride and Bridegroom, the book provides a model for woman's voice in love and, in fact, presents the Bride's desire as being as strong as that of the Bridegroom. This vision of reciprocal love has left its imprint on those few woman's songs which portray woman's love as similar to man's. In the Cambridge song, "Levis exsurgit zephirus,"[6] for instance, only the gender of the adjective *sola* identifies the speaker, alone and longing for her lover while spring burgeons around her, as being a woman; consequently, the poem has an emotional dignity lacking in those cynical abandonment laments which stress the practical consequences of love peculiar to woman's condition—pregnancy and social ostracism. Actual verbal echoes of the Song of Songs in the woman's songs serve to elevate the human love expressed by associating it with divine love. For, as everyone knows, the explicit eroticism of the book had been reconciled to the spirit of the Bible by allegorizations which identified the Bridegroom with Christ and the Bride, variously, with the Church, the Virgin Mary, or the individual human soul.[7] Thus the longing in the last line of "Levis exsurgit zephirus"—"nam mea languet anima"—gains seriousness from its allusion to the Bride's statement "quia amore langueo" ("because I languish with love") in Cant. 2:5.[8]

In a similar way, the invitation to the beloved, "Veni, dilectissime," also in the Cambridge Songs (no. 49), alludes to the most erotic passage of the Song of Songs in order to dignify the woman's physical passion:

Veni, dilectissime,
et a et o,
gratam me invisere,
et a et o et a et o!

In languore pereo,
et a et o—
Venerem desidero,
et a et o et a et o!

. . . .

Si cum clave veneris,
et a et o,
mox intrare poteris,
et a et o et a et o!

(Come, most beloved . . . visit me—I am
pleasing . . . I die of longing . . . I desire to
make love . . . If you come with your key . . .
you'll be able to enter soon.)[9]

Although the explicitness of this eroticism seems to have so distressed the clerical owners of the manuscript that they mutilated it
almost beyond legibility, the poem is in fact a close paraphrase of
the Song of Songs. The most physical reference, "If you come with
your key, you'll be able to get in soon" ("si cum clave veneris, . . .
mox intrare poteris") is an allusion to the Bride's statement, "My
beloved put his hand through the keyhole, and my bowels were
moved at his touch. I arose up to open to my beloved" ("Dilectus
meus misit manum suam per foramen, et venter meus intremuit ad
tactum ejus. Surrexi, ut aperirem dilecto meo," Cant. 5:4–5). The
metaphor of the key is a delicate, almost riddle-like expression of
desire, in contrast to the heavy-handed metaphors of spear and
fortress which produce a lewd and comic effect in a woman's song to
be discussed below.[10] Moreover, the words *veni, dilectissime,* and
languore, by echoing the Song of Songs, put the lyric in the world of
serious reciprocal love.

Peter Dronke has certainly helped us to see the Latin love lyric,
woman's song as well as man's, as far more spiritual and idealistic
than we had previously thought. Nevertheless, most of the lyrics,
particularly those in the *Carmina Burana,* follow the older stereo-
type of being at best good-naturedly, and at worst cruelly, sensual.
They portray woman as Other—a being whose erotic feelings are
different from those of men, and who is primarily a victim of male

predation. This dominant tradition has affinities with classical Latin love poetry, unlike the "Solomonic" tradition, whose affinities lie with the idealistic love lyrics of the medieval vernaculars. Past scholars might have called this tradition "Ovidian," but this is accurate only if we take into account the recently altered perception of Ovid as a proponent of serious, reciprocal love (however hard he believes it is to achieve) as much as of cynical seduction.[11] The unifying element in his two views of love, and the thing that distinguishes them from the view put forth in the Song of Songs, is their emphasis on the difference between the experiences of the two sexes in love: the men are presented as loving only until consummation, the women only afterward. While the man's songs either bewail frustration or boast of consummation, the woman's songs merely lament abandonment.[12]

The sympathetic strain of Ovidian woman's song in the medieval Latin lyric is strongly indebted to the *Heroides*, which, along with the *Metamorphoses*, is a source of the "romantic" Ovid of recent discovery. As a series of letters addressed by legendary women to their absent—usually faithless—lovers, the *Heroides* provided a model for woman's voice during the Middle Ages, when women themselves seldom gave literary expression to their own feelings.[13] A clear example of the influence of these letters on the woman's songs is a little known poem in the *Carmina Burana*, a lament of Dido after her desertion by Aeneas (no. 100, "O decus, O Libye regnum, Carthaginis urbem!"). Although ultimately based on Book IV of the *Aeneid*, the poem follows closely *Heroides* VII, which presents the situation from Dido's point of view, with none of Vergil's concern for the epic hero's historical imperative to found Rome. Poignant expressions of misery link the lyric to Ovidian lines such as "miseramque . . . Didon" (*Her.* VII),[14] as when Dido laments "me miseram!" ("wretched me," st. 2b), and "quid agam misera?" ("what shall I do, miserable as I am?" st. 4a). Following Ovid, she stresses the humiliation of having been left for another woman, rather than—as in the *Aeneid*—for imperial ambitions:

> regina spreta linquitur,
> et thalamos Lavinie
> Troianus hospes sequitur!
>
> (st. 4a)

> (A scorned queen is abandoned, and the Trojan guest seeks the bedchamber of Lavinia.)

Dido is outraged that she, a queen, should have been rejected.

Although, in fact, the lyric shows her situation to be like that of any woman in a medieval Latin abandonment lament, simply on a grander scale. Like the pregnant peasant girl who faces the neighbors' vicious gossip in a poem we shall see below, Dido must face the loss of her reputation among the Carthaginians, who mock her with the epigram:

> Dido se fecit Helenam:
> regina nostra gremio
> Troianum fovit advenam!
>
> (st. 4b)

> (Dido has made herself a Helen: our queen
> has fostered a Trojan stranger at her bosom.)

Concluding that there is no more hope, Dido says "hai, vixi nimium! / mors agat cetera!" ("Alas, I have lived too long, / let death do the rest!" st. 4a) and stabs herself.

This lament shows the strong influence of Ovid's *Heroides* on medieval Latin abandonment laments of a sympathetic nature—lyrics which portray woman as victim in a way that man never is but which give some imaginative credence to her suffering. The more familiar Ovid, however, the one who earned his reputation as a seducer in the *Ars Amatoria*, *Remedia Amoris*, and *Amores*, was influential on women's abandonment laments of a more cynical type. Since he wrote these works in the male voice, they are not a direct influence on the woman's song but, rather, an indirect contribution to the general literary attitude toward women. In the *Heroides*, Ovid denounces deceit in seducers from a female point of view, having his Dido call Aeneas *perfide* ("faithless," *Her*. VII. 79, 120), and rage against the "falsae periuriam linguae" ("perjury of his false tongue," 1. 67). Yet in the *Ars Amatoria*, his handbook for seducers, he actually recommends fraud (*fraudem*); for, women, being themselves treacherous, release men from the ethical injunction against fraud, and so he urges that men "fallite fallentes" ("deceive the deceivers").[15] The truth is that while Ovid had—for an Augustan Roman—an extraordinary ability to project himself into the mind of a woman, he could see her only as a victim rather than as an autonomous actor, and, when he projected himself into the mind of a man as he did in his cynical works, it was as a predator.

This cynical Ovid was influential on the witty, explicitly erotic medieval Latin learned verse of poets such as Serlo of Wilton, who also celebrated fraud.[16] In one poem Serlo, in the persona of a libertine, tells the audience, before recounting a virtual rape, that he intentionally deceived the girl, with the help of "Amor" who made

his words seem plausible.[17] In another, "Pronus erat Veneri Naso,
sed ego mage pronus" ("Ovid was prone to love, but I am more
prone"), his speaker insists that his interest lies entirely in the chase:
"I love only in the hope of the first union; that hope being satisfied,
what more should I hope for? . . . I love when I am rejected; when I
am loved, I reject. Those who pursue me, I hate; but I desire to
pursue each of them."[18] Such an attitude of approval of the deception and conquest of women lies for the most part behind the
goliardic man's songs in the *Carmina Burana*, which are themselves
indebted to Ovid and which treat women as pleasures to be enjoyed,
like food or wine. It is not surprising that there should be woman's
songs in the same tradition which invite the audience to find amusement in a woman's plight.

I would like to suggest that in such woman's songs the Latin
language itself is used as a metonymy for deception. Since women
were not generally trained in Latin, but rather, as Dante points out,
spoke and understood the vernacular language they learned in child-
hood,[19] they were excluded from the audience of the Latin lyric.
Poets using Latin, therefore, enjoyed a freedom from the pressures
which women exerted on the vernacular love poets to idealize love
and were able, by attributing the language to the female voice, to
achieve an irony at the expense of the speaker.

Such an irony is very evident in the bilingual lyric in the
Carmina Burana, "Ich was ein chint" (no. 185), in which the girl's
narration of her seduction proceeds much more rapidly in Latin
than in German, so that she appears either not to know what is
happening to her, or else to willfully soften it with the idealistic
diction of Minnesang:[20]

> *Er nam mich bi der wizen hant*,
>   sed non indecenter,
> *er wist mich div wise lanch*
>   valde·fraudulenter.

> *Refl.* Hoy et oe!
> maledicantur tilie
> iuxta viam posite!

> *Er graif mir an daz wize gewant*
>   valde indecenter,
> *er fûrte mih bi der hant*
>   multum violenter.

(st. 3–4)

(He took me by the white hand, but not
indecently; he led me along the meadow very

> fraudulently. Alas and oh! Cursed be the
> linden trees set along the road! He seized my
> white dress very indecently; he guided me by
> the hand, extremely violently.)

The girl's description of the man's "courtship"—his taking her by the "white" hand, showing her the meadow, etc.—is punctuated by a series of rhyming adverbs—*fraudulenter, indecenter, violenter*—which reveal the true manner of his actions. These words function in the same way as the Latin refrain, *maledicantur tilie*—a curse on those stock elements of the Minnesang landscape, the linden trees—which precludes a romantic interpretation of the poem as a whole.[21]

The use of Latin to connote the man's deception of the girl becomes even clearer in his blunt proposal, "ludum faciamus" (st. 7), which undercuts her interpretation that "Minne" forced him ("diu minne twanch sêre den man"). For it has been pointed out that the use of *ludus* or "game," the usual word for lovemaking in the medieval Latin lyric, underscores the frivolous nature of the act.[22] I would argue that the word also suggests a deception or joke at the girl's expense, since *ludos facere aliquem* means to make a mockery of someone, and *ludere* can mean "to deceive," as when Ovid, in the passage on fraud cited above, tells his readers "deceive [*ludite*] with impunity only girls, if you are wise" (*Ars Amatoria*, I.643). The girl, however, continues to use German to romanticize what is in fact a rape:

> *Er warf mir ûf daz hemdelin,*
>   corpore detecta,
> *er rante mir in daz purgelin*
>   Cuspide erecta.
>
>   (st. 9)

> (He threw up my little shirt, leaving my body
> uncovered; he battered my little fortress with
> his erect spear.)

With the diminutives *hemdelin* and *purgelin* for the "little shirt" and "little fortress," the girl brings an amusing, almost pathetic euphemism to the description; the corresponding Latin lines, however, are considerably more explicit. When we arrive at the concluding lines, we find, finally, that the girl's awareness has caught up with the events she has been narrating, for she laments that the man has betrayed (*betrogen*) her, quoting his parting remark, "ludus compleatur!" Thus the Latin, which in the woman's mouth lacks verisimilitude, has been used to provide a sophisticated commentary on the seduction. This technique of playing off the learned language against the vernacular to achieve humor at the expense of a woman is the same one that is used two centuries later in England to circumvent even stronger pressures from the female audience. Chaucer, for instance, has Chauntecleer gloss "Mulier est hominis confusio" as "Womman is mannes joye and al his blis," and the anonymous author of a lyric called "Abuse of Women" undercuts his ostensible praise with its Latin contradiction in the refrain: "Of all creatures women be best: *cuius contrarium verum est.*"[23]

Latin is clearly used to suggest the exploitation of women's ignorance in the bilingual "Ich was ein chint"; it is used more subtly in the same way, I think, in many woman's songs which are written entirely in Latin. This fact, together with a knowledge of cynical goliardic lyrics, can help us to understand the essentially comic nature of the famous lament of the pregnant girl, "Huc usque, me miseram" (CB, no. 126). Such an interpretation flies in the face of most of the poem's romantic critics; P. S. Allen, for instance, concludes that "in the length and breadth of medieval Latin singing we have no other poem on this theme which betrays half the sincerity and directness of this planctus," and Dronke remarks that the girl's fate is "truly seen as tragedy."[24] But the observations of Elizabeth Hardwick on the same theme in the nineteenth-century novel are all the more true of this medieval poem:

Those who suffer from a mere consequence of love, pregnancy, are implicated in their own fall. The consequence is mechanical, universal, repetitive; it will not alone make a tragic heroine or a heroine of any kind. Secret sympathy for the man is everywhere in literature when the mere fact of this sexual cause and effect is the origin of woman's appalling suffering.[25]

In fact, although the poem contains elements such as *me miseram* which are characteristic of serious laments, many of its most poignant details also occur in genres which make misfortune the subject of humor.

The poem's opening lament invites the audience's detachment from a stock situation by using word play in the manner of witty goliardic lyrics:

> Huc usque, me miseram!
> rem bene celaveram
> et amavi callide.
>
> Res mea tandem patuit,
> nam venter intumuit,
> partus instat gravide.

(st. 1–2)

(Up till now, woe is me, I hid the fact well
and loved cleverly. But at last my condition is
clearly seen, for my belly swells: labor
approaches pregnantly.)

Callide "cleverly," which seems to suggest the shrewdness of the
clerical seducer, is applied to the circumspection of the girl; it is
contrasted by rhyme and parallel syntax to *gravide*, which, despite
its usual translation as "grievously," can only be taken as "pregnantly." The effect is that the woman's attempt at shrewdness—at
aping her seducer by deceiving the world as he would deceive her—
is shown to be utterly foiled by the brute physical fact of pregnancy.
The Latin language makes the girl's description of her plight more
humorous even than in those popular Middle English woman's
songs which conclude accounts of seduction with laments such as
"my gurdul a-ros, my wombe wax out."[26]

The girl's reference to her mother's beatings and her father's
reproaches further links the poem with comic treatments of seduction in another Latin genre, the goliardic pastourelle, which reflects
the discrepancy in class between the man and woman by portraying
the seduction of a shepherdess by a wandering knight or scholar. As
W. T. H. Jackson has pointed out, not the speaker, the author, or
the audience of the pastourelle is much concerned about the fate of
the girl, and many of the examples in the *Carmina Burana* constitute a satire on the gullibility of country women.[27] The complaint of
the girl in "Huc usque, me miseram,"

Hinc mater me verberat,
hinc pater improperat,
ambo tractant aspere

(st. 3)

(Hence my mother beats me, hence my father
upbraids me; they both treat me harshly),

recalls in its wording the pastourelle "Vere dulci mediante" (CB
no.158). The ravished shepherdess in that poem rhymes *pater*,
frater, and *mater* (from all of whom she expects punishment) for
humorous effect:

Si senserit meus pater
vel Martinus maior frater,
erit michi dies ater;
vel si sciret mea mater,

cum sit angue peior quater,
virgis sum tributa!

(st. 6)

(If my father were aware of this, or my older
brother Martin, it would be a black day for
me; or if my mother knew, since she's four
times worse than snakes, I'd get my payment
with a switch.)

Although Jackson states that the "lamentation of the betrayed girl
over her fate" belongs to a genre entirely different from the
pastourelle,[28] it is clear that there is considerable overlap between
the two. If satirical pastourelles can incorporate lamentations, then
a lament like "Huc usque, me miseram" can, conversely, take on
pastourelle overtones.

A comparison, finally, of "Huc usque, me miseram" with another goliardic poem, the well-known lament of the roast swan
(separated by only three poems in the *Benediktbeuren* manuscript)
also points to the probability of comic distancing. In "Olim lacus
colueram" (CB no. 130), the swan bewails its singed and doomed
state, remembering its earlier freedom and beauty on the water:

Olim lacus colueram,
olim pulcher exstiteram,
dum cygnus ego fueram.

　　miser! miser!
Refl. Modo niger
et ustus fortiter!
　　. . . . .

Me rogus urit fortiter,
gyrat, regyrat garcifer;
propinat me nunc dapifer.
　　miser! miser!
Refl. Modo niger
et ustus fortiter!
　　. . . . .

Nunc in scutella iaceo
et volitare nequeo;
dentes frendentes video—
　　miser! miser!

Refl. Modo niger
et ustus fortiter!

(st. 1, 3, 5)

(Once I dwelt in a lake; once I was conspicuously beautiful, while I was a swan. . . . The
pyre burns fiercely, the spit turns and turns
again; now the serving boy hurries to me. . . .
Now I lie on a salver and cannot fly about. I
see gnashing teeth—woe is me! woe is me!
very black and burnt grievously!)

The refrain "miser! miser!" suggests that the poem is a parody of the
planctus, an extremely broad genre which includes laments for dead
rulers as well as for departed lovers.[29] I would argue that "Huc
usque, me miseram" operates as a similar parody, by pretending for
a moment to take seriously the sufferings of a creature alien to the
audience. Thus, just as the swan contrasts its past happiness on the
lake to its present blackness, suffering in the fire, and imminent
destruction in the mouths of the chewing guests, so the girl contrasts
the pleasures of love to her imminent confinement, her parents'
beatings, and the neighbors' scorn and gossip:

Cum foris egredior,
a cunctis inspicior,
quasi monstrum fuerim.

Cum vident hunc uterum,
alter pulsat alterum,
silent, dum transierim.

Semper pulsant cubito,
me designant digito,
ac si mirum fecerim.

(st. 5–7)

(When I go outside, I'm stared at by everyone, as if I were a monstrosity. When they see
this womb, one shoves the other; they don't
speak when I pass by. They always nudge
with their elbows; they point me out with
their finger, as if I had performed a miracle.)

In both poems a "rogus" ("pyre") is mentioned as an instrument of
torture: the fire by which, on the one hand, the swan is roasted, and
to which, on the other, the gossips would like to consign the girl

("dignam rogo iudicant, / quod semel peccaverim"—"They judge me worthy of the pyre, because I sinned just once," st. 8). The swan's lament is, finally, a striking use of the figure prosopopoeia—the attribution of speech to something which lacks it.[30] The intention is clearly comic, and the lyric was probably sung at feasts where swans were served. I believe that a similar technique is at work in "Huc usque, me miseram," and that it bears the same relation to the goliardic song of sexual conquest that the swan's lament does to the goliardic song of gluttony: it is a comic personification of a mute victim.

Medieval Latin woman's song, as a poetry whose audience as well as whose authors were male, thus presents a distinctly masculine view of woman's experience in love—the belief that it is essentially unhappy. The genre as a whole is, in a sense, an extended use of prosopopoeia, in that it is an attribution of thought and feeling to a group which was historically mute. A small number of the poems treat women's suffering in love—either frustration or desolation—as serious; they are indebted respectively to the Song of Songs and Ovid's *Heroides*, two important models for the female voice in western literature. The majority of woman's songs, however, are cynical, showing approval of the woman's abandonment. These show the influence of those works of Ovid which celebrate seduction, and they use the learned Latin language, which effectively excluded medieval women from the audience, to express a strong sympathy toward men and hostility toward women.

Notes

[1] Woman's Songs (*Frauenlieder*) were initially isolated by Theodor Frings, who saw them as proof of the "popular" origins of the courtly love lyric, *Minnesinger und Troubadours*, Deutsche Akademie der Wissenschaften zu Berlin, Vorträge und Schriften, 34 (Berlin: Akademie, 1949). More recently, the topic has been treated by Kemp Malone, "Two English *Frauenlieder*," *CL*, 14 (1962), 106–17; Peter Dronke, *The Medieval Lyric* (1968; rpt. New York: Harper & Row, 1969), pp. 86–108; Clifford Davidson, "Erotic 'Women's Songs' in Anglo-Saxon England," *Neophil*, 59 (1975), 451–62; and John F. Plummer, "The Woman's Song in Middle English, in this volume. Medieval Latin woman's songs have been mentioned, though not analyzed as a group, by Joseph Szövérffy, in *Weltliche Dichtungen des lateinischen Mittelalters: Ein Handbuch*, I, *Von den Anfängen bis zum Ende der Karolingerzeit* (Berlin: Erich Schmidt, 1970), pp. 42–43, and in Peter Dronke, *Medieval Latin and the Rise of European Love-Lyric*, 2nd ed (Oxford: Clarendon Press, 1968), I, pp. 273–77, and

Poetic Individuality in the Middle Ages: New Departures in Poetry 1000–1150 (Oxford: Clarendon Press, 1970), p. 27.

[2] Most of the essays in this volume attest to the fact that the woman's songs in the vernacular were written by men; in the absence of evidence to the contrary, this would seem to be all the more true of those written in Latin. F. J. E. Raby, in *A History of Secular Latin Poetry in the Middle Ages*, 2nd ed., (Oxford: Clarendon Press, 1957), I. p. 305, II, p. 275, makes the latter point in answer to P. S. Allen's romantic suggestion that women wrote some of the lyrics, *Medieval Latin Lyrics* (Chicago: Univ. of Chicago Press, 1931), pp. 71, 292–93. This suggestion was recently repeated by Dronke on the basis that nuns are known to have written love letters and verses in Latin, *Medieval Latin*, I, pp. 222–32. Hubert Heinen's work on persona in the German love lyric furnishes support for Raby: "Observations on the Role in *Minnesang*," *JEGP*, 75 (1976), 198–208.

[3] See Kenneth J. Northcott, "Some Functions of 'Love' in the 'Carmina Burana,'" *DBGÜ*, 6 (1970), 19.

[4] The "sensual" view is argued by Allen, p. 291, and Northcott, pp. 11–25. It has been popularized by George F. Whicher, *The Goliardic Poets: Medieval Latin Songs and Satires* (1949; rpt. New York: New Directions, 1965), pp. 4–6; and Edwin H. Zeydel, trans., *Vagabond Verse: Secular Latin Poems of the Middle Ages* (Detroit: Wayne State Univ. Press, 1966), pp. 20, 23–24. Dronke puts forth the "courtly" view in *Medieval Latin*, esp. I. pp. 264–331. The difference of opinion has been summed up by Szövérffy, p. 52.

[5] The general influence and in fact the fusion of the two sources in the Latin love lyric are pointed out by Dronke, *Medieval Latin*, I, pp. 163–68, 268–71, and Raby, I. pp. 303–05.

[6] Karl Strecker, *Die Cambridger Lieder* (Berlin: Weidman, 1926), no. 40.

[7] F. J. E. Raby, *A History of Christian-Latin Poetry from the Beginnings to the Close of the Middle Ages*, 2nd ed. (1953; rpt. Oxford: Clarendon Press, 1966), pp. 365–67, and Dronke, *Medieval Latin*, I, pp. 268–71. James Wimsatt, however, in "Chaucer and the Canticle of Canticles," in *Chaucer the Love Poet*, ed. Jerome Mitchell and William Provost (Athens: Univ. of Georgia Press, 1973), pp. 75–83, takes issue with Dronke and argues that such echoes are used parodically to point up the idolatrous nature of human love in contrast to divine—as in fact they are in the "Merchant's Tale." Though I disagree with Wimsatt—a lyric lacks the social context which in a fabliau directs our response—he underscores the difficulty of interpreting biblical allusion with certainty.

[8] Dronke cites this allusion in *Medieval Latin*, I, p. 275. Other serious woman's songs of longing with similar Solomonic allusions are "*Nam languens amore tuo*," an interpolation into *Cambridge Songs* no. 14, and "*Quia sub umbraculum*," printed in Dronke, *Medieval Latin*, II. p. 364.

[9] The lyric is reconstructed in Dronke, *Medieval Latin*, I. p. 274. The translation and all subsequent ones (except for the Douay version of the Bible) are my own.

[10] Wimsatt, however, sees the allusions as constituting a "take-off" on

the Song of Songs for the purpose of satirizing the woman's "concupiscent haste," in *Chaucer the Love Poet*, p. 75.

[11] See Brooks Otis, *Ovid as an Epic Poet*, 2nd ed. (Cambridge: Cambridge Univ. Press, 1970); Henry Ansgar Kelly, *Love and Marriage in the Age of Chaucer* (Ithaca: Cornell Univ. Press, 1975), pp. 71–75, 97–100; and Dronke, *Medieval Latin*, I, pp. 163–68.

[12] One exception to this statement, a lyric spoken by a man deserted by his lover, is *"Rumor letalis"* from *Carmina Burana*, ed. A. Hilka and O. Schumann, I. 2, *Die Liebeslieder* (1941; rpt. Heidelberg: Carl Winter, 1971), no. 83. But its tone is very different from that of women's abandonment laments, since, in dwelling bitterly on the faithless woman's character, it reflects hurt pride rather than a ruined life.

[13] Harold Jacobson, in *Ovid's Heroides* (Princeton: Princeton Univ. Press, 1974), pp. 319–49, and Ellen Moers, in *Literary Women* (Garden City, N.Y.: Doubleday, 1976), pp. 247–49, make similar points from somewhat different perspectives, but not in connection with the medieval period.

[14] Heinrich Dörrie, ed., *P. Ovidii Nasonis Epistulae Heroidum* (Berlin: Walter de Gruyter, 1971), p. 104, 1.9.

[15] Paul Brandt, ed., *P. Ovidi Nasonis De Arte Amatoria Libri Tres* (Hildesheim: Georg Olms, 1963), I. pp. 642, 645.

[16] On Serlo, see Raby, *Secular Latin Poetry*, II. pp. 113–14, and Dronke, *Medieval Latin*, I. pp. 239–43. The latter argues that Serlo's poems are not "obscene," as previous scholars have thought, but merely Ovidian *tours de force*.

[17] *Vultum / Finxit Amor, fictis verba dedere fidem*, Dronke, *Medieval Latin*, II, p. 505, ll. 3–4.

[18]   Spe tantum primi coitus amo, spe satiatus
         Ultra quid sperem? Spe nichil ulterius.

         . . . .

         Diligo dum spernor; dilectus sperno; faventes
         Odi, dum cupiam quamque favere tamen.
See Dronke, *Medieval Latin*, II, p. 504, ll. 9–10, 17–18.

[19] In arguing the merits of the "illustrious vernacular" over "grammar" (Latin), Dante stresses that the former is nobler because more natural: even women and children speak it, *De Vulgari Eloquentia*, ed. Aristide Marigo (Florence: Felice le Monnier, 1957), I.i.4.

[20] Although scholars believe that the series of dance songs in the *Carmina Burana* whose Latin stanzas are followed by German ones were designed to be sung and understood by unlearned women as well as learned men (Dronke, *Medieval Latin*, I. p. 302), the discrepancy in meaning between the German and Latin lines in CB no. 185 clearly makes the poem ironic at the girl's expense. This irony has been overlooked by critics who have otherwise recognized the satirical nature of the poem; e.g., Northcott, who argues that the satire is literary, directed against the conventions of Minnesang (pp. 20–23), and W. T. H. Jackson, who argues that it is social, expressing clerical contempt for the brutality of knightly lovemaking, "The Medieval Pastourelle as a Satirical Genre," *PQ*, 31 (1952), 163.

[21] See Northcott, p. 21.

[22] Northcott, p. 20. See C. T. Lewis and C. Short, *A Latin Dictionary*, s.v. *Ludus*, II B, *Ludo*, II G.

[23] *The Nun's Priest's Tale*, VII 3164-66, in the *Works of Geoffrey Chaucer*, ed. F.N. Robinson, 2nd ed. (Cambridge: Houghton Mifflin, 1961), and no. 38 in Rossell Hope Robbins, ed. *Secular Lyrics of the XIV*[th] *and XV*[th] *Centuries*, 2nd ed. (1955; rpt. Oxford: Clarendon Press, 1968).

[24] Allen, p. 274, and Dronke, *Medieval Latin*, I. p. 302. The only critic who sees the cynicism of the poem is E. Herkenrath, "*Tempus adest floridum*," *ZDA* 15 (1930), 135-40.

[25] "Seduction and Betrayal," in *Seduction and Betrayal: Women and Literature* (New York: Vintage, 1975), p. 196.

[26] Robbins, no. 28, 1. 43; similarly, no. 29, 1. 37 ("sone my wombe began to swelle"); no. 24, 1. 11 ("Now wyll not my gyrdyll met"); no. 25, 1. 17 ("I go with childe, wel I wot"); and no.27, 1. 20 ("alas, I go with schylde!").

[27] Jackson, pp. 162-63; Edgar Piguet points out that the shepherdess of the pastourelle was frequently a stock figure of humor, *L'Evolution de la pastourelle du XII*[e] *siècle à nos jours* (Basel: Société suisse des traditions populaires, 1927), p. 30, n. 1.

[28] Jackson, p. 162.

[29] See Dronke, *Poetic Individuality*, pp. 27ff.

[30] Geoffrey of Vinsauf, *Poetria Nova*, in *Les Arts poétiques du XII*[e] *et du XIII*[e] *siècle*, ed. Edmond Faral (Paris: Champion, 1962), pp. 211-13.

Kathleen Ashley

Voice and Audience:
The Emotional World
of the *cantigas de amigo*

After decades of preoccupation with the courtly love lyric whose dominant voice is male, critics have been turning their attention toward another type of medieval love lyric, the woman's song. The discovery a generation ago of the Mozarabic *kharjas* has led to increasingly sophisticated investigations of lyrics in the female voice, which are found throughout Europe in the Middle Ages and which may form an even more ancient genre in Mediterranean poetry.[1] Whereas early studies saw woman's songs as confirming the priority of "folk" or "popular" over courtly lyric in a search for the origins of vernacular lyric,[2] recent studies emphasize the cultural and poetic functions of the woman's voice. Whatever their ultimate origins, virtually all the examples of medieval woman's song we possess are, like the male love lyrics, products of an aristocratic context.[3] The relation between the two genres has been called one of "organized contrast" or "counterpoint," that is, the woman's voice is used to express an anti-institutional or non-courtly ethos by poets who also wrote in the traditional male voice of the courtly lyric.[4]

One result of the heightened interest in the genre has been a tendency to overlook distinctions between woman's songs from different countries and eras in order to arrive at a clearer understand-

ing of structures and attitudes common to all women's lyrics. However, such an approach, while both attractive and fruitful, may
obscure the very features which give each type of woman's song its
poetic individuality. In order to appreciate the unique features of
the *cantigas de amigo* as well as their indebtedness to generic and
courtly contexts, we will look at the emotional world conjured up by
the lyric voice as it addresses a fictional audience of mother, sisters,
lover, women friends, and natural objects. Far from portraying a
static and monotonal universe of wistful lament as some critics have
claimed, these poems evoke the complex emotional states of the
amiga, whose voice issues from a dynamic universe of arrivals and
departures, reports and rumors, shared joy, or the menace of uncertainty, misperception, and even betrayal. The tension of the best
poems—their mood of mingled desire and fear—often arises from
address to a figure or object ambivalent toward the love of the
amiga. This anxiety or insecurity about love, although achieved by
different means, is much closer to the view of love expressed in the
male love lyrics, the *cantigas de amor*, than has been acknowledged.
What I will suggest, then, is that neither the formulae of woman's
songs nor the expectations of a sophisticated audience are, by themselves, sufficient to illuminate the art of the *cantigas de amigo*, for it
is out of the relation of lyric voice to both fictive and actual audiences that the *cantigas'* unique emotional world is created.[5]

Perhaps the most widespread misapprehension about the
Gallego-Portuguese woman's song is that in it the woman always
expresses an intense and uncomplicated yearning for her absent
loved one, an emotion which the Portuguese now call *saudades*. The
first datable *cantiga de amigo*, attributed to King Sancho I who
lived at the end of the twelfth century, in fact does exemplify the
saudades mood:

> Ai eu coitada!
> Como vivo en gram cuidado
> por meu amigo que ei alongado!
> Muito me tarda
> o meu amigo na Guarda! (Nunes, DXII)[6]

> (Oh mournful me!
> How I live in great longing
> for my friend who is far away!
> He is tardy
> my friend in the Guard!)

Sancho's lyric is indeed a poignant cry of longing for an object separated from the speaker by time (*tarda*) and space (*alongado*). The

narrow universe of the lyric hardly contains even two persons, for the *amiga* addresses and describes herself as much as her absent lover.

Such quasi-solipsism is not, however, the norm among the Portuguese lyrics; even a cursory examination of the more than five hundred *cantigas de amigo* reveals that the great majority are addressed to a variety of named "others," and their tone is rarely that of pure lament. Often the poem is half of a conversation between the *amiga* and her confidante, with a fair number of lyrics turning into dialogues by including a response. The dialogue form is especially common when the conversation is between a woman and her mother.[7]

At times in the Portuguese lyric the mother is a sympathetic auditor of her daughter's confessions of love and complaints that the lover has overstayed his promised time away from her. More often, however, the mother is portrayed as hostile to the girl's emotions, as an old-fashioned repressive figure. The lyric result is a tense world of generational cross-purposes: accusations by the daughter that she is being deprived of her happiness and suspicion on the part of the mother that the daughter is somehow circumventing her prohibitions. In her role as chaperone, the mother is bent on keeping the lovers apart, while they scheme to meet. As one daughter complains:

> Non poss' eu, madre, ir a Santa Cecilia
> ca me guardades a noit' e o dia
> do meu amigo. (Nunes, CCCCLXXXVI)

> (I can't go, mother, to Saint Cecilia
> because you keep me night and day
> from my friend.)

The woman friend, in poems addressed to her, is invariably a more sympathetic confidante than the mother; however, she too inhabits a world where love maintains a precarious existence. The friend may take an active role as emissary to the lover, or as reporter of all that is rumored about him at court, or she may simply listen to descriptions of the lovers' emotional states. Typical of the extreme logic the friend hears is the final refrain of one lyric: "Mais, pois non ven, nen envia / mandad', é mort' ou mentia," (Nunes, VIII; "But since he does not come, nor sends a message, he's dead or he lied!"). The friend sometimes receives complaints about the mother; in one well-peopled lyric, for example, the *amiga* tells her friend of her mother's happiness and her own sadness when the lover left town in the king's service.

The *amigo* and even the poet himself are often among the cast of characters in the *cantigas*. The lover is present not just as a longed-for, but often as a threatening or disappointing figure in these lyrics. Of the many poems addressed to the lover himself, a surprising number are accusatory, addressing an "amigo fals' e desleal" (a false and disloyal friend) who has not kept his promise to return, who has failed to send an expected message, or who has chosen another mistress.[8]

The presence of the lover or the poet-as-lover, especially in poems addressed to girlfriends, sometimes provides the occasion for clever parody of love poetry, typically at the expense of the male love lyric and the male poet, not the female persona. The formulae of the male love lyric may be mocked, as in one poem where the exaggerated claims of the courtly lover that he loses his mind or dies for his mistress are held up to ridicule. The woman speaker tells her *amigas* that when she sees the lover turn up quite healthy after all his protestations she asks him, "Didn't you die for love?" (Nunes CLXXXIX). Such parody is also frequently suggested when the poet appears in the lyric. There are poems in which the woman discusses male love poetry, for example by describing love songs her poet-lover has created for her.[9] In one poem the friends agree that the countless troubadours in the kingdom of Portugal are a poor lot who no longer have the ability to praise beauty properly. The troubadours have, in short, lost their vocation and love suffers (Nunes, CXCV).

Other woman's songs in which the poet-lover is present seem to suggest parody not only of the male lyrics but of the social conditions of which they are a part. In a series of *cantigas*, the poet Joan de Guilhade brings himself and his art into the world of the poem, thus expanding its boundaries by making fiction that is conscious of itself and of an external courtly audience. In one poem he has the *amigas* describe him as a loyal lover who should be praised by them.[10] Conversely, in another poem, he has the girl complain to her friend that she has given Joan de Guilhade all sorts of tokens of love, but he wants another kind of gift![11] Whether presenting himself in a favorable or unfavorable light, the poet thus uses the woman's song to call attention to the world outside, to the courtly context itself, where the audience of Joan's peers could laugh at the poet's self-mockery.

All these lyrics are interesting as reminders that the same courtly poets were composing both male and female love lyrics and that the two genres were conceived as complementary types. But here I am especially intrigued by their portrayal of the poet as capable of the same ambivalent power over love that we see in the lyrics' other personnae. When the poet exercises his art properly, love prospers; when he fails to do so, love suffers.

We see, therefore, a considerably more complex and populous world than commonly supposed, one in which the dominant emotion would seem to be not longing but anxiety. Just as the male love lyric has its interfering jealous husband, its schemes and scandal-mongers at court, as well as the lady's potential coldness, so the female love lyric in Portugal has its cast of characters which jeopardize the love affair. The *amiga's* desires are threatened not only by the vigilance of her mother or the potential unfaithfulness of her lover, but also by a variety of other figures at court, the most prominent of which is the king himself.

Scholars have always spoken of the king's role in these poems in socio-economic or political terms, noting the lover's conventional absence in the king's war against the Moors. The frequent reference to the king also reminds us that the Portuguese woman's lyric is produced by court poets. However, here I will examine the king's *poetic* role as a force hostile to the existence of love, because that role, I would argue, is the reason for his importance in the *cantigas de amigo*. In innumerable lyrics, the king is portrayed as the power responsible for the lover's absence. Joan Zorro's sea lyrics[12] allude to the launching of the king's fleet into the Tagus estuary at Lisbon:

> El-rei de Portugale
> barcas mandou lavrar
> e la irá nas barcas migo
> mia filha, o voss' amigo. (Nunes, CCCLXXXIV)

> (The king of Portugal
> ordered ships built
> and there on the ships, my daughter,
> goes your lover.)

Occasionally the woman's antagonism to the king erupts into open rivalry, as in a poem by Joan Airas where the woman complains that her lover has deserted her to go live with the king; in justification of her pique, the refrain explicitly compares her ability to make the lover happy to the king's: "nunca lh' el-rei tanto ben fazer quanto lh' eu farei, quando mi quiser" (Nunes, CCCXVIII; "the king can never be as good to him as I can when I want to!")

Although in his role as separator of the lovers the king is usually an enemy, one poem by Pai Gomes Charinho dramatically reverses this expectation and transforms the king into a savior figure. The poem manages at once to evoke the fears which had tormented the *amiga* while her lover was "almirante do mar," and her joy and relief now that she has received the news that he is no longer away. It does this by recalling all the anxieties she will no longer have: she will not be sad when she sees high winds; she will not lose

sleep through tormented thought, nor fear every messenger who
arrives from the frontier as a potential bearer of bad tidings about
her lover. She ends each stanza with a grateful refrain:

> Se foi el-rei
> o que do mar meu amigo sacou,
> saque-o Deus de coitas que afogou. (Nunes, CCXXI).

> (If it was the king
> who rescued my lover from the sea, let God
> rescue him from the cares in which he drowns.)

While portraying the king here as the agent of reunion rather than
separation, the poem's power comes, I think, precisely from its
juxtaposition of the two possibilities. The *amiga's* present joy gains
depth when contrasted to her past traumas for which the king, at
least implicitly, was responsible. Therefore, although there are no
poems addressed directly to the king, I see his function as analogous
to that of the other addressees and personae in the *cantigas de
amigo* who objectify the potential of the woman's love to bring her
both *prazer* and *coita*, joy and sorrow.

Some of the most memorable *cantigas* are addressed not to
human beings but to objects in the natural world which stand for the
ambiguity of the love. Martim Codax's lyric calls on "ondas do mar
de Vigo" ("waves of the sea of Vigo"), asking "se vistes meu amigo?"
("Have you seen my friend?" Nunes, CCCCXCI). On the one hand,
the waves—described as stormy or high—may be implicated in the
lover's delay at sea; on the other hand, the waves can bring welcome
news of his return. The sea's importance as a setting in the Portuguese love lyric can be explained not only by Portugal's location on
the Atlantic Ocean, but also by the transformation of that geo-
graphical fact into a poetic metaphor for the experience of love. The
landscapes and seascapes of the *cantigas de amigo* are scenes of the
heart, and the objects or agents there come to symbolize the ambivalent power of love.[13]

In discussing the mother's role in the Portuguese woman's song
I cited a poem in which the daughter complains she can't go to Saint
Cecilia—that is, to the shrine dedicated to that saint—where the
faithful go to make special prayers for intercession. It is only one of
many shrines and pilgrimage spots mentioned in the Portuguese
lyrics,[14] and it is emblematic of the transformation of the external
world which takes place in these lyrics: a religious site is metamor-
phosed into a site for a love tryst, for it is there the daughter invariably hopes to meet her lover.

In poems addressed to the mother, the saint's shrine has a kind of negative valence, for it is usually a forbidden place. But the locale also occurs in poems addressed to female friends or sisters where it becomes the site for their *baile*, or dance of love.[15] In one lyric, for example, the *amiga* says to her girlfriends, "our mothers are going to the shrine of Saint Simon to burn candles; let's go with them and while they worship we will dance there for our lovers" (Nunes, CLXIX). Codax also has a limpid poem in the parallelistic style which unfolds with subtle humor. "At the shrine in Vigo the lovely one danced," the first two stanzas declare. "The lovely one danced who never had a lover," the next two stanzas tell us. However, in the final two stanzas the idea is humorously completed: "who never had a lover, except in the shrine at Vigo!" (Nunes, CCCCXCVI). Like her dancing in a sacred place, the girl's gestures, such as bathing in the ocean or mountain spring, binding or washing her hair, and washing her clothes, may also have erotic overtones.

> Quantas sabedes amar amigo
> treides comig' a lo mar de Vigo
> e banhar-nos emos nas ondas (Nunes, CCCCXCV)

> (All you who know how to love a lover,
> hurry with me to Vigo bay
> and we will swim in the waves),

one *amiga* calls to her friends, suggesting a connection between emotion and action.

Objects mentioned in the lyrics—letters from the lover, gifts like rings or belts—also take on a heavy emotional charge and function in the stark way familiar to us from ballads, epitomizing the forces acting on the human beings in their world. The ring of the lover which the *amiga* cries she has lost under the pine tree would seem to stand for her lost virginity; trees, especially the pine and the hazel, are associated with love in the *cantigas*.[16] In one of the most famous Portuguese lyrics, the girl asks the flowers of the green pine if they have any news of her lover, who appears to have lied about returning to her:

> Ai flores, ai, flores do verde pino,
> se sabedes novas do meu amigo?
> ai, Deus, e u é? (Nunes, XIX)

> (Oh flowers, oh, flowers of the green pine,
> do you have news of my friend?
> oh God, and where is he?)

The poem is a dialogue, with the pine flowers answering the *amiga* and reassuring her that the lover is alive and well and will be with her soon. The implication of the poem is that the lover's promise took place under the pine, which thus becomes a replacement for him.

Another poem demonstrates a similar strategy as the lover's gifts become talismanic objects which the *amiga* threatens when the lover does not return to her. Expressing her bewilderment at his desertion, she tells her hair she will not bind it with a silk band, her jewels that she will not wear them, her mirror that she will not look into it, and her belt that she will not fasten it (Nunes, CCLX).

As my final example of this technique of symbolizing the complexities of love through the objective world which provides the occasion and audience for the woman's lyric, I will take a group of poems by Pero Meogo. The setting is not the sea but a mountain forest where stags come to drink at the spring. In one poem the *amiga* addresses the female deer (*cervas*) as in the Codax poem she had addressed the waves:

> Ai cervas do monte vin vos preguntar:
> foi-s' o meu amigu' e se ala tardar,
> que farei, velidas? (Nunes, CCCCXIV)

> (Oh deer of the mountain, I come to ask you:
> my love went away and if he delays,
> what shall I do, my lovely ones?)

Clearly the logic of asking a wild creature for advice is a poetic logic, for the deer are objectifications of the *amiga*'s emotional state. In another poem, the stags (*cervos*) function explicitly as analogues to the lover:

> Tal vai o meu amigo
> com amor que lh' eu dei
> come cervo ferido
> de monteiro del-rei. (Nunes, CCCCXII)

> (There goes my lover
> with love that I gave him
> like the wounded stag
> of the king's huntsman.)

One edition of Meogo's poetry has provided a fifty page elucidation of the figure of the stag in sacred and secular love poetry as well as in the folklore of the Near East and Europe.[17] The resonances of all those traditions certainly contribute to the "rightness" of the symbol here, but I am even more struck by the likeness in technique between Meogo's lyrics and those of other Gallego-Portuguese poets, even where the latter fall below his in achievement. Typically, all use a technique of juxtaposition rather than exposition. The *amiga* defines her love by implication and objectification, not by overt statement or analysis. A parallel relationship is established between an action or object (that is, a natural fact) and a subjective exclamation of love (that is, an emotional fact) without, in most cases, the link between natural and emotional fact being made explicit. The effect is at once simple and sophisticated.

This technique owes much to the "popular" roots of the *cantigas de amigo*, and the internal audience of mother, friends, and even natural creatures or objects also appears to have had its origins in traditions of woman's songs. However, it is important to stress that these conventions of the Portuguese woman's song, if that is what they were, are present in the lyrics we possess because they were adopted by the courtly poets of the thirteenth century. The extant *cantigas de amigo* have been thoroughly domesticated so that the emotional world of the *amiga* is a counterpart to the emotional world of the male lover in his lyrics, the *cantigas de amor*. Both present a range of tones, from joy to sorrow, including humor and philosophical meditation. But their most characteristic tone is insecurity, for the perception that love exists in a universe of potentially hostile forces seems to have been one that especially appealed to the thirteenth-century courtly audience for which both genres of Portuguese love lyric were written.

   *Notes*

¹See Margit Frenk Alatorre, *Las Jarchas Mozárabes y Los Comienzos de la Lírica Románica* (El Colegio de México, 1975); Elvira Gangutia Elícegui, "Poesiá griega 'de amigo' y poesia arabigoespanola," *Emerità*, 40 (1972), 329–96.

²See, for example, Leo Spitzer, "The Mozarabic Lyric and Theodor Frings' Theories," *CL*, 4 (1952), 1–22; P. F. Ganz, "The 'Cancionerillo Mozarabe' and the Origins of the Middle High German 'Frauenlied,'" *MLR*, 48 (1953), 301–09.

³This is especially true of the *cantigas de amigo* which constitute the largest corpus of medieval woman's songs precisely because the genre was adopted by court poets of Iberia. To read these poems without reference to their courtly context would be highly misleading, as I have argued in "The Role of the Courts and the Thirteenth Century Portuguese Lyric," *ACTA III: The Thirteenth Century* (SUNY-Binghamton, 1976), pp. 65–78.

[4] John Plummer, "The Woman's Song in Middle English," included in this collection. I am also indebted to comments by Doris Earnshaw of The University of California at Berkeley, who is writing a dissertation on this topic.

[5] In stressing the distinctive poetic techniques of the *cantigas de amigo* I differ from C. P. Bagley who would obliterate *all* important differences between the two genres. Writing on "*Cantigas de Amigo* and *Cantigas de amor*" in *BHS*, 43 (1966), 243, he says: "Both genres have something in common with the Provençal tradition, and both seem to be influenced by what is assumed to be an ancient indigenous lyric. Both appear to represent a fusion of courtliness and tastes peculiar to the Peninsula. . . . A more satisfactory way of judging the two types of Peninsular love-lyrics is to see them as showing complementary aspects of the same situation; the *cantigas de amigo* and the *cantigas de amor* are two sides of the same cloth and the pattern shows through on the reverse side in the same colors."

[6] The edition cited throughout this essay will be that of José Joaquim Nunes, *Cantigas de Amigo dos Trovadores Galego Portugueses*, II (Lisboa, 1973).

[7] See, for example, Nunes, XVIII, LIX, LXXXII, LXXXV, XCIV, CXX, CCXIII, CCXLIV, CCLIX, CCLXXI, CCCXL, CCCLV, CCCLXXXI, CCCLXXXV, CCCXCVIII, CCCCXIII, CCCCXL. On the address to the mother in Mozarabic *kharjas* and woman's lyrics in other languages, see Linda Fish Compton, *Andalusian Lyrical Poetry and Old Spanish Love Song: The Muwashshah and its Kharja* (New York: New York Univ. Press, 1976), pp. 88–90.

[8] Nunes, XXXIV, XLVI, LXXIV, CIII, CXXXIV, CXXV, CLXIV, CCXVI, CCCXXXIV.

[9] Nunes, CXCIII, CCLXXXIV, CCCXXXVI, CCCCII, CCCCLXXV.

[10] "Lealment' ama Joan de Guilhade / e de nós todas lhi seja loado / e Deus lhi dê da por que o faz grado, / ca el de pran con mui gran lealdade" (Nunes, CLXXVI).

[11] "Sempr' averá don Joan de Guilhade / mentr' el quiser, amigas, das mias dõas, / ca ja m'end' el muitas deu e mui bõas / des i terrei-lhi sempre lealdade, / mas el demanda-m' outra torpidade" (Nunes, CLXXXI).

[12] Nunes, CCCLXXXII–CCCLXXXIX.

[13] Stephen Reckert has commented on the complex fears of the *amiga* symbolized by the waves in a sea lyric by Meendinho: "As ondas, como significado, *causam* o terror da 'fremosa'; como significante, *significam-no*: isto é, são o correlato objectivo do seu pânico crescente. Mas a outro nível significam também a paixão amorosa que a arrebatou até à ilha." *Do Cancioneiro de Amigo*, ed. Stephen Reckert and Helder Macedo (Lisboa: Assirio e Alvim, 1976), p. 132. See also his comments on a lyric by Fernando Esguio in which the birds are symbols for the *amiga's* ambivalent emotions (p. 230).

[14] See series of poems whose setting is San Servando, Nunes, CCCLXIV–CCCLXXIX; also Sant'Iago, Nunes, CXVII; Santa Maria da Leiras, Nunes, CLXXIV, LXXV; Santa Maria da Reca, Nunes, CCCXLII, CCCXLIII.

[15]Nunes, CCCCXCVIII, CCCCXCIX.

[16]See Nunes, CCLXII. The hazel tree—*avelaneira*—functions usually as the site for the *amigas* to dance. A lovely *cantiga* by Airas Nunes issues an invitation:

> Bailemos nós já todas, todas, ai amigas
> so aquestas avelaneiras frolidas,
> e quen fôr velida, como nós, velidas,
> se amig' amar,
> so aquestas avelaneiras frolidas
> verrá bailar. (Nunes, CCLVIII)

[17]Xosé L. Méndez Ferrin, *O Cancioneiro de Pero Meogo* (Vigo, 1966), pp. 54–110. See also Appendix I, "A Digression on the Stag and Doe Imagery of some Thirteenth Century Galician Poetry and the Question of its Ritual Origins," in A. T. Hatto, *Eos: An Enquiry into the Theme of Lovers' Meetings and Partings at Dawn* (The Hague: Mouton, 1965), pp. 815–19.

William E. Jackson

The Woman's Song
in Medieval German Poetry

I. The Medieval German Woman's Song in Scholarly Focus

Among the ancient genres of secular poetry in which the woman figures prominently as a speaking (or perhaps originally, singing) character, the dawn song and the pastourelle have traditionally been treated as separate entities. On these two genres has been focused an ongoing scholarly discussion that is recorded in a voluminous body of secondary literature.[1] I shall take this situation as a justification for excluding the dawn song and the pastourelle from my discussion in favor of other genres featuring the woman which have received a good deal less attention.

The poems which I shall treat here under the name woman's song—which term, along with its German counterpart *Frauenlieder*, I shall use as a general heading—fall under several categories. First, there is the poem in which the woman is the sole speaker. I shall call this form the woman's monologue (German *Frauenmonolog*) or usually, in keeping with its modest dimensions, woman's stanza. Secondly, there is the dialogue-poem (German *Dialoglied*) in which we hear the woman engaged in conversation with a second (usually male) character within the fiction of the poem. For the third cate-

47

gory I shall, for lack of a satisfactory English term, retain the German name *Wechsel* to designate a poem in which a woman and a man utter statements which are not made directly to each other but which seem to be connected in an apparently common fictional realm. The messenger-poem, a possible fourth category, poses something of a problem since the messenger appears, sometimes with a speaking role and sometimes as a silent addressee, in poems belonging to the other three groupings. It will prove easier to treat the messenger-poem as a special case than to establish a perfect system of categories.

That the woman's song in German literature has received so little and such unsatisfactory treatment has to do with the manner in which scholarship on medieval German secular love poetry, the *Minnesang*, has developed over the decades. In the nineteenth century, the poems of the *Minnesang* were viewed as confessions and revelations which could serve as a basis for conclusions about the lives of the authors of these poems. Since the woman's songs in German literature were composed as far as we know by male authors, they had somehow to be reconciled with the biographical assumptions about these authors which had been made on the basis of other poems by the same poets. In a still highly respected publication from the year 1838, Friedrich Heinrich von der Hagen interpreted some poems of Reinmar der Alte, in which man and woman address each other, as messages which were to be relayed back and forth between Reinmar and a woman at the court in Vienna, where Reinmar is thought to have been active.[2] Much more recently (1953), Helmut de Boor has spoken of a "Dame am Wiener Hof, der Reinmars reale Werbung galt" in a way which seems to echo von der Hagen.[3]

That medieval German love poetry depicted aspects of actual courtships in the lives of its authors continued to be the working assumption of scholars throughout the nineteenth century. In light of this view, the woman's song could only cause perplexity; for, whereas in the poems in which the speaker is a man—those we have come to associate with the terms "courtly" or "unrequited" love— the woman is portrayed as unresponsive, aloof, and pitiless in her treatment of the poet, in the woman's song the woman is depicted as an extremely infatuated creature who often seems to take the initiative in courtship. Since the former was assumed to be in harmony with the biography of the poet, the latter required special explanation.

In an article from 1877, Reinhold Becker proposed that the words of the woman in the *Frauenlied* should not be taken as the actual utterances or sentiments of the poet's lady, but rather as the vain imaginings of the poet in question, whose wishful thinking supplied the apparitions of a success at conquest of the female heart which reality belied.[4] A few years later (1882), in a book devoted largely to the early (mid twelfth-century) love poetry of Austria, Becker offered a somewhat different explanation without reconciling it entirely with the initial one. Here we find the suggestion that the woman's song was used by poets to present sentiments which they hesitated to express in their own persons, since it was held to be unsuitable for a knight to be too sentimental and emotional.[5]

Becker's sharpest critic, Konrad Burdach,[6] objected strongly to this suggestion, apparently because it appeared to imply dissimulation on the part of the poets in question. In a book first published in 1880, Burdach returns in essence to the position of von der Hagen, insisting that the poems of the *Minnesang* are not only based on real situations, but are also to be believed literally, statement by statement.[7] This very insistence on the literal interpretation of the *Minnesang* produces a serious difficulty for Burdach in his discussion of Reinmar when he moves from superficial summary to more thorough treatment of individual poems.[8] Then Burdach becomes aware, apparently to his surprise, of troubling features of the woman's song. At an earlier point in the book, Burdach had maintained that, except for the dawn songs of Wolfram von Eschenbach and a few poems by Heinrich von Morungen and Hartwic von Rute, the *Minnesang* of the twelfth century is devoid of overflowing passion.[9] After becoming aware of the passion of the woman's song, however, in which things are said plainly and bluntly,[10] Burdach sees himself caught up in a dilemma of his own making. Every time he reads Reinmar, he avows, in what seems to be bewilderment, he judges the poet differently.[11] Nowhere does Burdach resolve the dilemma; instead, in a later publication, he attributes the woman's song of Reinmar to the poet's female soul.[12] Meanwhile, Burdach's book of 1880 went on to become one of the standard works of scholarship on the *Minnesang* and ultimately was published in a second, expanded, edition in 1928.[13]

Some of the studies indebted to Burdach have in turn themselves become influential, in some cases eclipsing him. There will be sufficient occasion to draw on or take issue with these studies during the course of the present discussion. For the moment, however, I would like to concentrate briefly on those studies, all from the twentieth century, which focus expressly on the woman's song of the categories indicated above.[14]

The first of these to claim our attention is the dissertation on the *Wechsel* by Adolar Angermann published in 1910. Angermann sees the *Wechsel*, which he separates strictly from the dialogue-poem, as a specifically German creation and takes issue in particular with the derivation of the *Wechsel* from the French and Provençal

woman's song.[15] Ultimately, Angermann would credit the creation
of the *Wechsel* as a genre to a single poet in its prehistory, a
suggestion which—perhaps not coincidentally—is quite similar to
John Meier's proposal for the explanation of the German folk-
song.[16] It is doubtful whether Angermann's strict separation of the
Wechsel either from the dialogue or from the French and Provençal
woman's song is entirely justified. Theodore Frings expresses quite a
different view, which will raise the question whether Angermann has
done justice to the remarkable similarity among examples of the
woman's song from various literary traditions. However
Angermann did deal in commendable fashion with certain issues
whose importance seems later not to have been appreciated. I would
emphasize in particular three points made by Angermann which I
consider especially important.

First, he breaks emphatically with the tradition which sees in
the poems of the *Minnesang* a record of, or at least a reference to,
actual events and situations in the lives of the poets.[17] He insists that
the situations depicted in the *Wechsel* are completely fictional and
have nothing to do with actual relationships. Second, Angermann
stresses, just as emphatically, the importance of seeing the *Wechsel*
as a poetic creation composed to be performed before an audience.
With this proposal he anticipates by several decades an approach to
the interpretation of medieval German poetry which was to become
the occasion for a lively discussion among students of the *Minnesang*.[18] The third point which I want to underscore is his suggestion
that the *Wechsel* may have been performed with the participation of
more than one performer as a kind of theatrical presentation with
assigned roles. Angermann makes this proposal in connection with
historical records of participation of women both as poets and as
performers in the age in which the *Wechsel* is known to have
thrived.[19] Here Angermann addresses himself to aspects of the
woman's song which have remained unexplained and for the most
part unnoticed until the present day—features which have to do
with the importance, not to say dominance, of dialogue in the
woman's song.

We next turn our attention to Carl von Kraus, whose studies of
Reinmar der Alte, Walther von der Vogelweide, and the *Minnesang*
in general have influenced and often determined a good deal of what
has been said and written about the *Minnesang* down to the present.
And yet, perhaps characteristically, the one discussion which von
Kraus devoted to the woman's song, a lecture from the year 1930, is
possibly the least influential of all his writings. Unfortunately, it
shares some important weakness with his better known writings.
First, the lecture, like his other works, contains glaring errors. Possibly excusable is von Kraus' assertion that there is no direct address

from one character to another in the *Wechsel*, an assertion made to support the statement that this genre cannot be based on actual conversations.[20] This is a case of a poor statement made in a good cause, namely the refutation of biographical interpretation of the *Wechsel*. The erroneousness of the statement stems from the tendency to separate the *Wechsel* too strictly from similar genres often cultivated by the same poet, a tendency which we also noted in Angermann. The fact is that, as we shall see, some poems which fit the description of *Wechsel* do contain cases in which one figure in the fiction addresses another directly. Nevertheless, we must take into account that von Kraus makes the assertion in keeping with a tradition of long standing and in reference to a question (distinction between genres) which is not without complications.

Much less excusable, indeed bewildering, is a statement which von Kraus makes in an apparent attempt to confine the importance of the German *Frauenlied* to the early period of medieval German poetry. To be contrasted with these earlier years is the age of the important poets—mentioned by name are "Reinmar und Morungen" —concerning whom von Kraus makes two false and absurd claims. First he insists that the woman's song occurs rarely in the works of these "bedeutenden Dichtern." Particularly inexcusable in the case of this claim is von Kraus' failure to note that the opus of Reinmar, the very poet to whom the same von Kraus had dedicated a three-part study a decade before, contains more lines of woman's song than that of any other medieval German poet.[21] Burdach, whom von Kraus quotes repeatedly and profusely, had said as much.[22] But von Kraus continues just as wrongly by stating that the woman in the *Frauenlied* of the "bedeutenden Dichtern" is never allowed to declare her love unilaterally; that her declarations of affection for the beloved man are always accompanied by his for her.[23] This false statement is made in the face of comparatively abundant evidence to the contrary, some of which we shall investigate below.

That such an error could be made, and indeed insistently, is surely related to other claims which von Kraus makes in this discussion as well as others—claims which he apparently held to be important enough to justify challenging the evidence to the contrary. For one thing, he adheres to the idea that the *Minnesang*, including the woman's song, was composed to teach the society of that age exemplary feeling.[24] Poems which he could not reconcile with this idea, he tended to relegate to a period of youthful wildness which is supposed to have taken place before the poet came into his own as a teacher of model emotions. This conjecture, which originated with Erich Schmidt, is incorporated in von Kraus' Reinmar study of 1919.[25] What von Kraus could not use in support of his own theories, he tended either to explain away or ignore. As a result, the step from Angermann to von Kraus, particularly in reference to the woman's song, can, on balance, only be characterized as a giant step backwards.

Four years after the publication of von Kraus' lecture appeared a dissertation devoted to the woman's monologue by Heinz Fischer. It is a discussion which begins very strongly only to encounter difficulties which will not be unfamiliar. In contrast to von Kraus, Fischer does not attempt to convince us that the woman's song becomes less well represented and less important as one progresses from the age of Der von Kürenberg (c. 1160) to the age of von Kraus' "bedeutenden Dichtern." On the contrary, Fischer points out emphatically that the medieval German woman's song not only accompanies the development of the *Minnesang* in its entirety—this may be a little overstated—but also provides a unique insight into the *Minnesang* itself.[26] Fischer also alleges as an important aspect of the woman's songs their supposedly greater age, an assertion which we shall encounter again from Theodor Frings though its correctness is not entirely certain.[27] Downright inaccurate are Fischer's attempts to show that there is a development in the thematic material of the woman's song from the earliest women's laments about unrequited love to the great women's monologues of the high courtly age.[28] Fischer would have us believe that the woman's song underwent major changes in the course of this alleged development, and that this development was unified and continuous. We shall see below that, while the woman's song does indeed take on different forms at different times, one cannot speak of a consistency in progression, nor is the change always in the direction of "courtliness" as Fischer assumes.[29]

The next study devoted to the woman's song is that of Alfred Götze. Götze addresses himself to the question of whether the poets of the *Minnesang* granted the same level of artistic excellence to the woman's song as to their other poems; after all, he continues, as well-bred and as sensible as the women were, they clearly could not attain to the artistic heights of the poet in question, as daily experience must have shown him.[30] I find it difficult to comment comfortably on Götze's article. Whether his assertion that the woman's song is more simple than the man's will hold for the texts of the *Minnesang* as a whole is difficult to say, especially since simplicity is not always easy to measure. He is clearly correct in some degree. And whether the poets of the *Minnesang* would have agreed with him about the inferior artistic capabilities of the women of their society is also a statement that I cannot weigh. One year after the appearance of Götze's article, Herbert Grundmann published a study which gives a much more flattering picture of the literary capabilities of the German-speaking women of that age.[31] And while

Grundmann offers a wealth of material to substantiate his claims, Götze offers practically none that can serve as a basis for comparison.

Erika Mergell's dissertation on the language of the woman in the *Minnesang*, which appeared two years after Götze's article, may well be a case of less being more. Her thesis is anything but spectacular. Her main point is that in the *Minnesang* the language of the woman contrasts with that of the man in that the former is concrete, direct, open, simple, and passionate.[32] Because of these features, the speech of the woman, particularly in the early *Minnesang*, has the quality of a confession.[33] In presenting her observations, she limits herself on the whole to description, though she does not distort. Furthermore, her ideas seem to anticipate in some ways those of Elisabeth Lea and Meg Bogin.[34] If I read them correctly, all three seem to imply that the stated characteristics make the language of the woman in some way more basic, more down-to-earth, more real, and, it seems, more honest than that of the man who, by contrast, tends to be more non-commital and not without dissimilation. I think that such a view is clearly supported by the texts which we shall discuss below. However, I cannot help but wonder if either Mergell or Lea does justice to the fact that the medieval German woman's song (in which, I submit in their support, the stated contrast is by and large clearly maintained) was composed, as far as we know, exclusively by men. I also wonder if Bogin would not have commented differently had she given attention to the similarities between the German woman's song and the Provençal compositions of female poets. Poems featuring women and composed in a direct, passionate, and bold language by male authors are, after all, also preserved in the poetry of China, India, and the Omaha tribe of North America.[35] It is thus not a simple matter to draw conclusions which bear on knowledge about the sexes from the texts of the woman's song, lest one risk attributing to sexual make-up what may actually be due to tradition.

Theodor Frings, whose work is frequently noted in the essays in this volume, has come to be recognized as something of a founding father of modern study of woman's song. I have already noted that it is Frings who has directed our attention to the woman's song as an international phenomenon.[36] It is also Frings who is best known for having proposed that the woman's song preceded that of the man in the history of poetry.[37] Unfortunately, Frings takes his cue from Carl von Kraus, particularly in assuming a progressive development in the history of the medieval German woman's song from open confession of female enamorment to studied reserve toward a male suitor.[38] In addition, he has expanded this idea in such a way as to address the question of the origins of medieval love poetry not only in German-speaking areas, but also in Provence. According to Frings, the woman's song originates in folk poetry, an old proposal which, interestingly enough, had been expressly rejected by Carl von Kraus in the study discussed above.[39] This is all the more interesting since it is quite clear that Frings was very familiar with von Kraus' lecture, which made a substantial impression on him and may have provided the germ of Frings' own interest in the woman's song.[40] Frings' implicit disagreement with von Kraus on the basic issue of the origins of the woman's song may have been occasioned by the appearance in the same year as von Kraus's article of the epoch-making study by André Jolles entitled *Einfache Formen* ("simple forms").[41] The term "einfache Formen" or variations of it occur repeatedly in the works of Frings.[42] From the woman's song, itself derived from the folksong, is derived in turn, according to Frings, the man's song of courtly love, a development which Frings, very much in keeping with the proposals of von Kraus and Fischer, interprets in connection with cultural developments in the society of that age. With the advance of refinement in courtly society, the woman's song is supposed to have given way increasingly to the poems of courtly love featuring the devoted man.[43] Thus Frings also fails to come to grips with the fact that the songs of man and woman coexist side by side in the works of the same poets and continue to do so in the works of those who, for Frings as well as for earlier scholars, represent a new age in courtly refinement.

The only remaining study known to me which is devoted explicitly to the medieval German woman's song—except for discussions of individual authors[44]—is the dissertation of Gerhard Pomassl from 1958. This study treats various ways in which women portrayed in the *Minnesang* react to amorous love as a phenomenon. According to their various attitudes, the women who make their appearance in the *Minnesang* are divided by Pomassl into six main categories which are assigned the following labels: the lustful woman ("Die Begehrliche"), the loving woman ("Die Liebende"), the educator ("Die Erzieherin"), the plaintive woman ("Die Klagende"), the fearful woman ("Die Furchtsame"), and the refusing woman ("Die Ablehnende").[45] In most cases these have sub-categories totalling over twenty. As one can see, the labels are not without moralistic overtones and in some cases border on the condemnatory. Pomassl's study has the distinct aura of a specimens gallery. His scholarly purpose is apparently to show how studies on the *Minnesang* have credited women of the society of that age with a concern for the courtly love establishment which they did not have, and that the German *Minnesang* was basically a man's affair.[46] We shall see that Pomassl is possibly right in the first instance—at least as far as the poetry is concerned—and seems clearly to be right in the second. Thus one can only regret that Pomassl, like others already mentioned, did not give more consideration to the important fact of apparent male authorship of the woman's song in medieval German poetry. This fact has a definite bearing on how one is to apply Pomassl's categories and may even render them useless.

The relationship of the woman's song to reality, personal or social, remains problematic. What is clear and will become clearer in the present discussion is that the poems of this genre were composed for artistic presentation before an audience. It is to the credit of Angermann to have seen this fact and recognized its importance more clearly than any other critic discussed above, and it is regrettable that Angermann's study did not have a greater impact on the scholarly tradition in its development since his time.

II. The Medieval German Woman's Song: Poems and Poets

The following pages contain a survey of poems in medieval German literature which present the woman as a speaking character.[47] Since the authors of these poems, so far as they are identifiable, are among the best known poets of medieval German literature, the main manuscripts and the standard text editions of the *Minnesang* are also the main sources for texts of the woman's song, but the survey will begin with poems which are preserved anonymously and usually thought to be among the oldest which have been transmitted. The contents of each poem will be briefly summarized, and a note will be supplied indicating recommended English translations. Summaries of stanzas which feature a male speaker will be supplied only in those cases where there seem to be clear relationships between those stanzas and accompanying woman's songs (e.g., in the *Wechsel*). Following the summaries, an attempt will be made to characterize the woman's song as written by medieval German poets up to, and including, Walther von der Vogelweide, excepting only those written by Hartmann von Aue which are treated elsewhere in this volume.

Anonymous Poems[48]

1. "Dû bist mîn" (1 stanza): The speaker informs her beloved that he is enclosed in her heart and that the key to it has been lost (MFMT, p. 21; MF 3, 1).[49]

2. "Uvere div werlt alle min" (1 stanza, belonging apparently to a *Wechsel*): In the accompanying stanza, a speaker of indeterminate sex praises secret love ("tougen minne"). The woman of

our stanza claims that she would gladly exchange wealth and power for an opportunity to lie beside the king of England (CB 145a, p. 247; MFMT, p. 21; MF 3, 7).[50]

3. "Gruonet der walt allenthalben" (1 Latin plus 1 German stanza with a mixed Latin and German refrain): While viewing the greening of the forest, the speaker grows concerned about her absent beloved (CB 149, p. 253; MFMT, p. 20).[51]

4. "Eine wunnechliche stat" (1 stanza): The speaker recalls a love-bed of flowers and grass prepared in expectation of her arrival (CB 163a, p. 275).[52]

5. "Chume, chume, geselle min" (2 stanzas): An impatient call goes out to the beloved friend ("geselle") to come and heal the waiting speaker with a kiss (CB 174a, p. 292).

6. "Ich wil truren varen lan" (2 stanzas with refrain): An invitation to a proud man ("stolzer man") to accompany the speaker to the heath and pick flowers to make a wreath for him (CB 180a, p. 303).[53]

7. "Ich was ein chint so wolgetan" (10 stanzas, mixed German and Latin): A seduction by force is recounted by the victim (CB 185, p. 310).[54]

8. "Mich dunket niht sô guotes" (1 stanza): A man whose love is compared to a rose is awaited midst surroundings of estival beauty not fully enjoyed in his absence (MFMT, p. 22; MF 3, 17).[55]

9. "Diu linde ist an dem ende" (1 stanza): An apparently two-fold complaint about antipathy ("mich vehet") on the part of the beloved plus alienation of his affection on the part of unstable ("unstaeter") women (MFMT, p. 22; MF 4, 1).[56]

10. "Mir hât ein ritter" (1 stanza): Determination to reward a knight for service rendered according to the speaker's wishes is coupled with joyous expectation of the fulfillment of her intent (MFMT, p. 22; MF 6, 5).[57]

Of the above poems, only one can be dated with any certainty, and that only approximately. The first selection, "Dû bist mîn," is transmitted in the Tegernsee Manuscript Clm 19411 which, according to Helmut Plechl, was collected and written between 1178 and 1186.[58] It is conceivable that the ten remaining selections, or at least some of them, may date from the same period or even earlier, but it is impossible to establish this with certainty since they are preserved only in manuscripts of a later time. The Benediktbeuren Manuscript (*Carmina burana*), from which selections 2-7 are taken, is dated by Bernard Bischoff around the year 1230.[59] The remaining selections, 8-10, are recorded earliest in the smaller Heidelberg Manuscript A (*Die kleine Heidelberger Liederhandschrift*) which Walter Blank dates "etwa um 1275."[60] In both cases the *terminus ante quem* post-dates most of the poets whose works are to be discussed in the present study.

Among the poets to be treated below who are known to us by name, five are dated by de Boor between the years 1150 and 1175—Der von Kürenberg, Meinloh von Sevelingen, Der Burggraf von Regensburg, Der Burggraf von Rietensburg, and Dietmar von Eist.[61] If this dating is correct—and we shall find much that supports it—then the activity of all five of these poets precedes the composition of "Dû bist mîn," and the possibility can thus not be excluded that this poem, which is attested earlier than any of the other anonymous German *Frauenlieder*, may have been composed at a later date than some of the *Frauenlieder* of poets known to us by name. Another instructive example of the difficulty of dating these poems is a woman's song preserved in the *Carmina burana* (CB 113a, p. 186) which is not listed above since it turns out to be a variant of a poem by Dietmar von Eist (item 1 below). If one assumes that Dietmar is the composer of the original version, then we have a second possible case of an anonymous poem making its appearance later than one identified with an author.

The point is that while anonymity may be suggestive of greater age, it is not proof.[62] It would be tempting to view the anonymous poems as examples of a tradition which poets whom we shall presently encounter came to know and drew upon for their own (sometimes individualistic) artistic purposes. We shall find that such a view is probably not wholly inaccurate but useful only so long as one does not trust it without discretion. The anonymous poems could in some cases also be versions of poems composed either by contemporaries of the five poets named above, or conceivably by one or more of these poets themselves.

Der von Kürenberg[63]

1. "Vil lieben vriunt" (1 stanza in a *Wechsel* of 2 stanzas): Decrying betrayal among friends, the speaker asks a third party (presumably) to admonish her beloved to remember her and remain true (MFMT I, 1; MF 7, 1).[64]

2. "Leit machet sorge (1 stanza): Complaint of a woman who has been deprived by spies (*merker*) of a handsome knight (MFMT II, 1; MF 7, 18).[65]

3. "Ich stuont mir nehtint spâte" (1 stanza in a *Wechsel* of 2 stan-
    zas): A knight's song in the "wîse" (melody?) of Kürenberg has
    aroused the yen of a woman listening from a turret (MFMT II,
    2; MF 8, 1). A defiant negative response to the woman's wooing
    is recorded in MFMT II, 10 (MF 9, 29).[66]

4. "Jô stuont ich nehtint spâte" (dialogue of 1 stanza): Nocturnal
    shyness on the part of a man provokes his lover's ire (MFMT II,
    3; MF 8, 9).[67]

5. "Swenne ich stân aleine" (1 stanza): Thoughts of a noble knight
    cause wistful blushes (MFMT II, 4; MF 8, 17).[68]

6. "Ich zôch mir einen valken" (2 stanzas): The escape of a falcon,
    seen again sometime later, provokes a longing for reunion
    (MFMT II, 6 and 7; MF 8, 33 and 9, 5).[69]

7. "Ez gât mir vonme herzen" (1 stanza): A sad parting caused by
    liars ("lügenaere") provokes grief and a wish for reunion
    (MFMT II, 8; MF 9, 13).[70]

There is general agreement that the poet known only by the
name Der von Kürenberg (i.e., the one from Kürenberg) was probably an Austrian.[71] This assumption is supported by the similarity
between his poetry and that of other poets discussed below whom
we can also link with Austria. The Austrian Kürenbergs were
ministeriales of the Bavarian counts of Burghausen who were
related by marriage to the Babenberg family to which belonged the
margraves and (after 1156) the dukes of Austria.[72] The poets Der
Burggraf von Regensburg and Der Burggraf von Rietenburg also
belonged to a family which was related to the Babenburgs by
marriage (see below). According to Anton Wallner, the Kürenbergs
of Austria owned two castles about which we know, namely "bei
Melk (Purchard, Magins, Otto 1132-66) und bei Linz (Konrad,
Walther 1140-61)."[73] These locations will be of significance for us
later in reference to Reinmar der Alte.
    The two metrical forms used by Der von Kürenberg vary only
slightly from each other and are essentially the same as that of the
Nibelungenlied.[74] This heroic epic by an unknown author was composed at the beginning of the thirteenth century in the same general
area as the residences of the Austrian Kürenbergs.[75] The Nibelungen-
stanza and the Kürenberg-stanza are both variations of the long line
(*Langzeile*) with caesura and end-rhyme, which was popular in German and Latin poetry of the twelfth century.[76] Several of the
anonymous poems above also use variations of this long line, specifically selections 8, 9 and 10 (all from the secular manuscript A) and
4 (from the CB). Also characteristic of the Kürenberg and

Nibelungen-stanza is the so-called *Schlussbeschwerung*, the inser-
tion of an additional metrical foot in the last half of the concluding
long line of the stanza.[77] This feature appears in the anonymous
item no. 8 above, while in 9 the fuller half-line occurs in the second
and fifth as well as in the closing half-line.

Of the fifteen stanzas of poetry which Manuscript C attributes
to Kürenberg, seven and possibly an eighth—I did not list MFMT
II, 5; MF 8, 25 because the sex of the speaker is not entirely certain—
are woman's songs. There is considerable similarity in content as
well as form between the anonymous woman's song and that of
Kürenberg. In both cases, attention is focused on the separation of
the woman from her beloved. An exception is the anonymous item
7, as my summary indicates. This poem is apparently also an exception in a wider sense, for I know of no other poem in medieval
German literature which portrays the use of force in seduction,
although it is depicted a few times in the epic. Indeed, in the wom-
am's song it is generally the woman herself who contemplates or
takes the initiative in courtship, as here in both the anonymous
poems and those of Kürenberg. Common to both cases is also the
plaintive tone of the poems, a tone which is often tinged with a note
of desperation. On the other hand, such themes as jealousy of competitors and defiance of society, which we hear in the Kürenberg
selections 2 and 7, and which we shall hear often in poems still to be
discussed, are to be found among the anonymous poems only in
those which are preserved in lay manuscripts, specifically in items 9
and 10.[78]

One feature which is typical of Kürenberg's poetry is not apparent in any of the anonymous poems. Kürenberg consistently depicts
man and woman in confrontation with one another. The confrontation is sometimes indirect, as it is in selection 1 where the woman
addresses her beloved through a third party. In the accompanying
stanza, the man speaks to the woman directly, at least according to
the wording of the text. In the dialogue-poem no. 4, the confrontation produces a clash of some severity, or perhaps more correctly,
an attack on the part of the woman. In no. 3, a collision is also
indicated, although the confrontation is indirect, and a collision
itself is avoided only by the man's decision—this time the man
addresses a third party—to flee the country rather than give in to the
woman's wishes. Furthermore, even among the poems in Kürenberg'
opus which are not *Frauenlieder*, there are interesting instances of
eye-to-eye contact between man and woman, specifically in MFMT
II, 9 (MF 9, 21)[79] and MFMT II, 11 (MF 10, 1).[80] Also, in item 5 by
Kürenberg, the words of the woman are directed to a "ritter edele,"
a fact which deserves much more attention than it has received.[81]

In sum, Kürenberg's poetry involves to a considerable degree situations in which man and woman speak to each other face to face. These situations have a dramatic character which we shall find to be quite common in the poetic tradition of early Austria to which Kürenberg belonged.

Meinloh von Sevelingen[82]

1. "Sô wê den merkaeren" (1 stanza): Invective against spies is mingled with defiant affirmation of continued devotion to the man whom the speaker courts to their dislike, but also with assurances that she has not lain with the man in question (MFMT I, 7; MF 13, 14).[83]

2. "Mir erwelten mîniu ougen" (1 stanza): Complaints that other women envy the speaker because of her success (through service!) with an attractive (*kindeschen*) man give way to a revelation that she has taken him from another less fortunate (MFMT I, 8; MF 13, 27).[84]

3. "Ich hân vernomen ein maere" (1 stanza from a *Wechsel* of 2 stanzas): Following a "dull lecture on the theory of love"[85]— and especially on keeping it a secret—by the man, we hear from the woman words of joy at the news of her handsome (again *kindeschen*) man's arrival and at the prospect of his nearness and his service (MFMT II, 2; MF 14, 26).[86]

Meinloh von Sevelingen belonged to a family whose members served as vassals (*Truchsessen*) of the counts of Dillingen.[87] Sevelingen (now Söflingen) is a surburb of Ulm, hence located near the Swabian stretch of the Danube River. The only member of the poet's family who is attested under the name Meinloh makes his appearance in 1240, which is, of course, rather late to be reconciled with the work under discussion. Thus one must assume either that Meinloh reached great age or that the poet was an ancestor of the historically attested Meinloh.

Anton Wallner and J. W. Thomas date the poetry of Meinloh no later than about 1170, Pörnbacher about 1180.[88] The latter also offers an explanation for the similarity between Meinloh's works and those of the other poets of this age, all of whom seem to have lived a good distance to the north and east of Meinloh's home. It seems that members of the Dillingen family who come into question as liege lords of Meinloh and his relatives during the years when, according to the above datings, we assume the poet to have been active, had personal connections through marriage and otherwise with families farther east, in addition to the associations necessitated by regional and imperial affairs.[89]

The recorded metrical structures—three in number—used by Meinloh are based, like those of Kürenburg, on the long line with caesura and end-rhyme. The stanzas of Meinloh are longer than those of Kürenberg, containing respectively seven, six, and nine lines per stanza. In this they are similar to the anonymous poem number 8 above. Dronke notes in particular the similarity between this anonymous poem and our selection 2 by Meinloh.[90]

The selections by Meinloh belong to a total of twelve stanzas attributed to him. There are a few poems among them in which the sex of the speaker cannot be determined. Thematically, Meinloh's poems are, as a whole, quite different from those of Kürenberg. The theme of secrecy and deception in courtship, which Kürenberg touches on only once and with marked indirectness (MFMT II, 11; MF 10, 1),[91] receives prominent treatment in the poems of Meinloh, interestingly, only in the words of a male figure (MFMT I, 3; I, 4; I, 9 and II, 1 = MF 12, 1; 12, 14; 14, 1 and 14, 14).[92] In addition, the woman's song figures much less prominently in the opus of Meinloh than in Kürenberg's where it amounted to over half the total, and the man in Meinloh's poetry is portrayed quite differently from his counterpart in Kürenberg's works.

By contrast, the woman is portrayed much the same way by both poets. The harsh words aimed at the social environment which were heard in the verses of Kürenberg are present again in poems by Meinloh, and in the case of the latter they are considerably more explicit. Themes not treated by Kürenberg but introduced by Meinloh are jealousy (no. 2) and concern for one's reputation (no. 1).

Meinloh is usually depicted as a transitional figure between the age of Kürenberg and an age of new refinement in courtly attitudes.[93]

Der Burggraf von Regensburg[94]

1. MFMT I, 1; MF 16, 1:[95]
    I am subject to a good knight in all constancy.
    How sweet is it to my heart when I have him in my embrace!
    He who by his many virtues
    Has engratiated himself to the whole world can well afford
        to be of good cheer.

2. MFMT I, 2; MF 16, 8:
    They simply cannot take from me the one whom I have received
    Into my heart in all constancy, who affords me much delight.
    And even if they all lay dead of vexation,
        Yet I will always be fond of him. They are defeated without
        any trouble.

62   *Vox Feminae*

3.   MFMT II, 2; MF 16, 23:
     Now they are ordering me to avoid a certain knight:
         I cannot.
     When I think of how I lay so sweetly
     And secretly in his arms, I ache with longing.
     Parting from him is always harsh, my heart knows it
         all too well.

The poet known by the name Der Burggraf von Regensburg
belonged to a family which held the office of burgrave in that city
from 1045 to 1185.[96] The poet known as Der Burggraf von
Rietensburg (see below) belonged to the same family. Given the
scarcity of the information at our disposal, it is impossible to prove
incontestably that the two names do not belong to one and the same
person. However, it has come to be assumed generally that there are
indeed two poets involved, a consensus which, I think, will be borne
out by the nature of the poetry preserved under the two names. I
shall thus treat them as two poets, while reserving judgement on de
Boor's (cautious) attempt to identify the family members behind the
two names.[97]

The two metrical forms used by Regensburg are similar to
those employed by Kürenberg, being in all cases stanzas of four long
lines with caesura and end-rhyme.

In the first item the relationship between the speaker and her
knight is depicted in terms of subjection: the woman is in subjection
to the man. It is not clear whether this relationship is to be seen as a
reversal of the service-and-reward relationship which we know from
the poems of the courtly love tradition—but where the man is subject to his lady—or whether the metaphor refers to some other kind
of subjection (e.g., serfdom). The fact that the woman praises the
man for his many good virtues might suggest the influence of the
courtly love tradition. This suggestion seems to find support in the
second stanza where the woman speaks of her constancy in reference to her own devotion to the man. This also seems to be a
reversal of the courtly love relationship.[99] Nos. 2 and 3 take up the
theme of defiance of society now familiar to us from Kürenberg and
Meinloh. Selection 3, with its memories of a time of pleasure spent
with the beloved, calls to mind our anonymous item 4. It is not usual
to hear such revelations from a male figure.

Der Burggraf von Regensburg seems to have been capable of
considerable originality in his treatment of traditional themes. One
must also wonder if his unusual portrayal of the relationship between man and woman is only coincidentally a reversal of the traditional courtly love relationship, or if perchance Regensburg composed with that tradition in mind. It is unfortunate indeed that not

enough poetry by him is preserved for one to judge confidently his artistic intentions.

Der Burggraf von Rietenberg[100]

MFMT I, 1; MF 18, 1:
No one may rebuke me now
For wanting very much to see him.
This I shall try to do. [conjectured line]
What does it matter if I said in anger
That someone else is just as dear to me?
I will not give him up because of their envy;
They are all wasting their trouble,
He will never lose my favor.

The six metrical structures used by Rietenburg depart noticeably from those we have encountered up to this point. None of the seven stanzas attributed to him uses the long line employed by the preceding poets. In his single woman's stanza Rietenburg uses a structure of eight lines of which seven seem to have four metrical feet—the scansion is not lucid—and the eighth, five metrical feet. These lines rhyme alternately, but read very much like long lines with inner rhymes added at the ends of half-lines that would normally have no rhyme.

The theme of defiance of society dominates this one woman's stanza of Rietenburg almost completely. The fourth and fifth lines, the meaning of which is not entirely clear to me—my translation is as literal as I could make it—may introduce a different theme of antagonism between the woman and her friend, a theme which we shall encounter frequently below.

The translated stanza is part of a *Wechsel*. In the accompanying man's stanza (MFMT I, 2; MF 18, 9), we hear words very similar to those of the woman. The man also insists that he does not fear the threats of his enemies ("ir aller drô"), as long as his lady—presumably the speaker in our woman's stanza—wishes his happiness. However, he also asserts that he has earned her favor, a statement which is typical of the man in courtly love poetry but, as we have seen, not typical of the early *Minnesang* and certainly not of the early woman's song. The remaining stanzas of Rietenburg also use the language of courtly love in a manner suitable to that tradition. I thus subscribe to de Boor's suggestion that Rietenburg is a poet who has learned from the West.[101] However, I wonder if his relative, Der Burggraf von Regensburg, did not learn from the West also, but reacted differently to what he had learned.

Dietmar von Eist[102]

1. "Waz ist vür daz trûren guot" (1 stanza): Beset by sadness and watched all too closely, the speaker thinks longingly and constantly of a beloved man (MFMT I, 1; MF 32, 1).

2. "Genuoge jehent" (1 stanza): Two women, for whom constancy (*staete*) has not proved to be the help (*trost*) that it is reputed to be, express the wish to be free of love (MFMT II, 2; MF 32, 9).

3. "Nu sage dem ritter edele" (1 stanza in a group of 3): The speaker addresses a messenger with words of instruction and affection for her beloved but reserves her complaints about his absence for a personal meeting (MFMT II, 2; MF 32, 21).[103]

4. "Ez dunket mich vol tûsent jâr" (1 stanza—as part of a *Wechsel*?): The speaker thinks plaintively of a dear man who has not held her since the departure of the birds and flowers, which seems to her like a thousand years. (MFMT 11, 5; MF 34, 3).[104]

5. "Ez stuont ein vrouwe alleine" (1 stanza): After being introduced in an epic opening, the speaker contrasts her situation with that of a free-flying falcon. This leads to complaints about beautiful (!) women who envy her because of her choice of a friend (MFMT IV; MF 37, 4).[105]

6. "Sô wol dir, sumerwunne" (1 stanza): After an opening lament on the passing of summer and on the similar passing away of her happiness, a woman addresses her beloved and demands that he give up other women (MFMT V; MF 37, 18).[106]

7. "Wie tuot der besten einer sô" (1 stanza): The speaker is puzzled and hurt about the cool treatment of her by a man who deserves more wrath than she can maintain in his presence (MFMT VII, 2; MF 35, 24).

8. An example of *revocatio* which I translate as follows:[107]
   Whoever furthers my knowledge,
   Him will I serve if I can;
   And yet I will keep my distance from men,
   For I have a longing heart.
   It would be a great misfortune for me
   If I fell deeply in love with him.
   And it would be well for me to die
   If he did not let me enjoy it (MFMT VII, 3; MF 35, 32).

9. "Diu welt noch ir alten site" (1 stanza): The speaker complains that the world continues to mistreat her by demanding (and apparently seeing to it) that she stay away from the best friend in existence (MFMT VIII, 1; MF 36, 5).

10. "Ich muoz von rehten schulden" (1 stanza of 4 in this meter): A woman exults about a man who loves her secretly (*verholn*) and who rewards (*gelônen*) her great toil (*grôzer arbeit*) according to her wishes (MFMT XI, 2; MF 38, 5).

11. "Jâ hoere ich vil der tugende sagen" (1 stanza of three in this meter): The speaker praises an unforgettable knight of many virtues because of whom she must surrender (contact with?) the whole world (MFMT XII, 2; MF 39, 4).

12. "Slâfest du, vriedel ziere" (dialogue of 3 stanzas): Possibly a dawn song. Conversation at the parting of lovers.[108]

13. "Wir hân die winterlangen naht" (1 stanza of 3 in this meter): The speaker rejoices about a long winter night spent with a knight (MFMT XIV, 2; MF 40, 3).

14 "Ich solde zürnen" (1 stanza, same meter as the previous): Anger about the long absence of the beloved[109] (MFMT XIV, 3; MF 40, 11).

15 "Waz wizet mir der beste man" (1 stanza of 3 in this meter): The speaker indignantly refutes uncomplimentary words from a man from whom she also withdraws her favor (*hulde*). She admits that he lay with her—like a fool (*toerschen*), to be sure—but denies having become his lover (*sîn wîp*), which was thus apparently the offending claim (MFMT XV, 3; MF 40, 35).

A "Dominus" Dietmar von Eist, "vir illustris," is recorded in several historical documents of the Bavarian-Austrian area between the years 1143 and 1161.[110] Kurt Rathke, whose study of Dietmar deserves a new assessment, placed his death "um 1170."[111] This would make Dietmar about the same age as Der von Kürenberg and possibly a little older than the two burgraves and Meinloh von Sevelingen. However, some of his poems betray the influence of the poetry of courtly love. Because of this, scholars have been hesitant to credit the historical Dietmar with all of the poems preserved under that name, since it has been usually assumed that the influence of the courtly love tradition reached Austria later than the dates at which the historical Dietmar is recorded. De Boor assumes the hand of more than one poet at work in these poems.[112]

But there are two reasons, in particular, for questioning the necessity and validity of such an assumption. First of all, there is the matter of the uncertainty of dating. We must resign ourselves to rather generous approximations in the dating of individual poets, for we are not entirely certain when the ideas of the courtly love doctrine began to make themselves felt in the eastern part of the German language area. Anton E. Schönbach suggested quite some time ago, in specific reference to the poetry of early Austria, that it happened quite early,[113] and more recently critics have tended to agree.[114] If the earliest known poets of the German love lyric were familiar with the new ideas about *minne*, then there would be no difficulty in reconciling the presence of them in the work of Dietmar with the dates recorded for the historical person by that name. My second reservation has to do with the fact that the presence of two views of love, sometimes in apparent conflict with one another, is not confined to the work attributed to Dietmar von Eist. We have already noted in the poems of Der Burggraf von Rietenburg and Meinloh von Sevelingen a similar tendency to depict courtship very differently according to the sex of the speaker. The significance of this tendency cannot be underestimated for the later period of MHG verse. In short, I know of no convincing reason to challenge the attributions in the manuscripts, so far as Dietmar is concerned, that would not also apply to numerous other poets. To be sure, there is also no possibility of proving that the manuscripts are correct. But, here again, this could apply to numerous other poets, and particularly in reference to the woman's song. Thus, without necessarily considering the matter closed, I shall discuss the poems under the name Dietmar as the poems of one poet.

The fifteen selections listed above for Dietmar appear among a total of forty-one stanzas preserved under that name. The woman's songs of Dietmar continue the trend toward variety in metrical structure which we noted in the verses of Rietenburg, though Dietmar's corpus does include poems composed in the old long line (selections 1–5, 10, 11). Others are composed in rhyming couplets (selections 5 and 6)[115] which, as in the case of Rietenburg, read very much like developments out of the long line with rhyming of the first half-line.

It is often difficult to determine if a given woman's stanza in Dietmar's poetry is part of a *Wechsel* and, if so, to ascertain which or how many stanzas should be connected with the woman's stanza in an interpretation of the latter. Stanzas of the same metrical pattern occur with conspicuous frequency in groups of three. Involved in such a tri-strophic grouping are selections 1–3, 7, 8–11, and 13–15. The groupings occur in varying combinations; in a few cases, two of the three stanzas feature the words of a woman, specifically in items 1, 2, 7, 8, 13 and 14. Rathke sees this grouping in threes as a conscious innovation of Dietmar.[116]

A few of Dietmar's *Frauenlieder* are different in their conception from anything we have seen up to this point. First of all, selection 2 features two female speakers in the same stanza. This poem is an anticipation of the *Gespielinnen*-poem of Neidhart von Reuenthal who, incidentally, also spent a good part of his life in the

Danubian area of Lower Austria.[117] This connection is thus hardly coincidence. One particularly interesting poem by Dietmar (no. 6) depicts what I would call a half-dialogue: the words of the poem are addressed to a non-speaking character in the fiction who is clearly visible to the speaker. Examples of the same kind of composition are to be found in works of Der von Kürenberg not discussed in this study (MFMT II, 1 and 11 = MF 9, 21 and 10, 1) and in a poem by Reinmar der Alte—"Lieber bote" (no. 8)—to be discussed later.

The subject matter of Dietmar's woman's songs is basically the same as that of nearly all of the poems which we have encountered up to now. Here also we hear the woman complain of loneliness, betrayal, and desertion. Further, she berates those who threaten to hinder her amorous successes and in particular her competitors who vie for the affection of her knight. However, there are fresh details in Dietmar's work. One that is no longer entirely new, but unusual enough to single out again, is the statement in no. 10 about the man's reward for the woman's great toil ("grôzer arbeit") on his behalf (cf. the handling of this apparent reversal of the courtly love situation in Meinloh, no. 2, and Der Burggraf von Regensburg, no. 1). In item 15 by Dietmar as in Meinloh, no. 2, the speaker makes a revelation which we must surely assume to be unintentional. Meinloh's woman exposes herself as a victimizer instead of the victim which she had pictured herself to be at the beginning of the poem, while Dietmar's woman all but reveals the falsity of her denial of the man's claim that she has become his lover; for in order to believe her, the hearer must also believe that, to be sure—and this is the unfortunate revelation—the man did indeed lie beside her, but not with the results that he had asserted.

Otherwise, the cleverish revocatio-poem (no. 8), the scene of the parting and squabbling lovers (no. 12), and the psychologically quite interesting admissions of a woman (no. 7) that, to borrow a phrase from Brecht's *Mother Courage*, her anger is simply not long enough—such varied subject matter rounds out work of notable color and complexity.

Kaiser Heinrich[118]

1. "Ich hân den lîp gewendet" (1 stanza from a *Wechsel* of 2): The speaker exults over her good knight and rails against nagging competitors (MFMT I, 2; MF 4, 26).

2. "Rîtest dû nu hinnen" (1 stanza, apparently belonging to a *Wechsel*): Parting from the dearest man a woman ever had causes distress and provokes a plea for a hasty return, lest she die (MFMT II, 1; MF 4, 35).

The name "Kaiser Heinrich" can only be taken to refer to the Emperor Henry VI, son of Frederick Barbarossa, who lived from 1165 to 1197. In one of the poems of this Kaiser Heinrich (MFMT III, 2; MF 5, 23), the poet plays on the theme of imperial rule, maintaining that the realms and lands ("diu rîche und diu lant") are subject to him whenever he is with his beloved ("der minneclîchen").

De Boor takes the words of this poem as an indication that the poet is indeed Emperor Henry VI, here making use of his position for creative purposes.[119] Wapnewski is skeptical and reserves judgment on the question of the poet's identity while amassing a good deal of evidence on the traditional use of imperial rule as a topos in love poetry, including its use in our anonymous item 2.[120] More recently, Eugen Thurnher has made a strong case in favor of de Boor. Thurnher points out, first of all, that the misgivings about attributing the poems under the name Kaiser Heinrich to the historical Emperor Henry stem basically from assumptions that the statements of the poems should somehow reflect the historical circumstances of the poet, which would, in this case produce an incongruity.[121] This is indeed, in part, the case with Wapnewski who betrays considerable consternation about certain aspects of the poetry which seem to him scarcely suitable (and believable) for the historical emperor.[122] However, Thurnher continues by pointing out that, contrary to the beliefs of earlier scholarship—to which I referred above—the *Minnesang* does not contain revelations about the personal experiences of a given poet, but rather presents fictional creations for presentation to a courtly audience.[123]

Thurnher points our further, in support of the attribution of Kaiser Heinrich's poems to Emperor Henry VI, one circumstance which is of no little pertinence to our study. The poem by Kaiser Heinrich, the so-called *Kaiserlied*, in which the poet refers to himself as emperor, is composed in a dactyllic meter which, it is generally agreed, must be of western (Romance) origin. The remaining poems attributed to Kaiser Heinrich are the two *Wechsel* to which our selections belong which are composed in the long line with caesura and end-rhyme now familiar to us. Thurnher explains this mixture quite plausibly in terms of the age in which we would assume the historical Emperor Henry to have been active. Henry VI married Constance of Sicily in the year 1186, which Thurnher thus proposes as the *terminus ante quem* of Kaiser Heinrich's poems.[124] The reasoning here is not flawless, since we know that after marriage some medieval German poets composed, or continued to compose, love songs which were not dedicated to the spouse, Ulrich von Liechtenstein being a particularly flamboyant case in point. Nevertheless, Thurnher's proposal does conform in other respects to much that we have already seen. 1186 is one year after the death of the last of the burgraves of Regensburg. The poetry of one member of this family, namely Der Burggraf von Regensburg is, as we saw, composed in the long line; that of the other, Rietenburg, employs a variety of meters which may in part go back to the long line, but which otherwise—as also in the content—betrays obvious influence from Romance poetic traditions. One member of Rietenburg's family, namely Henry IV—possibly the poet Rietenburg himself—has been located in the company of the emperor-to-be Henry VI in Italy during the year 1184.[125] There is thus the distinct possibility of a direct connection. In any case, the dating confirms resoundingly Thurnher's depiction of Kaiser Heinrich as a poet active in a period of transition.

Kaiser Heinrich portrays the woman in terms now more than familiar to us. There may even be verbal reminiscences of poems discussed above. The expression "Rîtest dû nu hinnen" which opens the second selection by Kaiser Heinrich is strikingly similar to the phrase "du rîtest hinnen" from the third stanza of no. 12 by Dietmar, while the words "daz nîdent ander vrouwen" in Kaiser Heinrich's no. 1 occur verbatim in our no. 2 by Meinloh. There are other less exact echoes of the older *Minnesang* in the stanzas of Kaiser Heinrich which shed an interesting light on his relationship with the Danubian tradition. There are also a number of phrases in this corpus which call to mind lines from the poetry of Rietenburg. The man in Rietenburg's poems characterizes his devotion to his lady in such terms as *gedinge* ("hope"), *staeten dienest* ("faithful service") and *swaere* ("despondence"); similar terms used by the male figure in Kaiser Heinrich's poetry are *staetez herze* ("faithful heart"), *senden kumber* ("pining") and *klage* ("lament"). Since it is more than probable that Kaiser Heinrich and Rietenburg travelled in the same circles, these similarities should surely not surprise us.

Kaiser Heinrich also depicts the *minne*-relationship differently according to whether the speaker in a given stanza is male or female. Wapnewski sees in this a discrepancy which causes him to doubt the unity of the work transmitted under Kaiser Heinrich's name.[126] However, we have already seen that this divergence in the view of courtship between male and female speakers belongs to the poetic tradition Kaiser Heinrich used with remarkable faithfulness.

Friedrich von Hausen[127]

1. "Sie waenent hüeten mîn" (1 stanza from a *Wechsel* of 2): The speaker warns that her guardians will turn the Rhine into the Po before she gives up the man who has served her (MFMT IX, 2; MF 49, 4).[128]

2. "Wol ir, si ist ein saelic wîp."

Version a (3 stanzas): Torn between the desire to satisfy the wishes of a wonderful (*saelic*) man and the fear of consequences, the speaker laments her plight (MFMT XVIIa; MF 54, 1).

Version b (5 stanzas): Torn between the desire to satisfy the wishes of her "saelic man" and the fear of repercussions, the speaker decides to risk all to reward him (MFMT XVIIb; MF 54, 1).[129]

Friedrich von Hausen was a prominent man who was active as soldier and administrator in the service of Frederick Barbarossa in whose army he lost his life on the Third Crusade on May 6, 1190.[130] Of the fifty-eight stanzas of poetry (my count) preserved under Hausen's name, only four or six stanzas, depending on the version of selection 2, feature a woman as speaker. Except for these verses of woman's song, Hausen's poetry is typical of poetry in the courtly love tradition.[131]

The influence of this tradition can be perceived in at least one of the above selections. The first seems not to be affected by the new ideal of refinement. To be sure, we do hear the woman praise her friend for having served her, but this is not a conclusive sign of the new love ideal, since both Meinloh (no. 3) and Dietmar (no. 11) have the woman speak of a suitor's service to her. Otherwise, Hausen's heroine in selection 1 is typical of what we have encountered in the older woman's song.

In selection 2, however, we hear attitudes and tones which are new to our study. For one thing, the relationship between the womman and society has changed noticeably. Before now, we have heard, by and large, only vituperation of society; here, we hear concern for its demands and fear of its displeasure. The relationship between woman and man has also changed. The woman's love for him is expressed in words of perplexity and misgiving rather than defiance and determination. Indeed, the woman of the a-version of selection 2, preserved in the fourteenth-century manuscript C, leaves us at the end of the poem with the distinct impression that she has succumbed to social pressures. For the first time, we hear of surveillance (*hüeten*) as something positive and indeed as something which the woman imposes upon herself (MFMT XVIIa, 3, 8 = MF 54, 26). In the b-version, preserved in the fifteenth-century manuscript F,[132] this mention of self-imposed *hüeten* occurs earlier in the song (MFMT XVIIb, 2, 8) and turns out to be only a temporary resolve.

Curiously, Carl von Kraus considered selection 1 to be an authentic poem by Hausen while condemning the much more "courtly" selection 2 as "unecht."[133] Given the recent criticism which the views of von Kraus have encountered, it would seem that this poem by Hausen, the first stanza of which is attributed to him in three manuscripts, deserves a new assessment.[134]

Heinrich von Veldeke[135]

1. "Ich bin vrô" (a-version in 5 stanzas) or "Mir hete wîlent" (b-version in 3 stanzas); The speaker expresses her anger and disappointment concerning a man whom she believed courtly but whose demands proved him to be boorish (MFMT IIa and IIb; MF 57, 10).[136]

2. "Durch sînen willen" (1 stanza from a *Wechsel* of 2): The speaker is willing to do only one thing (not clearly indicated) and nothing more for her suitor because of her concern for its effects on other beautiful women who have undergone such suffering (MFMT XXX; MF 67, 17).

Heinrich von Veldeke was a native of the Maastricht area of the Netherlands. He was active as a poet during the last quarter of the twelfth century and took part in the festivities at Mainz in 1184 which accompanied the knighting of the aforementioned Henry VI, son of Frederick Barbarossa.[137] The selections listed above are two of thirty-three lyrics attributed to Veldeke in MFMT. One additional woman's song of a rather different nature is considered to be a "Pseudo-Veldeke" and is printed on page 149 of MFMT.

As might be expected of a poet so close geographically to the Romance countries, Veldeke's poetry, like that of Hausen, is very much under the influence of the courtly love tradition, in form and in content. Unlike Hausen, however, Veldeke portrays the woman in a manner which departs drastically from the older woman's song and conforms closely to the new ideals. The woman in Hausen's poem (no. 2 above) was torn between the desire to fulfill the wishes of her suitor and the pressures of social decorum. Her counterpart in Veldeke's poems has made the view of a refined society her own. She is determined to take no risks on behalf of her suitor and is incensed that he should dare expect of her any such consideration. She berates him harshly and repeatedly for even mentioning the idea of actions which could jeopardize her reputation. We seem to have come full circle. The alliance between lovers against society has become an alliance between woman and society against the man.[138] We shall see, however, that the future—in any case, the immediate future—did not belong to Veldeke's approach to the woman's song.

Albrecht von Johansdorf[139]

1. "Wie sich minne hebt" (3 stanzas from a *Wechsel* totalling 4):

The woman ponders the nature of *minne*, in particular its gen-
esis, and even more the pain of parting. In the accompanying
stanza, the man speaks of his service and devotion to his lady
(MFMT VIII; MF 91, 22).[140]

2.   "Ich vant si âne huote" (dialogue-poem of 7 stanzas): To the
     man's pleas for the rewarding of his singing and service, the
     woman responds that his reward is to be even more worthy than
     he is and to be in high spirits to boot (MFMT XII; MF 93, 12).

3.   "Guote liute" (1 woman's stanza as the third in a complex of
     four): While the man exhorts to bravery (presumably in refer-
     ence to the crusade), makes an unsuccessful attempt to free
     himself from love, and praises the woman who supports her
     crusader, the woman gives vent to her anguish about the pros-
     pect of her beloved's departure and of her subsequent loneliness
     (MFMT XIII; MF 94, 15).[141]

Turning to Johansdorf, we are again in the eastern part of the
German-speaking world. Johansdorf's home was the present-day
Jahrsdorf on the Vils River, a small town located northwest of
Passau in Lower Bavaria. There is considerable uncertainty about
the dates of the poet's life since men by the name of Albrecht von
Johansdorf appear in historical documents over a lengthy period.[142]
However, it is fairly certain that the poet lived in the last quarter of
the twelfth century (like Veldeke), possibly a few years into the
thirteenth, and that he belonged to a family of *ministeriales* in the
service of the bishoprics of Passau and Bamberg.[143]
    The above selections belong to a corpus of thirteen songs. Like
Hausen and Veldeke, Johansdorf composed poems of considerably
greater length than the earlier poets, whose works tended to feature
stanzas that were by and large independent of each other. The metrical patterns used by Johansdorf show an interesting and—considering his age and homeland—perhaps characteristic mixture.
Selections 1 and 3, for instance, are composed in a western *canzone*,
the latter in a long and complex version which reminds one of some
of Reinmar's extensive stanzas. Selection 2 with its extended final
line looks very much like a development of the strophic forms which
we encountered in the anonymous poems and in the works of
Dietmar.[144]
    Thematically, Johansdorf's poems are also a mixture. Remi-
niscent of the older Danubian tradition is, in particular, the dialogue: man and woman confront each other directly in two of the
three selections. Typically Danubian, also, is the articulation of the
old familiar fears of parting in selections 1 and, now relating to the
crusades, 2. But western influence is also clearly evident. New is the

argumentative, almost theoretical approach to the subject of love in selection 1. Reminiscent of Veldeke, but considerably less pointed, is the pedagogical tone in selection 2 used by a cornered woman to fend off the advances of a stalking man.[145]

Heinrich von Rugge[146]

1. "Vriundes komen" (1 woman's stanza in a complex of 5): The coming of the speaker's friend would be good if it were not for the thought of parting (MFMT I, 4; MF 100, 23).

2. "Vil wunneclîchen hôhe stât" (1 woman's stanza in complex of 4): The speaker rejoices about a knight who banishes her care and serves her well (MFMT VI, 4; MF 103, 27).

3. "Ein reht unsanfte lebende wîp" (1 woman's stanza in a complex of 10): The speaker declares that no one surpasses her in faithfulness to a man whom no one exceeds in her favor; she then pleads for him to reward her service (MFMT VII, 11; MF 106, 15).

4. "Solt ich an vröiden nu verzagen" (1 woman's stanza in a complex of 4): The speaker complains to a messenger about the distress of separation from the man whom she would like very much to see (MFMT VIII, 4; MF 107, 17).

5. "Dem ich alsolher êren şol" (1 woman's stanza in a complex of 6): The woman expresses the need to examine her suitor before granting him his desire (MFMT XI, 5; MF 110, 8).

6. "Mîn lîp in ein gemüete swert" (fragment of 1 woman's stanza in a complex of 3): (The stanza is, unfortunately, too poorly preserved to determine the meaning) (MFMT XII, 3; MF 111, 5).

Heinrich von Rugge belonged to a family of *ministeriales* in service to the counts of Thuringia. A "Heinricus de Rugge" who may be the poet is attested in chronicles of the counts between the years 1175 and 1178.[147]

Of the six selections listed above, the first four are attributed in the manuscripts partly to Rugge and partly to Reinmar, while the last two are credited only to Reinmar. It is therefore possible, and, I think, even probable, that one or more of the above woman's stanzas may actually have been composed by Reinmar.[148] Furthermore, there is substantial disagreement both among the manuscripts and in the scholarly discussion as to the development of Rugge's corpus over the years.[149]

Under these circumstances, it is not possible to give an assessment of Rugge's contribution to the woman's song with any confidence. The compositions which I have summarized have the same features which we encounter in the work of Reinmar der Alte, and the great similarity may account for the confusion—if indeed the above poems were not written by Reinmar himself.

Heinrich von Morungen[150]

1. "Owê des scheidens" (2 woman's stanzas alternating with 2 man's stanzas in a *Wechsel*): While the man praises his beloved as the dawn of his heart and pronounces a curse against any who would speak against her, the woman recalls a tearful parting from her beloved, then defends him against two-faced backbiters (MFMT X; MF 130, 31).

2. "Gerne sol ein rîter ziehen" (2 woman's stanzas in a complex of 3): Maintaining that a knight should keep company with good women and avoid the bad, the speaker attacks her own knight for doing the opposite and, after a few itemized complaints, claims the right to be angry (MFMT XXVIII, 2 and 3; MF 142, 26 and 142, 33).

3. "Owê, sol aber mir iemer mê" (2 woman's stanzas alternate with 2 man's stanzas in a *Wechsel*): Man and woman remember vividly a night of pleasure (MFMT XXX; MF 143, 22).[151]

Morungen's home was located near Sangerhausen near the Harz mountains in upper Thuringia. In 1217, he entered the convent of St. Thomas in Leipzig where he died in 1222.[152] His poetry is thought to have been composed before 1200.

The three selections introduced above belong to a corpus of thirty five poems printed under Morungen's name in MFMT. The corpus contains a great variety of meters generally based on the *canzone* form.

In keeping with a pattern which we have noted now in several cases, Morungen portrays courtship differently according to whether the speaker is male or female. In the former case, we see—literally: the visual element fascinates Morungen— the man looking up to his beloved lady in religious adoration. By contrast, the woman in selection 2 gives the impression that her beloved's affection is not concentrated on her, but is shared by other women: this is, of course, the old motif of jealousy which we heard so frequently in earlier poetry. Our selection number 1 is a bit different. There we hear man and woman defend each other against enemies. This kind of mutual defense alliance is a new motif, although the hostile tone and the biting words are standard in the tradition.

Reinmar der Alte[153]

1. "Si koment underwîlent her" (2 woman's stanzas separated by 2 man's stanzas in a *Wechsel*): While the man brags of his amorous successes—at least as far as I can understand from the text—and tells of his long period of service, the woman complains of unwanted guests and the absence of the desired one (MFMT II; MF 151, 1).[154]

2. "Ich wirde jaemerlîchen alt" (1 woman's stanza in complex of 4): The speaker, addressing a messenger, expresses the fear that another woman could supercede her in the favor of her beloved and tells the messenger to convey her fear of betrayal (MFMT III, 1; MF 152, 15).

3. "Ich lebte ie nâch der liute sage" (1 woman's stanza in a complex of 4): The woman laments her failure to please people of conflicting inclinations and expresses the fear that her beloved, apparently a man of splendid reputation, may be dealing with her in bad faith (MFMT IV, 1; MF 152, 25).

4. "Owê trûren unde klagen" (1 woman's stanza as last in a complex of 5): After 4 stanzas in which the man recounts his loneliness at daybreak, the woman expresses her exasperation at the burden of grief caused by her beloved's absence (MFMT VIa, 5[155]; MF 155, 38).

5. "Si jehent, der sumer der sî hie" (3 stanzas): The speaker mourns the death of her beloved (MFMT XVI; MF 167, 31).[156]

6. "Ich bin sô harte niht verzaget" (1 woman's stanza in a complex of 5): In supposed response to the man's threat of a damage suit—charging her with having robbed him of his joy and his senses (stanza 3 = MF 171, 38)—the woman responds that she will be quite able to defend herself (militarily?) (MFMT XXI, 3; MF 172, 5).

7. "Sage, daz ich dirs iemer lône" (dialogue of 5 stanzas): The woman attempts unsuccessfully to enlist the help of a messenger in reestablishing a courtship broken because of indiscretions committed by the intended addressee of the message (MFMT XXVII; MF 177, 10).[157]

8. "Lieber bote" (6 stanzas): Generally the same content as 7 except the messenger does not speak (MFMT XXVIII; MF 178, 1).[158]

9. "Ungenâde" (5 stanzas): The speaker reveals that her coolness

toward her dear good man is due not to her dislike for him, but to her concern for her reputation (MFMT XXXVII; MF 186, 19).

10. "Dêst ein nôt" (5 stanzas): A man of very eloquent speech has gained so much power over the speaker that she is worried about her own inability to resist him (MFMT XLIV; MF 192, 25).

11. "War kan iuwer schoener lîp" (1 introductory stanza plus 5 by the woman): Responding to a sympathetic inquirer, the featured speaker relates how unrequited love has affected her physical appearance and her psychological state (MFMT L; MF 195, 37).

12. "Er hât ze lange mich gemiten" (1 woman's stanza in a *Wechsel* of 2): The woman complains about the absence of her beloved and her great desire to see him; the man rejoices about a meeting with his beloved and promises to reward her goodness as best he can (MFMT LIII; MF 198, 4).

13. "Ane swaere" (6 stanzas): Such is the devotion of this lady for her friend that she would gladly give up anything for him, even her salvation, a matter which, she admits in the last line of the poem, causes her concern (MFMT LV; MF 199, 25).

14. "Zuo niewen vröuden" (2 stanzas): A beautiful woman rejoices that a knight is now doing her will and making her life a time of bliss (MFMT LIX; MF 203, 10).

As we already heard above, there are more lines of woman's song attributed to Reinmar der Alte than to any other medieval German poet. The fourteen selections summarized above belong to a corpus of sixty poems credited to him in MFMT.

The metrical structures employed by Reinmar are varied and complex, betraying the influence of the traditions which have been mentioned continuously in the course of our discussion but using these traditions in an original and, in part, unusual manner. The rather extended length of his stanzas reminds one of Johansdorf whom, however, he not infrequently surpasses in this regard. One poem by Reinmar, not among the above selections (MFMT VII; MF 156, 10) is composed in a meter that reminds one very much of that used in numbers 5 and 6 by Dietmar.[159]

In those poems by Reinmar in which the speaker is a man, we hear a view of *minne* which is very much in keeping with the ideas and ideals of courtly love. These are the poems which are usually considered typical for Reinmar and which have even been used to characterize him.[160] However, as in the case of several of the poets discussed previously, Reinmar presents a quite different view of *minne* in those poems in which the speaker is a woman. And it is here that, as de Boor correctly notes, Reinmar's works betray clearly the influence of the older poetic tradtion represented by the poems and poets with which our survey opened.[161] The same themes which occur in the woman's song of Kürenberg, Dietmar and the burgraves, also occur in the woman's song of Reinmar der Alte. Here also we hear complaints about the absence of the beloved man (nos. 1, 4, and 12), suspicions about the man's ill intent and betrayal (2, 3, 7 and 8), attacks against society (1,11,13 and 14), and rejoicing about the pleasure of the beloved man's company (10, and 14). Reinmar also portrays the cautious woman concerned about decorum and reputation as in poems by Veldeke and Hausen (Reinmar 3 and 7–9). The woman offended by a remark made by her friend, met in Dietmar, we encounter again in Reinmar's number 6.

However, Reinmar also makes contributions which, as far as we know, are original. There is, for instance, the theme of aging in no. 2 which, to my knowledge, is not mentioned in the *Minnesang* before Reinmar's time, at least not in relation to the woman. Then there is the portrayal of the woman worried about her enslavement to a lover who dominates her (10 and 13) which, to my knowledge, is also new in the *Minnesang*. Unprecedented in the *Minnesang*, finally, is the depiction in Reinmar's no. 11 of the woman suffering adverse physical effects of unrequited love, a motif which reminds one of the figure of Sigune in Wolfram von Eschenbach's *Parzival*.

It has usually been assumed that Reinmar der Alte was a native Alsatian. It is also generally believed that the works of Reinmar which bear the greatest similarity to the old Danubian tradition were composed in his youth, that is, while he was presumably still in Alsatia. Reinmar is supposed to have come from Alsatia to Austria as an established poet. This is the way in which de Boor (following the traditional view) pictured him, in perhaps the most widely used handbook on medieval German literature.[162]

It is surely obvious that I disagree with this view. Reinmar was, in all probability, an Austrian, a member of the illustrious and powerful Hagenau-family whose members are to be found in the same circles as those frequented by a number of poets introduced above.[163] The Austrian Hagenaus owned two castles known to us, one each in the same general area of Upper and Lower Austria, respectively, in which were located castles belonging to the Austrian Kürenbergs.[164]

Walther von der Vogelweide [165]

1. "Under der linden" (4 stanzas): The speaker recounts a time of pleasure spent with her beloved on the heath (L 39, 11).[166]

2. "Ich hoere iu sô vil tugende jehen" (2 woman's stanzas alternate with 2 man's stanzas in a dialogue): Man and woman exchange views about what makes the opposite sex attractive (L 43, 9).[167]

3. "Genâde frowe" (2 woman's stanzas alternate with 2 man's stanzas in a dialogue): The man begs forgiveness and understanding for his unfaithfulness, and the woman rejects his petition (L 70, 22).

4. "Mich hât ein wünneclîcher wân" (1 woman's stanza between 2 man's stanzas): Man and woman recount a time together (L 71, 35).

5. "Frowe'n lât iuch niht verdriezen" (2 woman's stanzas alternate with 2 man's stanzas in a dialogue): The woman agrees to listen to the man's words but does not agree to his proposed exchange of bodies (L 85, 34).

6. "Ich bin ein wîp" (1 woman's stanza in a complex of 2): Apparently echoing the preceding man's stanza, the woman rebukes and ridicules an admirer for wanting to steal a kiss (L 111, 32).[168]

7. "Frowe, vernemt dur got" (1 woman's stanza as the last in a dialogue of 4): The pleas of a messenger on behalf of his love-sick client provoke a rebuff based on distrust of the deceitful ways of the world and determination to keep to the godly ways of right (L 112, 35).[169]

8. "Got gebe ir iemer guoten tac" (2 woman's stanzas between 2 man's stanzas in a *Wechsel*): The man complains in one stanza that his beloved speaks affectionately of him to others, but differently in his presence; in the other, the man laments that the world has become worse than it used to be. The woman praises, in one stanza, a man whose wishes she wants to fulfill but cannot find the opportunity; in the other, a (the same?) woman complains that she has no friend and expresses concern about social pressures (L 119, 17).

The controversy about the homeland of Walther von der Vogelweide has not yet been settled.[170] Suffice it to say that, according to his own assertion, Walther learned "singen unde sagen" in Austria (L 32, 14) and that he showed a continuing affection for that country (especially for Vienna) as well as frustration at his inability to attain to permanent residence there.[171]

A characterization of Walther's corpus is currently much less feasible than in the case of most of the poets introduced above. This is true not only because of the variety of that corpus, but also because of important recent studies which challenge traditional conceptions about the poet and his work.

In any case, Walther's *Frauenlieder* contain a few features which will remind us of poems which we encountered above. No. 1 by Walther, "Under der linden"—surely the best known woman's song in medieval German poetry—is very similar to the anonymous poem which I listed above as no. 4: in both a woman describes an outdoor love-bed made of grass and flowers—the phrase "bluomen unde gras" occurs in both poems—which her lover prepares while awaiting her arrival. In the anonymous poem no. 6 above, the woman invites her beloved to go with her to pick flowers on the heath to make a wreath for him; a similar invitation, likewise involving a wreath, is extended in Walther's poem "Nemt, frowe, disen kranz" (L 74, 20) which I have not included here because it is not certain—though I consider it likely—that the invitation is issued by the woman.[172]

Interestingly enough, both of these poems by Walther have been linked with the (Latin) pastourelle tradition, and in both cases the similarity is to an anonymous poem transmitted in the *Carmina burana*.[173] The atmosphere in both cases is quite different from that which we sense in most of the *Frauenlieder* preserved in lay manuscripts under the names of authors belonging to the lay nobility. Conspicuously absent in the woman's song composed by Walther is, for instance, the motif of deeply felt emotional attachment of the woman to the man.

To be sure, there is at least one poem by Walther which is strikingly similar to that of a lay author. His no. 5 calls to mind no. 2 by Johansdorf: in both cases, an attempted seduction by the man is parried by a woman in full command of her wits—incidentally, a theme which is not typical of the traditional woman's song and, even in the poetry of Johansdorf, seems to be somewhat isolated. While Johansdorf has his heroine handle the matter by appealing to the higher principles of courtly love, the woman in Walther's poem simply ridicules the man by pretending to interpret literally what the man intends figuratively: the man proposes the exchange of bodies as a metaphor for mutual devotion in the sense in which Gottfried von Strassburg uses it in his *Tristan* (ll. 18334)[174]; however, Walther has the woman interpret the proposal literally and express an ostensibly naive fear of pain.

Martha M. Hinman has pointed out that it is typical of Walther to attack a hallowed tradition by "introducing a realistic rationale into the closed world of fiction."[175] No. 5 by Walther is, in my opinion, clearly a case in point. Another is, in all probability, Walther's no. 6 which is supposed to belong to the feud which he carried on with Reinmar. In a poem not belonging to our study

(MFMT X, stanza 3; MF 159, 37), Reinmar expresses as a gallant whim the desire to steal a kiss from his beloved. Walther has the woman in no. 6 react to that suggestion in reference to its moral-legal implications (stealing a kiss is theft).

Walther seems, in general, not to have had a great deal of sympathy and patience with traditional genres. John A. Asher has argued compellingly in favor of seeing his dawn song "Friuntlîchen lac" (L 88, 9) as a parody of that tradition.[176]

III. The Woman's Song after Walther von ver Vogelweide

The woman's song is a delicate fictional complex which cannot endure a great deal of scrutiny. To spell out the implications or possible consequences of the events and situations depicted there amounts to a violation of a brittle genre. To be sure, the fictional realm of the woman's song is, indeed, a realm which includes sorrow, betrayal, disappointment, and looming disgrace as well as exultation in pleasure and heart-warming memories; however, it can contain them only as long as they are treated in a manner that is suitable to a relatively self-contained fiction. What the realm of the woman's song could apparently not endure was a challenge from the outside, such as the moral-religious criticism implicit in Vogelweide's no. 7 or the moralistic attack implied in his nos. 2, 3 and 6. Also a simple refusal to play along with metaphorical games, such as that in no. 5, surely boded ill for this genre, especially when it is portrayed in the work of a gifted and influential poet such as Walther von der Vogelweide.

Even less could the traditional woman's song survive an opening up to include plurality of class such as that which occurs in the works of Neidhart von Reuenthal.[177] Of course, as I have already implied, Walther himself was clearly an outsider to the circles in which the woman's song was cultivated. As far as we can tell, all of the poets discussed previously belonged to the in-group which met at the courts of medieval Germany and Austria.[178] Walther also frequented these courts but did not really "belong" even though, to all appearances, he wanted to very much.[179] His poetry is focused very much on the courts, although, as I have pointed out, Walther seems not to have been prepared to go along with the art-games which were cultivated there for the insiders by noble dilettantes.

By contrast, Neidhart's view is no longer fixed on the court. As we noted above, Neidhart, like Walther, was a poet of the Danubian area, having spent the last years of his life in generally the same area of Austria in which were located the home castles of the Kürenbergs, the Eists, and the Hagenaus.[180] Women play a major role in the fiction of Neidhart's poetry and particularly in his summer songs.[181] We have already noted, in connection with no. 2 by Dietmar, that the *Gespielinnen*-poem is a genre which, perhaps under Dietmar's influence, was also cultivated by Neidhart.[182] More numerous in Neidhart's poetry, however, are the mother-and-daughter poems in which a girl, infatuated with an irresistible knight from "Riuwental" and determined to go off with him, encounters resistance from her mother.[183] In these as in the *Gespielinnin*-poems, the world of courtly fiction has been opened up to include the world of the village peasantry.

It was to songs such as these that the future of the later thirteenth century belonged, not to the traditional woman's song and, perhaps ironically, not to the songs of Walther von der Vogelweide.[184] When the voice of the infatuated woman is heard in the poetry which immediately followed the age of Walther and his younger contemporary Neidhart, it is usually heard in tones which betray, for the most part unmistakably, the influence of the latter.[185]

IV. Conclusion

As noted previously, the degree to which the woman's song reflects reality is uncertain. It is also not generally obvious to what extent the portrayals in the poems discussed above show some basic attitude toward women on the part of a given poet. Conspicuously, the woman is presented in a number of cases—particularly in the poems of Reinmar—in a manner which seems intended to elicit sympathy for the plight of a woman in dire straits stemming from actions or attitudes on the part of a man who is depicted in terms which can hardly be considered flattering. But there are also poems—again by Reinmar, and also in the works of Kürenberg, Meinloh and Dietmar—in which the woman makes compromising disclosures and commits blunders.[186]

We are on much firmer ground when we view the woman's song in terms of its capacity as a medium of performance before an audience. In two poems by Reinmar, nos. 5 and 9, the audience is addressed directly: "râtent unde sprechent" (MFMT XVI, 1, 4; MF 167, 34) and "rât ein wîp" (MFMT XXXVII, 1, 4; MF 186, 22). One could easily add to such examples, particularly from the works of Reinmar.[187] More common in the woman's song, however, is the situation where words in a given poem are addressed to a second character within the fiction of that poem. Usually these words are uttered in a tone of striking intensity which gives the scene a markedly dramatic, not to say melodramatic, character.

I have already referred to Angermann's and Frings' suggestion that such characteristics of the woman's song may indicate the performance of these poems, with the assigning of roles and the participation of women.[188] Unfortunately, these two scholars are among the very few who have addressed themselves to the specifics of performance and audience in medieval German society.[189] Perhaps future studies on the woman's song will provide greater clarity on this important issue.

   *Notes*

[1] E.g., *Eos*, ed. A. T. Hatto (The Hague: Mouton, 1965); Jonathan Saville, *The Medieval Erotic Alba* (New York: Columbia Univ. Press, 1972); Próspero Saíz, *Personae and Poiesis* (The Hague: Mouton, 1976).

[2] Friedrich Heinrich von der Hagen, *Minnesinger* (Leipzig: Barth, 1838), IV, p. 142.

[3] Helmut de Boor, *Die höfische Literatur* (Munich: Beck, 1953), p. 292. Hereafter cited as de Boor, HL.

[4] R. Becker, "Über Reinmar von Hagenau," *Germania*, 22 (1877), 76. Hereafter cited as Becker, "R.v.H."

[5] R. Becker, *Der altheimische Minnesang* (Halle: Niemeyer, 1882), pp. 60-61. Hereafter cited as Becker, AhM.

[6] See Burdach's review of Becker's book in *ADA*, 10 (1884), 13 ff.

[7] K. Burdach, *Reinmar der Alte und Walther von der Vogelweide*. 1st ed. (Leipzig: Hirzel, 1880), pp. 76 ff. Hereafter I shall cite—in the form: Burdach, *RuW²*—the second edition of this book, an expanded version of the first (mentioned later in my discussion) which is identical with the first edition for the first 172 pages.

[8] Burdach, *RuW²*, pp. 43 ff.

[9] Burdach, *RuW²*, p. 26.

[10] Burdach, *RuW²*, p. 45.

[11] Burdach, *RuW²*, p. 45.

[12] Burdach, "Reinmar der Alte," in *Allgemeine deutsche Biographie* (1889, rpt. Berlin: Duncker & Humblot, 1970), XXVIII, p. 97. Rpt. RuW², p. 371.

[13] See note 7 above.

[14] Merely an echo of Burdach, and therefore not included in this discussion, is E. Lesser, 'Das Verhältnis der Frauenmonologe in den lyrischen und epischen deutschen Dichtungen des 12. und angehenden 13. Jahrhunderts," *BGDSL*, 24 (1889), 361–83.

[15] A. Angermann, *Der Wechsel in der mittelhochdeutschen Lyrik*, Diss. Marburg 1910 (Bielfeld: A. von der Mühlen, 1910), pp. 8, 70 ff., 74 ff.

[16] Angermann, p. 98. J. Meier, *Kunstlieder im Volksmunde* (Halle: Niemeyer, 1906), p. xvi.

[17] Angermann, pp. 80 ff., 85 ff.

[18] See the articles in *Der deutsche Minnesang*, ed. Hans Fromm (Darmstadt: Wissenschaftliche Buchgesellschaft, 1963), and *Formal Aspects of Medieval German Poetry*, ed. Stanley N. Werbow (Austin and London: Univ. of Texas Press, 1969). See also the readable and stimulating discussion of the role of performance in E. Joseph, *Die Lieder des Kürenbergers* (Strassburg: Trübner, 1896), pp. 35 ff., 41, 57–58.

[19] Angermann, pp. 54 ff., 104–05.

[20] C. von Kraus, *Unsere älteste Lyrik* (Munich: Verlag der Bayerischen Akademie der Wissenschaften, 1930), p. 10. Hereafter cited as Kraus, *Lyrik*.

[21] C. von Kraus, *Die Lieder Reinmars des Alten*. 3 pts. (Munich: Verlag der Bayerischen Akademie der Wissenschaften, 1919) = Abhandlungen der Bayerischen Akademie der Wissenschaften. Philosophisch-philologische und historische Klasse, vol. 30, Abhandlungen 4, 6, 7). Hereafter cited as *RU* I, *RU* II and *RU* III.

[22] See note 12 above.

[23] Kraus, *Lyrik*, p. 15.

[24] Kraus, *Lyrik*, p. 5.

[25] Erich Schmidt, *Reinmar von Hagenau und Heinrich von Rugge* (Strassburg: Trübner, 1874), pp. 32–33. Hereafter cited as Schmidt, *RuR*. See also RU II, 5, 42–43.

[26] H. Fischer, *Die Frauenmonologe in der deutschen höfischen Lyrik*, Diss. Marburg 1934 (Mainz: Schneider, 1934), p. 5.

[27] Cf. Peter Dronke, *Medieval Latin and the Rise of European Love-Lyric* (Oxford: Clarendon Press, 1968), I, pp. 8–9.

[28] Fischer, pp. 12, 44.

[29] Fischer, pp. 20–21.

[30] A. Götze, "Gewollte Unkunst im Frauenlied," *BGDSL*, 61 (1937), 183.

[31] H. Grundmann, "Die Frauen und die Literatur im Mittelalter," *AKG*, 26 (1936), 129–61.

[32] E. Mergell, *Die Frauenrede im Minnesang*, Diss. Frankfurt 1939 (Limburg/Lahn: Limburger Vereinsdruckerei, 1940), pp. 24 ff., 129 ff.

[33] Mergell, pp. 24, 43.

[34] E. Lea, "Die Sprache lyrischer Grundgefüge," *BGDSL*, 90 (Halle, 1968), 308 ff., 340 ff.; M. Bogin, *The Women Troubadours* (London, New York, Ontario: Paddington, 1976), pp. 67 ff.

[35] Hans H. Frankel, *The Flowering Plum and the Palace Lady* (New Haven and London: Yale Univ. Press, 1976), pp. 56 ff.; *Eos*, p. 144; Alice C. Fletcher and Francis la Flesche, *The Omaha Tribe* (1911; rpt. Lincoln: Univ. of Nebraska Press, 1972), II, pp. 320 ff.

[36] T. Frings, *Minnesinger und Troubadours* (Berlin: Akademie, 1949); rpt. in *Der deutsche Minnesang*, ed. Hans Fromm (Darmstadt: Wissenschaftliche Buchgesellschaft, 1963), pp. 1–57. Hereafter cited as, Frings, "Minnesinger," according to the latter publication whose page numbering deviates from that in the publication of 1949; Frings, "Erforschung des

Minnesangs," *Forschungen und Fortschritte*, 26 (1950), 9; Frings, "Namenlose Lieder," *BGDSL*, 88 (Halle, 1967), 309–10.

[37] Frings, "Minnesinger," pp. 13 ff; "Erforschung des Minnesangs," loc. cit.; Frings, "Altspanische Mädchenlieder," *BGDSL*, 73 (1951), 193; "Namenlose Lieder," 307.

[38] Frings, "Minnesinger," pp. 15, 23; Frings, "Frauenstrophe und Frauenlied in der frühen deutschen Lyrik," in *Gestaltung-Umgestaltung: Festschrift für H.A. Korff*, ed. Joachim Müller (Leipzig: Koehler & Amelang, 1957), p. 19.

[39] Frings, "Minnesinger," pp. 12–13, 15–16; "Erforschung des Minnesangs," pp. 10, 43; "Frauenstrophe," p. 14. On the last-named page, Frings makes a distinction, perhaps with von Kraus in mind, between "Volkslieder" and "volkstümliche Lieder." I must confess that the implications of this distinction are not clear to me. Perhaps the term "volkstümliche Lieder" has implications of individual artistry as opposed to origins in the folk as masses.

[40] Von Kraus' assertion that the function of the *Minnesang* was to serve society and to teach exemplary emotions (Kraus, *Lyrik*, p. 5) is repeated in the exact terms ("der Gesellschaft dienen" and "vorbildlich empfinden") in Frings, "Frauenstrophe," p. 14.

[41] A. Jolles, *Einfache Formen*, 1st ed. (Halle: Niemeyer, 1930).

[42] E.g., Frings, "Minnesinger," p. 12; "Erforschung des Minnesangs," p. 9; "Frauenstrophe," p. 21. I should note in all fairness, however, that I have not been able to locate a single refrence to Jolles's book in studies by Frings which I have quoted.

[43] Frings, "Minnesinger," p. 15; "Erforschung des Minnesangs," pp. 42–43; "Frauenstrophe," pp. 15 ff., 19 ff.

[44] Very helpful general observations on the woman's song are to be found, for example, in Gustav Ehrismann, "Die Kürenberg-Literatur und die Anfänge des deutschen Minnesangs," *GRM*, 15 (1927), 328–50, esp. pp. 347 ff. Only for reasons of consistency did I not make this article the focus of special attention, and would like to recommend it strongly.

[45] G. Pomassl, *Die Reaktion der Frau auf Minnesang und Minnedienst in der dt. Lyrik des 12. und 13. Jhs.*, Diss. Jena 1958 (microfilm), pp. 7, 33, 52, 61, 74, 93.

[46] Pomassl, p. 144.

[47] For bibliography on the *Minnesang* and the individual poets of this tradition, see Helmut Tervooren, *Bibliographie zum Minnesang und zu den Dichtern aus des Minnesangs Frühling* (Berlin: Schmidt, 1969). For general discussions in English on the history of medieval German poetry, see Margaret F. Richey, *Essays on Mediaeval German Poetry*, 2nd ed. (New York: Barnes & Noble, 1969); W.T.H. Jackson, *The Literature of the Middle Ages* (New York: Columbia Univ. Press, 1960), pp. 255–75; M. O'C. Walshe, *Medieval German Literature* (Cambridge: Harvard Univ. Press, 1962), pp. 97–133; Paul Salmon, *Literature in Medieval Germany* (New York: Barnes & Noble, 1967), pp. 92–114.

Other introductory surveys to be highly recommended (all with substantial bibliography) are Gustav Ehrismann, *Geschichte der deutschen*

Literatur (Munich: Beck, 1935), II ("Schlussband"), pp. 180–219; Carl von Kraus, *Des Minnesangs Frühling. Untersuchungen* (Leipzig: Hirzel, 1939); André Moret, *Les débuts du lyrisme en Allemagne* (Lille: Bibliothèque Universitaire, 1951); de Boor, *HL*, pp. 215–376; Hugo Kuhn, "Die Klassik des Rittertums in der Stauferzeit," in *Annalen der deutschen Literatur*, ed. Heinz Otto Burger, 2nd ed. (Stuttgart: Metzler, 1971), pp. 99–177.

[48] Studies devoted to the early *Minnesang* include Wilhelm Scherer, "Deutsche Studien II. Die Anfänge des Minnesangs," in *Sitzungsberichte der philosophisch-historischen Classe der Wissenschaften* (Vienna, 1874), vol. 77, Heft 1, pp. 437–516; Anton E. Schönbach, *Die Anfänge des deutschen Minnesangs* (Graz: Leuschner & Lubensky, 1898); Hennig Brinkmann, *Entstehungsgeschichte des Minnesangs* (Halle: Niemeyer, 1926); Max Ittenbach, *Der frühe deutsche Minnesang* (Halle: Niemeyer, 1939); Jean Fourquet, "La chanson chevaleresque allemande avant les influences provençales," in *Mélanges de linguistique romane et de philologie médiévale offerts à Maurice Delbouille* (Gembloux: Duculot, 1964), II, pp. 155–64; Elisabeth Lea (see note 34); Rolf Grimminger, *Poetik des frühen Minnesangs* (Munich: Beck, 1969); and Derk Ohlenroth, *Sprechsituation und Sprecheridentität* (Göppingen: Kümmerle, 1974).

[49] The poem "Dû bist mîn" is used as the conclusion of a letter in the Tegernsee Manuscript which is addressed by a nun to an admirer. The text of the letter can be found in *Des Minnesangs Frühling*, ed. Carl von Kraus, 30th ed. (Zurich: Hirzel, 1950), pp. 318–20; see also Friedrich Ohly, "Du bist mein," in *Kritische Bewahrung. Beiträge zur deutschen Philologie. Festschrift für Werner Schröder*, ed. Ernst-Joachim Schmidt (Berlin: Schmidt, 1974), pp. 371–415.

MFMT = *Des Minnesangs Frühling*, ed. Hugo Moser and Helmut Tervooren, 36th ed. in 2 vols. (Stuttgart: Hirzel, 1977). Unless otherwise indicated, MFMT = vol. I (Texts). The numbering which follows the abbreviation MF is based on the first edition of *Des Minnesangs Frühling*, ed. Karl Lachmann and Moriz Haupt (Leipzig: Hirzel, 1857) and is used in all editions of MF prior to that of 1977. Quoted here as MF is the 35th edition, ed. Carl von Kraus (Stuttgart: Hirzel, 1970).

"Dû bist mîn" is translated in J.W. Thomas, *Medieval German Lyric Verse in English Translation* (Chapel Hill: Univ. of North Carolina Press, 1968), p. 13.

[50] CB = *Carmina Burana*, ed. Alfons Hilka and Otto Schumann (Heidelberg: Winter, 1941), vol. 1, pt. 2: "Die Liebeslieder." Translations of "Uvere div werlt alle min" can be found in Thomas, p. 41. Thomas's translation follows a version of this poem which results from a scribal alteration of an original woman's song. See Peter Dronke, *The Medieval Lyric* (London: Hutchinson, 1968), p. 83, footnote; generally in favor of the alteration are Max Wehrli, "Diu künegin von Engellant," *GR*, 31 (1956), 5–8; Günther Jungbluth, "Diu künegin von Engellant," *Neophil*, 41 (1957), 117–19; F. Norman, "Eleanor of Poitou in the Twelfth-Century German Lyric," *GL&L*, 3/4 (1963), 248–55.

[51] Trans. Thomas, p. 39.

[52] The stanza resembles the woman's song "Under der linden" by Walther von der Vogelweide which will be discussed below.

[53] This stanza is likewise similar to a poem by Walther von der Vogelweide, "Nemt, vrouwe, disen kranz," which I shall discuss briefly below in my treatment of that poet.

[54] Trans. Thomas, pp. 42–43.

[55] Trans. Frank C. Nicholson, *Old German Love Songs* (London: Unwin, 1907), p. 1; Thomas, p. 61.

[56] Trans. Thomas, p. 61.

[57] Trans. Nicholson, pp. 1–2.

[58] Helmut Plechl, "Die Tegernseer Handschrift Clm 19411," *DAEM*, 18 (1962), 419.

[59] B. Bischoff, "Einführung," *Faksimile-Ausgabe der Carmina Burana und der Fragmenta (Clm. 4660 und 4660a) der Bayerischen Staatsbibliothek in München* (Munich: Prestel, and Brooklyn, N.Y.: Institute of Medieval Music, 1967), II, pp. 14, 17 and (English translation): 28, 30. Here Bischoff argues against the dating late 13th century which stems from Otto Schumann and is followed in F. J. E. Raby, *A History of Secular Latin Poetry in the Middle Ages*, 2nd ed. (Oxford: Clarendon Press, 1957), II, p. 257. The difference is not crucial for my discussion.

[60] W. Blank, "Einleitung," *Die kleine Heidelberger Liederhandschrift Cod. pal. Germ. 357* (Wiesbaden: Reicher, 1972), p. 14.

[61] De Boor, *HL*, p. 242.

[62] As noted above, this is the assumption of Frings, especially in the article "Namenlose Lieder"; cf. Richey, *Essays*, p. 20; Walshe, pp. 100–01; Dronke, *The Medieval Lyric*, p. 95.

[63] For older studies on Kürenberg, see the bibliographies provided by the sources listed in notes 47 and 48; more recent discussions include Rudolf K. Jansen, "Mittelalterliche Hochzeitsliturgie und die Lyrik Kürenbergs," *Ostbairische Grenzmarken*, 12 (1970), 111–17; Jansen, "Randbemerkungen zum ersten Troubadour und ersten Minnesänger," *DVLG*, 48 (1974), 767–71; Peter Wapnewski, "Stern und Blume, Dorn und Klein. Zur Bildersprache des Kürenbergers," in *Geist und Zeichen. Festschrift für Arthur Henkel*, ed. Herbert Anton, Bernard Gajek and Peter Pfaff (Heidelberg: Winter, 1977), pp. 443–51.

[64] Trans. Nicholson, p. 4 (based on amended text); Thomas, p. 51; cf. Günther Jungbluth, "Zu Minnesangs Frühling 7, 1–18," *Neophil*, 37 (1953), 237–39.

[65] Trans. Thomas, pp. 51–52; Frederick Goldin, *German and Italian Lyrics of the Middle Ages* (Garden City, N.Y.: Anchor/Doubleday, 1973), p. 6/7 (synoptic); see also H.B. Willson, "Der von Kürenberg; MF 7, 18," *MLR*, 50 (1955), 321–22.

[66] Trans. Margaret F. Richey, *Medieval German Lyrics* (Edinburgh and London: Oliver and Boyd, 1958), p. 34. Hereafter cited as Richey, *Lyrics* to be distinguished from Richey, *Essays = Essays on Mediaeval German Poetry* (note 47). Trans. also in Dronke, *The Medieval Lyric*, p. 113; Goldin, p. 6/7.

[67] Trans. Dronke, *The Medieval Lyric*, p. 113; Thomas, p. 52.

[68] Trans. Nicholson, p. 5; Richey, *Lyrics*, p. 34; Thomas, p. 51; Goldin,

p. 6/7; cf. Wolfgang Stammler, "Bogenfüllsel (zu MF 8, 22)," *ZDP*, 73 (1954), 128.

[69] Trans. Nicholson, pp. 5–6; Richey, *Lyrics*, pp. 34–35; Dronke, *The Medieval Lyric*, p. 113; Thomas, p. 52; Goldin, p. 8/9. A survey of literature on Kürenberg's falcon poem can be found in Grimminger, *Poetik*, pp. 91–118; more recent discussions include Rudolf K. Jansen, "Das Falkenlied Kürenbergs," *DVLG*, 44 (1970), 585–94; Gerhard Eis, "Zu Kürenbergs Falkenlied," *GRM*, 52, N.F. 21 (1971), 461–62; Stephen J. Kaplowitt, "A Note on the 'Falcon Song' of Der von Kürenberg," *GQ*, 44 (1971), 519–25; Jansen, "De Arte Vanandi cum Avibus," *GQ*, 48 (1975), 187–89.

[70] Trans. Richey, *Lyrics*, p. 35.

[71] See de Boor, *HL*, p. 24.

[72] See *Des Minnesangs Frühling*, ed. Friedrich Vogt (Leipzig: Hirzel, 1911), p. 268. Hereafter cited as *MFV*.

[73] A. Wallner, "Der von Kürenberg," in *Die deutsche Literatur des Mittelalters. Verfasserlexikon*, ed. Wolfgang Stammler (Berlin and Leipzig: de Gruyter, 1936), II, p. 991.

[74] See Otto Paul and Ingeborg Glier, *Deutsche Metrik*, 8th ed. (Munich: Hueber, 1970), p. 84; Richey, *Essays*, pp. 15 ff.; D.G. Mowatt and Hugh Sacker, *The Nibelungenlied* (Toronto: Univ. of Toronto Press, 1967), pp. 16–18.

[75] See de Boor, *HL*, p. 157; Walshe, pp. 223–24.

[76] Paul-Glier, pp. 84, 67 ff.; Walshe, p. 76.

[77] See Paul-Glier, p. 68; Richey, *Essays*, p. 16; Walshe, p. 81.

[78] See Grimminger, *Poetik*, pp. 60–63, 68–69.

[79] Trans. Richey, *Lyrics*, p. 35 (# v); Thomas, p. 50; see also H. B. Willson, "Der von Kürenberg: MF 9, 21–8," *MLR*, 53 (1958), 552–53; Antonín Hrubý, "Die Kürenbergerstrophe MF 9, 21–28," *OL*, 18 (1963), 139–54; Jansen, "Mittelalterliche Hochzeitliturgie," loc. cit.

[80] Trans. Nicholson, p. 6 (# 6); Richey, *Lyrics*, p. 35 (# vi); Thomas, pp. 50–51; Goldin, p. 8/9.

[81] See Wapnewski, "Stern und Blume," pp. 447, 449–50.

[82] For older literature on Meinloh, see Tervooren's and the bibliographies in the sources listed in notes 47 and 48. As far as I know, the only recent study devoted to Meinloh is Karl-Heinz Schirmer, "Die höfische Minnetheorie und M.v.S.," in *Festschrift für Fritz Tschirch*, ed. Karl-Heinz Schirmer and Bernhard Sowinski (Cologne: Böhlau, 1972), pp. 52–73.

[83] Trans. Thomas, pp. 53–54.

[84] Trans. Dronke, *The Medieval Lyric*, p. 95; Thomas, p. 53.

[85] J.K. Bostock, "Herr Meinloh von Sevelingen," *MLR*, 50 (1955), 509.

[86] Trans. Thomas, pp. 54–55.

[87] *MFV*, p. 277; Hans Pörnbacher, "Meinloh von Sevelingen," in *Lebensbilder aus dem Bayerischen Schwaben*. ed. Götz Freiherr von Pölnitz (Munich: Hueber, 1959), VII, pp. 3, 5–6.

[88] A. Wallner, "M.v.S.," in *Die deutsche Literatur*, ed. Stammler, III, p. 336; Thomas, p. 53; Pörnbacher, p. 6.

[89] Pörnbacher, pp. 6–7.

[90] Dronke, *The Medieval Lyric*, p. 95.

[91] Trans. Nicholson, p. 6 (# 6); Richey, *Lyrics*, p. 35 (# vi); Thomas, pp. 50–51; Goldin, p. 8/9.

[92] Trans. Nicholson, pp. 8–9; Richey, *Lyrics*, p. 39; Thomas, p. 54.

[93] See de Boor, *HL*, p. 248; Walshe, pp. 104–05; Richey, *Essays*, pp. 22–23.

[94] For secondary literature on Der Burggraf von Regensburg, see the sources in notes 47 and 48. I know of no recent studies devoted to this poet.

[95] Due to the unusual subject matter of Regensburg's poems and the unavailability of any translation, as far as I know, I offer my own. The translation of the poem by Der Burggraf von Rietenburg is also mine.

[96] See *MFV*, p. 282; de Boor, *HL*, p. 242; Manfred Mayer, *Geschichte der Burggrafen von Regensburg*, Diss. Munich 1883 (Munich: Rieger, 1883).

[97] De Boor, *HL*, p. 242.

[98] See Walshe, p. 98; Richey, *Essays*, p. 3; de Boor, *HL*, p. 217.

[99] See Walshe, p. 93.

[100] For literature on Der Burggraf von Rietenburg, see the sources listed in notes 47 and 48. I know of no recent study devoted to this poet.

[101] De Boor, *HL*, p. 242.

[102] For older literature on Dietmar, see the sources listed in notes 47 and 48. More recent studies include Helmut Tervooren and Regine Weidemeyer, "Reimkonjekturen bei Dietmar von Eist und Friedrich von Hausen," *ZDP*, 90 (1971 Sonderheft), 46–65; P. Wapnewski, "Zwei altdeutsche Frauenlieder," in *Waz ist minne*, by P. Wapnewski (Munich: Beck, 1975), pp. 9–22.

[103] Trans. Richey, *Lyrics*, p. 38; Thomas, p. 57.

[104] Trans. Richey, *Lyrics*, p. 36; Thomas, p. 60.

[105] Trans. Nicholson, p. 15; Richey, *Lyrics*, pp. 36–37; Thomas, p. 57.

[106] Trans. Richey, *Lyrics*, p. 37; Thomas, p. 56.

[107] See Heinrich Siekhaus, "Revocatio—Studie zu einer Gestaltungsform des Minnesangs," *DVLG*, 45 (1971), 237–51.

[108] Trans. Nicholson, pp. 15–16; Richey, *Lyrics*, pp. 37–38; Thomas, pp. 58–59.

[109] The editors of MFMT construe only the first two lines of this stanza as the words of the woman since the speaker of the third line mentions having departed. According to MFMT II, p. 73, it is customary in the *Minnesang* only to speak of the man as departing.

[110] *MFV*, pp. 305–06; Theodor von Grienberger, "Dietmar von Aist," *ZDA*, 37 (1893), 419–24.

[111] K. Rathke, *Dietmar von Aist* (Leipzig: Eichblatt, 1932), p. 20.

[112] De Boor, *HL*, p. 245; cf. Richey, *Essays,* loc. cit.

[113] Schönbach, *Anfänge*, pp. 78 ff.

[114] F. Panzer, "Der älteste Troubadour und der erste Minnesänger," *Dichtung und Volkstum*, 40 (1939), 143; A. Hrubý, "Die Kürenbergstrophe" (see note 79), p. 151.

[115] See Walshe, p. 77; Paul-Glier, p. 40; cf. Richey, *Essays*, pp. 19 ff.

[116] Rathke, pp. 62–63.

[117] See Eckehard Simon, *Neidhart von Reuental* (Boston: Twayne, 1975), pp. 25 ff.

[118] For older literature on Kaiser Heinrich, see the sources in notes 47 and 48; more recent studies include Peter Wapnewski, "Kaiserlied und Kaisertopos," in *Waz ist minne*, pp. 47–64; Ulrich Pretzel, "Kaiser Heinrichs 'Köngislied,'" in *Sagen mit sinne. Festschrift für Marie-Luise Dittrich*, ed. Helmut Rücker and Kurt Otto Seidel (Göppingen: Kümmerle, 1976), pp. 79–94.

[119] De Boor, *HL*, pp. 250–51.

[120] Wapnewski, "Kaiserlied," pp. 52 ff., 63.

[121] E. Thurnher, "König Heinrich (VII.) und die deutsche Dichtung," *DAEM*, 33 (1977), 525.

[122] Wapnewski, "Kaiserlied," pp. 53–61.

[123] Thurnher, p. 525.

[124] Thurnher, p. 525.

[125] *MFV*, p. 282; Kuhn, "Die Klassik des Rittertums," p. 113.

[126] Wapnewski, "Kaiserlied," p. 51.

[127] For older literature on Friedrich von Hausen, see the sources listed in notes 47 and 48. More recent studies include A.T. Hatto, "The Earliest Extant Middle High German Political Poems," in *Mélanges pour Jean Fourquet*, ed. P. Valentin and G. Zink (Munich: Hueber, and Paris: Klincksieck, 1969), pp. 137–45; D.G. Mowatt, *F.v.H.* (Cambridge: Cambridge Univ. Press, 1971); Hermann Deuser and Knut Rybka, "Kreuzzugs- und Minnelyrik. Interpretationen zu F.v.H. und Hartmann von Aue," *WW*, 21 (1971), 402–11; Ulrich Müller, "F.v.H. und der Sumer von Triere (MF 47, 38)," *ZDP*, 90 (1971, Sonderheft), 107–15; Hugo Bekker, "F.v.H.: *Lichte ein unwiser man verwüete*," *Seminar*, 8 (1972), 147–59; Bekker, "F.v.H.: *Ich muoz von schulden sîn unfrô*," in *Husbanding the Golden Grain: Studies in Honor of Henry W. Nordmeyer*, ed. Luanne T. Frank and Emery E. George (Ann Arbor: Univ. of Michigan, Dept. of Germanic Languages and Literatures, 1973), pp. 24–45; Hans-Herbert S. Räkel, "Drei Lieder zum dritten Kreuzzug," *DVLG*, 47 (1973), 508–50; W.T.H. Jackson, "Contrast Imagery in the Poems of F.v.H.," *GR*, 49 (1974), 7–16; Norbert Wagner, "Zum Wohnsitz des F.v.H.," *ZDA*, 104 (1975), 126–30; Arne Holtorf, "Zu F.v.H. und das Trierer Schisma von 1183–1189," *Rheinische Vierteljahresblätter*, 40 (1976), 72–102; Volker Mertens, "Der 'heisse Sommer' 1187 von Trier," *ZDP*, 95 (1976), 346–56; H. Becker, *F.v.H.* (Chapel Hill: Univ. of North Carolina Press, 1977).

[128] Trans. Thomas. p. 65; Goldin, p. 24/25.

[129] All editions of *Des Minnesangs Frühling* prior to MFMT print a mixture of the two versions.

[130] Primary sources documenting some of Hausen's activities and the circumstances surrounding his death are recorded in *MFV*, pp. 323–24.

[131] See de Boor, *HL*, pp. 254–59; Richey, *Essays*, pp. 33–38.

[132] Cf. MFMT II, pp. 50–51.

[133] Von Kraus, *Des Minnesangs Frühling. Untersuchungen*, pp. 116–17, 127. Hereafter cited as Kraus, *MFU*.

[134] See MFMT II, pp. 13–14, 16–17; see also Friedrich Maurer, *Die "Pseudoreimare"* (Heidelberg: Winter, 1966), pp. 15 ff.; Mowatt, *F.v.H.*, pp. 48 ff. On page 156 of this study, Mowatt excludes our selection 2 by Hausen from his discussion for reasons which are not clear to me. In view of his criticism of earlier scholarship, I find the dismissal astonishing. Hugo Bekker, in his Hausen book of 1977, also dismisses the poem with a very brief reference to Mowatt (Bekker, *FvH*, p. 126, footnote 9).

[135] For older literature on Veldeke, see the sources in notes 47 and 48. More recent studies—not including those explicitly devoted to Veldeke's epic works—are Stanley N. Werbow, "Veldeke's 'My Fool Heart' (MF 56, 1)," in *Germanic Studies in Honor of E.H. Sehrt*, ed. F. Raven, W. Legner and J. King (Coral Gables, Florida: Univ. of Miami Press, 1968), pp. 241–49; Werner Schröder, *Veldeke-Studien* (Berlin: Schmidt, 1969); *Heinrich von Veldeken. Symposium Gent*, ed. Gilbert A.R. de Smet (Antwerpen and Utrecht: Nederlandsche Boekhandel, 1971); Thomas Klein, "Veldeke und die scholastische Logik," *ZDP*, 90 (1971, Sonderheft), 90–107; Cola Minis, "Epische Ausdrucksweisen insbesondere mit *sehen* in Veldekes Liedern," *ZDP*, 90 (1971, Sonderheft), 80–90; Minis, "Zu dem Genter Veldeke-Symposium," *ABäG*, 2 (1971), 193–211; John R. Sinnema, *Heinrich van Veldeke* (New York: Twayne, 1972); W. Sanders, *H.v.V.* (Bonn, 1973); Stephen J. Kaplowitt, "H.v.V's Song Cycle of 'Hohe Minne,'" *Seminar*, 11 (1975), 125–40.

[136] Trans. Thomas, pp. 75–76 (stanzas 1, 2 and 4 of the a-version).

[137] See Josef Fleckenstein, "Friedrich Barbarossa und das Rittertum," in *Festschrift für Hermann Heimpel* (Göttingen: Vandenhoeck & Ruprecht, 1972), II, pp. 1023–41; rpt. *Das Rittertum im Mittelalter*, ed. Arno Borst (Darmstadt: Wissenschaftliche Buchgesellschaft, 1976), pp. 392–418.

[138] An interesting interpretation of this change is presented in Horst Wenzel, *Frauendienst und Gottesdienst* (Berlin: Schmidt, 1974), pp. 81 ff.

[139] For older secondary literature on Johansdorf, see the sources listed in notes 47 and 48. More recent discussions include Karl-Heinz Schirmer, "Rhetorisches im Kreuzlied," in *Mediaevalia litteraria. Festschrift für Helmut de Boor*, ed. Ursula Hennig and Herbert Kolb (Munich: Beck, 1971), pp. 229–53; Räkel, "Drei Lieder" (see note 127); Hugo Bekker, "A.v.J.: *Mîn erste liebe,*" *Seminar,*" II (1975), 10–24; David P. Sudermann, *The Minnelieder of A.v.J.* (Göppingen: Kümmerle, 1976).

[140] Trans. Richey, *Lyrics*, pp. 47–48.

[141] Trans. Nicholson, pp. 29–30.

[142] See Sudermann, pp. 16–25.

[143] De Boor, *HL*, p. 274 and Sudermann, p. 16.

[144] See Robert Bergmann, *Untersuchungen zu den Liedern As.v. J.*, Diss. Freiburg 1963 (Freiburg: Krause, 1963), pp. 238 ff., 253 ff.

[145] See Sudermann, pp. 321 ff.

[146] For literature on Heinrich von Rugge, see the sources listed in notes 47 and 48. I know of no study of Rugge more recent than Tervooren's bibliography.

[147] *MFV*, p. 365; de Boor, *HL*, p. 262; Kuhn, "Die Klassik des Rittertums," p. 119.

[148] In my forthcoming book on Reinmar, I argue for Reinmar's authorship of some of these poems.

[149] See Schmidt, *RuR*, pp. 5 ff; Maurer, "Die 'Pseudoreimare,'" pp. 106 ff; Franz Joseph Paus, "Heinrich von Rugge und Reinmar der Alte," *DU*, 19, Heft 2 (1967), 17–31.

[150] For older secondary literature on Heinrich von Morungen, see the sources in notes 47 and 48. More recent studies include Antonín Hrubý, "Historische Semantik in Morungens 'Narzissuslied,'" *DVLG*, 42 (1968), 1–22; several articles in *ZDP*, 87 (1968, Sonderheft); Franz Rolf Schröder, "H.v.M.," *GRM*, N.F., 18 (1968), 337–48; several articles in *Interpretationen mittelhochdeutscher Lyrik*, ed. Günther Jungbluth (Bad Homburg: Gehlen, 1969); Frederic Tubach, "In sô hôe swebender wunne," *DVLG*, 43 (1969), 193–203; Hugo Stopp, "Zu Morungens Tageliedwechsel," *Euphorion*, 64 (1970), 51–58; Peter Börner, "Zu MF 131, 25 f," *ZDP*, 90 (1971, Sonderheft), 115–23; Peter Frenzel, "The Beginning and End in the Songs of H.v.M.," in *Husbanding the Golden Grain*, pp. 97–109; Klaus Brandes, *H.v.M.* (Göppingen: Kümmerle, 1974); W.T.H. Jackson, "Persona and Audience," *Mosaic*, 8 (1974/75), 147–59; Rüdiger Schnell, "Andreas Capellanus, H.v.M. und Herbort von Fritzlar," *ZDA*, 104 (1975), 131–51; Hans-Herbert Räkel, "Das Lied von Spiegel, Traum und Quell des H.v.M.," *LiLi*, 7, Heft 26 (1977), 95–108.

[151] Trans. Nicholson, pp. 47–48; Richey, *Lyrics*, pp. 53–54; Dronke, *The Medieval Lyric*, p. 180; Thomas, pp. 83–84; Goldin, pp. 54–56.

[152] De Boor, *HL*, p. 277; Richey, *Essays*, pp. 41–42.

[153] For older literature on Reinmar, see the sources in notes 47 and 48. More studies include Karl Bertau, "Überlieferung und Authentizität bei den Liedern Rs.d.A.," *ZDP*, 88 (1969), 389–400; Xenia von Ertzdorff, "R.v.H.," in *Interpretationen mhd. Lyrik*, ed. Jungbluth, pp. 137–52; Bert Nagel, "Hartmann 'zitiert' Reinmar," *Euphorion*, 63 (1969), 6–39; Friedrich Neumann, "Reinmars Lied: *Ein wîser man*," in *Interpretationen mhd. Lyrik*, pp. 153–68; Günther Schweikle, "War Reinmar 'von Hagenau' Hofsänger zu Wien?" in *Gestaltungsgeschichte und Gesellschaftsgeschichte*, ed. Helmut Kreuzer (Stuttgart: Metzler, 1969), pp. 1–31; Helmut Birkhan, "Manger zu den vrouwen gât," *Sprachkunst*, 2 (1971), 81–92; Birkhan, "Reimar, Walther und die Minne," *BGDSL*, 93 (Tübingen, 1971), 168–212; Jeffrey Ashcroft, "Crabbed Age and Youth," *GL&L*, 28 (1974/75), 187–99; William E. Jackson, "R.d.A. in Literary History," *CollG* (1975), 177–204; Wiebke Schmaltz, *R.d.A.* (Göppingen: Kümmerle, 1975); Albrecht Hagenlocher, "Das 'Tagelied' Rs.d.A.," *ZDP*, 96 (1977), 76–89; Manfred

92   *Vox Feminae*

Stange, *Reinmars Lyrik* (Amsterdam: Rodopi, 1977); William E. Jackson, *Reinmar's Women* (Amsterdam: Benjamins; forthcoming in German Language and Literature Monographs, ed. W. W. Moelleken); Christian Gellinek, "Zu R.d.A.," in *Staufer Zeit*, ed. R. Krohn, B. Thum, P. Wapnewski (Stuttgart: Klett, 1978), pp. 260–69.

[154] My forthcoming study on the woman's song of Reinmar, *Reinmar's Women* (see previous note), will include texts and translations of Reinmar's *Frauenlieder*.

[155] MFMT VIb, 2 is a different version of this stanza (based on Manuscript E) featuring a male speaker.

[156] Trans. Nicholson, pp. 53–54; Thomas, pp. 103–04; Goldin, pp. 88–91. Presumably, the "Liutpolt" of this poem is Duke Leopold V of Austria. See de Boor, *HL*, p. 268; see also the skeptical view in Schweikle, "War Reinmar 'von Hagenau' Hofsänger zu Wien?" pp. 23–28.

[157] Trans. Richey, *Lyrics*, pp. 57–58.

[158] Trans. Thomas, pp. 105–06.

[159] Cf. Gerhard A. Vogt, "Die Technik der Reimverklammerung," in *'Getempert und gemischet' für Wolfgang Mohr*, ed. Franz Hundschnurscher and Ulrich Müller (Göppingen: Kümmerle, 1972), pp. 71 ff., 74 ff.

[160] See de Boor, *HL*, pp. 285 ff; Walshe, p. 112; Salmon, pp. 104–05; a dissenting view in Richey, *Essays*, pp. 65 ff.

[161] De Boor, *HL*, pp. 289 ff.

[162] De Boor, *HL*, pp. 282–92.

[163] See Friedrich Wilhelm, "Zur Frage nach der Heimat Rs. d. A. und Walther von der Vogelweide," *Münchener Museum*, 3 (1917), 11 ff.

[164] See Joseph Ernst, Ritter von Koch-Sternfeld, "Die Dynastie von Hagenau," *Archiv für Kunde österreichischer Geschichts-Quellen*, 1 (1848), Heft 4, 127–28; Theodor Mayer, "Einige Bemerkungen über die Familie der Stifter von Seitenstetten," *Archiv für Kunde österreichischer Geschichts-Quellen*, 21 (1859), 365; Kamillo Trotter, "Über die Stifterfamilien von Seitenstetten," *Mitteilungen des österreichischen Instituts für Geschichtsforschung*, 43 (1929), 114 ff; Rudolf Büttner, *Burgen und Schlösser* (Vienna: Birken, 1969), pp. 196–97.

[165] For older secondary literature on Walther, see the sources in notes 47 and 48. More recent studies include George Fenwich Jones, *W.v.d.V.* (New York: Twayne, 1968); Gert Kaiser, "Walthers Lied von *wünschen unde waenen* (L. 184, 1 . . .)," *BGDSL*, 90, 2/3 (Tübingen 1968), 243–79; D.R. McLintock, "Walther's *Mädchenlieder*," *OGS*, 3 (1968), 30–43; several articles in *Interpretationen mhd. Lyrik*, ed. Jungbluth; Hedwig Heger, *Das Lebenszeugnis Ws.v.d.V.* (Vienna: Schendl, 1970); John A. Asher, "Das Tagelied Ws.v.d.V.," in *Mediaevalia litteraria*, pp. 279–86; *W.d.v.V.*, ed. Siegfried Beyschlag (Darmstadt: Wissenschaftliche Buchgesellschaft, 1971); Helmut Birkhan, "Reimar, Walther und die Minne" (see note 153); Edith Hermann and Horst Wenzel, "Her Wîcman," *Euphorion*, 65 (1971), 1–20; Michael Curschmann, "*Waltherus cantor*," *OGS*, 6 (1971/72), 5–17; Peter Frenzel, "Order, Function and Convenientia," *JEGP*,

71 (1972), 165–76; Alois Kircher, *Dichter und Konvention* (Düsseldorf: Bertelsmann, 1973); Hubert Heinen, "Walthers Mailied," *ABäG*, 6 (1974), 167–82; Martha Kimmna, "Minne in a New Mode," *DVLG*, 48 (1974), 249–63; Jeffrey Ashcroft, "Crabbed Age and Youth," *GL&L*, 28 (1974/75), 187–98; several articles in *Studien zur deutschen Literatur und Sprache. Festschrift für Hugo Moser*, ed. W. Besch et al.; Ashcroft, "*Min trutgelle*," *Euphorion*, 69 (1975), 197–218; Arthur Gross, "Shall I Compare Thee to a Morn in May," *PMLA*, 91 (1976), 398–405; Uwe Stamer, *Ebene Minne bei W.v.d.V.* (Göppingen: Kümmerle, 1976); Hubert Heinen, "Lofty and Base Love," *GQ*, 51 (1978), 465–75.

166 L = *Die Gedichte Walthers von der Vogelweide*, ed. Carl von Kraus, 12th ed. (Berlin: de Gruyter, 1962). Trans. of L 39, 11 in Ian G. Colvin, '*I saw the world*' (London: Arnold, 1938), pp. 41–42; Richey, *Lyrics*, pp. 69–70; Jones, pp. 46–47; Thomas, pp. 111–12; Goldin, pp. 124–27.

167 Jones, pp. 35–37.

168 Both stanzas are involved in the feud between Walther and Reinmar. See *RU* II, pp. 5 ff; de Boor, *HL*, pp. 295–96.

169 Jones, pp. 31–32.

170 The most recent treatment known to me of the questions concerning Walther's homeland is that in Rudolf Bayerlein, "Von Kreuzgang zu Kreuzgang," *Zeitschrift für bayerische Landesgeschichte*, 38 (1975), 425–85; see also Alfred Kracher, "Walthers Heimat: Franken oder Österreich?" in *Mediaevalia litteraria*, pp. 255–78.

171 See Helmut de Boor, "Zu der Strophe 185, 31," *BGDSL*, 90 (Tübingen 1968), 283; Günther Jungbluth, "Thesen," in *Studien zur deutschen Literatur und Sprache des Mittelalters*, pp. 105 ff.

172 See Peter Wapnewski, "Walthers Lied von der Traumliebe," *Euphorion*, 51 (1957), 113–50.

173 See McLintock, "Walther's *Mädchenlieder*," pp. 42–43; Jones, pp. 44 ff.

174 See Gottfried von Strassburg, *Tristan*, trans. A.T. Hatto (Middlesex, England, Baltimore, Maryland, and Victoria, Australia: Penguin, 1960), p. 282.

175 Hinman, "Minne in a New Mode," p. 253.

176 Asher, "Das Tagelied," p. 285.

177 Simon, *N.v.R.* (see note 117), pp. 16–17, 26–27.

178 See Humphrey Milnes, "The Minnesinger and the Court," *GL&L*, 21 (1968), 279–86; Ursula Peters, "Niederes Rittertum oder hoher Adel?," *Euphorion*, 67 (1973). 250 ff.

179 See Hermann-Wenzel, "*Her Wîcman*," pp. 15 ff; Curschmann, "*Waltherus cantor*," pp. 12–13.

180 Simon, *N.v.R.*, pp. 25 ff.

181 Simon, *N.v.R.*, pp. 36 ff.

182 Simon, *N.v.R.*, pp. 44 ff.

183 Simon, *N.v.R.*, pp. 39 ff.

[184] See Simon, "Neidhart und die Neidhartianer," *BGDSL*, 94 (Tübingen, 1972), 153 ff., 187 ff.

[185] E.g., *Deutsche Liederdichter des 13. Jahrhunderts*, ed. Carl von Kraus (Tübingen: Niemeyer, 1952), I, pp. 39–40, 47–48 (Burkhart von Hohenfels VII and XV); 79 (Gedrut-Geltar IV); 403–04 (Von Scharpfenberg I and II); 461–62 (Ulrich von Lichtenstein XXX); 551 (Ulrich von Winterstetten XXXVII, cf. his number IV). More traditional examples of the woman's song in this collection are number IV by Niune (p. 301) and—with some reservations—number II by Heinrich von der Muore (pp. 157–58).

[186] See Andrée Kahn Blumstein, *Misogyny and Idealization in the Courtly Romance* (Bonn: Bouvier Verlag Herbert Grundmann, 1977), pp. 13 ff.

[187] See Richey, *Essays*, pp. 67, 69–70; Schmaltz, *R.d.A.*, pp. 20–21; see also Hubert Heinen, "Observations on the Role in *Minnesang*," *JEGP*, 75 (1976), 198–208.

[188] See Angermann, p. 104; Frings, "Frauenstrophe und Frauenlied," p. 19.

[189] Studies on performance which have been particularly helpful to me are Edmond Faral, *Les Jongleurs en france au moyen âge* (1910; rpt. New York: Franklin, 1970); Walter Salmen, *Der fahrende Musiker im europäischen Mittelalter* (Kassel: Innenthal, 1960); Piet Wareman, *Spielmannsdichtung* (Amsterdam: Van Campen, 1951); Curschmann, "*Waltherus cantor*."

Hubert   Heinen

The Woman's Songs
of Hartmann von Aue

An increasing awareness of the use of roles in medieval lyrics, doubtless derived in part from our present-day understanding of the function of role playing in human behavior, and a similarly contemporary concern with the status of women have broadened and deepened scholarly investigation. The realization that the poet/ performer is presenting a role is not new—throughout the twentieth century scholars have been warning against the biographical fallacy—but the aesthetic implications of such roles are becoming more obvious.[1] The use of roles does not preclude the poet/ performer's projecting his own understanding of human responses into situations within the conventions of society, and woman's songs, despite their artificiality as conceived and sung by a male performer, are frequently among the most direct and genuine of the medieval period. This characteristic led Alfred Jeanroy, among others, to view the woman's voice as the most original and popular. In more recent years Theodor Frings and Peter Dronke have seen at least the early woman's songs as typical of folk poetry.[2] The songs of Hartmann von Aue, however, are very much of a piece. His three woman's songs and the dialogue/ *Wechsel* which is at least possibly his exhibit a treatment of themes and a technique clearly linked to his other courtly lyrics.

The dialogue/ *Wechsel* "Dir hat enboten" (XII) is attributed to Hartmann in two manuscripts. Another manuscript attributes an expanded version of it to Walther von der Vogelweide, to whom are also ascribed sententious strophes isolated from the multistrophed song. The *Wechsel*, a form which apparently antedates the dialogue in German, contains a set of strophes presenting independent monologues related to a central topic. 'Hartmann's' version of "Dir hat enboten" presents three roles: in a strophe each, the messenger and the lady engage in a dialogue about the knight's service and its appropriate reward; the singer *qua* knight follows with a strophe of his own in the style of the *Wechsel*.

1 To you has sent, kind Lady,
       his service one who wishes you to have it,
   a knight, who gladly does
       the best his heart knows how to.
           He wants to be, if you will, throughout this
                                                   summer
           in exceedingly high spirits in eager anticipation of
                                                   your favor.
           You are to accept this pleasantly
               so that I depart with good tidings.
           Then I'll be welcome there.

2 "You are to tell him I'm at his service.
       Whatever may happen that causes him delight,
   that could please no one better
       who has so seldom seen him.
           And ask the worthy knight to direct himself
           toward someone who will reward him—I am not
                                                   the right woman
           to accept words of this nature.
               Whatever else he desires
           I'll do, for he is worthy of it."

3 The first words of mine she ever heard
       she accepted in a manner which seemed positive
                                                   to me
   until she had me close to her—
       then all at once another spirit possessed her.
           However much I'd like to, I cannot leave her.
           My grand love has increased so mightily
               that it will not let me go.
           I'll always have to be her serf.
           Never mind, that is also my desire.[3]

The infelicities of my translation stem in part from my desire to stay as close as possible to the original in order to give some notion of the distribution of the key phrases. The translation does, however, mirror a remarkable attribute of the original. All three speakers use a stiff and formal diction that lacks the ease and fluidity of much of Hartmann's verse. Rather than conclude that the difference is an indication that the strophes are spurious, I prefer to believe that Hartmann, a master of style and tone in epic and lyric, is characterizing his speakers through their use of language. This contention seems remarkably anachronistic—consistent language characterization is a later development, and Hartmann's robbers in his *Erec*, for example, use speech easily as refined as that of his hero and heroine—but the fact remains that all three speakers here are on their best behavior but do not speak alike. A certain directness and ingenuousness frequently helps differentiate woman's strophes from man's, though more often they are indistinguishable and even interchangeable. But here the messenger's words are extremely stilted, the lady's only slightly less so, and the knight's come closest to a direct and natural style.

The messenger transmits an offer of service in exchange for reward and declares that her response will determine how he will be received back home. The lady is recalcitrant, protesting that she scarcely knows her suitor, and though she esteems him, she cannot love him. This straightforward statement is complicated in its presentation. In the *Aufgesang* (the first four lines) she answers his offer of service with her own and appears willing to grant him her favors, though, she comments, she has rarely seen him. Such a statement is calculated to puzzle an audience: how is it to reconcile the statement of the first *Stollen* (the first two lines) with that of the second? One solution would be that the lady is chiding her knight, through his messenger, for staying away so long. However, in the *Abgesang* (the last five lines) it quickly becomes apparent that she literally means that he is practically a stranger to her (or that she prefers to treat him as such). He should choose another lady to importune with requests for *genâde* ("favors," especially sexual ones), though she is glad to grant him more innocuous requests in recognition of his worthiness.

When the knight states his understanding of their relationship, it becomes clear that the lady's denial that any sign of love was ever exchanged perplexes him. "First I thought she was swayed by my words," he muses, "and now I find she's assumed another stance. We were so close till we got close together." According to the lady it was a chance encounter, but that is not the way he remembers it— and the contrasting accounts are presented to the audience indirectly but in such a way that the knight's seems more plausible. Only in the *Abgesang* does he turn to her suggestion that he seek another lady. Now, despite (or because of) her recalcitrance, he declares himself enthralled. He is in the service of the lady who has offered him any service but that which he desired; indeed, he is not her vassal (with the freedom that implies) but her serf—and he is so willingly.

Though the traces of the *Wechsel* are an archaic element, the content of the song recalls not the themes of Danubian *Minnesang* but rather the Provençal cliché of the abject suitor and the haughty lady—a cliché which was never, in Romance or in German song, an absolute, but, rather, simply the most common stance of the lover and his mistress. The lady's demurrer, if genuine and not a coquett- ish ploy, is perfectly sensible; love is not an appropriate enterprise for virtual strangers, the motifs of love from afar and especially love by hearsay notwithstanding. But that does not keep us from viewing her, on the basis of her own words, as either cruel or lacking in sentiment, or both. Her role is too distant to evoke the audience's sympathy. Especially if we accept the suitor's account (and he does have the last word), the lady is hard hearted. As seen through his eyes, she is feigning unfamiliarity with him to facilitate her refusing him. Her gracious offer of limited favors becomes coquetry or scorn. By having the suitor so color the audience's perception of the lady's stance, the author, at the same time, exposes the futile and demeaning nature of the suitor's subjugation. It is rather as if Hartmann were aware—and expected his audience to be aware—of the notion he expressed to another purpose in his crusade song "Ich var mit iuwern hulden": "Ir minnesinger, iu muoz ofte misselingen, / daz iu den schaden tuot, daz ist der wân" ("You minnesingers, you'll always fail; / What brings you to shame and grief is the vanity of your hope").[4] And yet there is a positive power in accepting the rigors of love service. A playful irony is no evidence that Hartmann rejects the values of the courtly game.[5] Rather, by presenting in- numerable nuances in a subtle (or, occasionally, blatant) manner, he heightens the delight of his audience that it has understood him, regardless of which side of the multicolored cloak of irony it perceives.

The lady in Hartmann's poem "Swes vröide hin ze den bluomen stât," however, is as consummate a game player as the singer/knight, the role most frequently assumed by the poet/performer.

1 Whoever finds joy in the flowers
   must soon mourn the sorrowful season.
However, solace comes to the lady
   who lies through the long night with her beloved.
Thus I, too, plan to shorten

the long winter without birdsong.
If I am to do without that, it is not by my will.

2 My friends have set up a game for me
   in which my choice, whichever it is, is wrong:
   —although I'll pick one of the choices
   without a real option, it would have been best left
                            alone—
   they say: if I want to love
   I must do without love.
   Nevertheless, my spirit recommends both courses
                            to me.

3 If I should follow my friends' advice,
   by God, why should he then owe thanks to me?
   Since he has earned it well
   I think he has had to wait too long,
      for I want to risk for him
      life, reputation, and mind—
   Then I will have to win, if fortune wills it.

4 He is well worth all of that
      —if I wish to keep my loyalty to him—
   which a man desires of a lady.
   In truth, no honor is too much for him.
   He is a man who understands so well how
                            things are
      —if I can keep it for him—
   that if I love him I'll never come to grief for it.

Here again some of the subtleties of the original are lost in my translation. For example, the dichotomy of joy and sorrow is expressed in the original in the subject (literally, the joy of whoever is inclined toward flowers) and in the verb rendered here with "mourn." "The hard or distressful season" forms an antithesis to the spring/summer implied by the flowers. The linked antitheses prevail throughout the first strophe. The "shortening" of the long winter night carries with it the contrast between amusement (*kurze wîle*) and boredom (*lange wîle*) in addition to the overt sexual connotation. The lady proposes to alleviate the anguish and boredom of winter and restore the joy of spring or summer by sleeping with her lover. Such a proposal corresponds to the desires of many of the ladies of Middle High German woman's song and those of virtually all the men in the more common songs with a male persona, but there is generally a catch, a reason why this desire cannot be fulfilled. An audience whose attention has been aroused by a skillful use of rhetorical figures, an audience which can perceive the intentional cleverness of the learned poet behind a role which seems to present all the urgency of a woman's desire, will expect the next strophe to explain why love cannot be consummated.

The audience's expectation is not denied. The beginning of the second strophe describes the hindrance which makes the desired fulfillment difficult, if not impossible. A third party—the friends and relations (the MHG word implies both), the fellow members of the court—is introduced, for whom a simple love between man and woman is contrary to the rules of the game. The lady recognizes the problem. Her friends want her to accept a no-win situation, to love only when she is willing to refrain from love at the same time. The alternative choice is, implicitly, not to wish to love in the first place. The two paths her spirit urges her to follow are (1) the praiseworthy abnegation recommended by the court, and (2) gratification of her desires, a direction for which she has already stated a preference. The subsequent arguments support her choice of the latter course.

By employing game or contest terminology in the third strophe, the lady lends legitimacy to her choice, obscuring the fact that this choice was not recognized as a possible one by her friends. She wants to reward her lover for his service and is impatient for him to claim his reward, even though she realizes she is risking everything by playing this game. In playing for such high stakes she places herself at the mercy of chance—again a legitimatizing action, since, we may assume, only a just choice will succeed.

The phrase *jâ herre* must either be a trivial exclamation ("by God"), an address to God (making the game into one for the very highest stakes, which seems unlikely), or an address to a courtier, perhaps the singer who is presenting her song. Though the last possibility would create an interesting interaction within the performance situation, there is neither functional need nor literary precedent for such an address from role to performer, and the trivial explanation is probably best. Nonetheless, the third strophe is remarkable for the intensity and radical commitment the lady expresses and the high degree of identification it elicits between the role and her statement. Unless we assume an unprecedented aside in the words *jâ herre*, the persona of the song has become more and more isolated from the audience; her musings are increasingly internalized rather than debated with the audience. The decision has been made; the die is cast.

The final strophe justifies the lady's choice of sensual delight over courtly restraint by assigning her lover a power beyond that which the court can give. In this strophe she eschews society as the honor-bestowing institution—the custodian of one's reputation—and assigns society's function to her lover. This transfer is not presented straightforwardly, however; if it were, it would not convince an audience. Rather, through a series of words such as *wert* ("worthy"), *triuwe* ("loyalty"), *êren* ("honor," "bestowing honor"), and *bescheiden* ("knowledgeable in the ways of the court"), she insinuates an assertion of her lover's personal worthiness. His value is placed so high that it sheds honor on her (a situation which more commonly obtains in the suitor's praise of his lady).

A logical examination of the lady's arguments in favor of her choice—especially undertaken from the viewpoint of an audience which could most nearly identify with the friends whose game the lady has declined to play—reveals that they are specious. Within the framework of the song, however, the lady wins, and we may assume the audience accepts her victory. Although the persona of the song is more and more introspective, the relationship between song and audience—the function of the song as a social event—remains. As an almost accidental side effect of the song as an instrument with which the poet/performer evokes and maintains a sense of belonging to a refined and clever elite among his auditors, the lady's expression of complex self-justification awakens the audience to an appreciation of the dilemma created for her by the rival claims of desire and propriety and to an awareness that women are no less capable of complex conceits on love than men.

A different dilemma is the basis of Hartmann's poem "Diz waeren wunneclîche tage."[6] Here, the lady is pondering two states—that of a woman who has lost her lover (or husband) on a crusade (or through his death),[7] and that of a woman who has never had one.

1 These would be happy days
   for a woman who could live them joyfully.
   Now God has given me a sad lament
      in this splendid season
         which I'll, unfortunately, never be rid of:
         I have lost such a man
      that I in truth must say indeed
         that no woman ever had a dearer lover.
            When I took care of him he caused me joy:
            now may God take care of him—He'll do so
                                 better than I.

2 No one could know the damage done me fully
      without recognizing it worthy of loud lament.
   The man in whom I always found loyalty and honor
      and whatever a woman desires in a man
         has been taken from me suddenly.

Therefore nothing can help me
ever till I die,
    without my having to suffer lovesick distress.
    A woman who has experienced something
better
    should let it be seen in her expression.

3 God has treated that woman well—
    since love causes such a sorrowful end—
who has refrained from both:
    for her the season (time) passes joyfully.
    I must lament so many a dazzling day
    and her mood is such
    that she cannot believe me.
    I have grown joyful through love:
    if I grow old in years,
    this will be repaid with sorrow a
thousandfold.

Of the options, the lady prefers to have lost rather than not to have
loved at all, and thus, despite differences in tone, the option rejected
here is the one implicitly rejected in "Swes vröide"—a refusal to
enter into any love relationship.

A preference for the pain of love to the stoic pleasure of an
existence without love or pain is a common avowal for a male
persona to make, and the superfluity of cueing in this song suggests
that Hartmann wanted to insure that his audience realized its persona was a woman. Her concept of what love should entail can be
sketched by citing a few phrases: "he caused me joy"; "I always
found loyalty and honor and whatever a woman desires in a man" in
him; love is, despite its necessary linkage with sorrow, a positive,
joyful force which is connected with such principles as *triuwe* ("mutual loyalty," as of liege and liege lord) and *êre* ("honor," "reputation")—the prime prerequisites of courtly existence. There is also all
the sensuality suggested by "whatever a woman desires."

The structure of the lady's lament is worth examining. Though
the first four lines appear to form an *Aufgesang* with two-line
Stollen and a six-line *Abgesang*, only the last strophe reflects this
form syntactically. The sense divisions of the first two strophes
group the lines 2 3 3 2; those of the last, 4 3 3 (or 5 2 3). In all
probability, the musical form heightened the strophic form in
presentation.[8] Here, a tension is created between the *Aufgesang* and
the first line of the *Abgesang* which emphasizes the fifth line of the
first two strophes. This effect probably carries over to the last
strophe, in which, in fact, lines 4 and 5 may be bound together by

sense. If the final couplet is, as the syntax of the first two strophes suggests, not only a metrical but also a musical entity, then the strophic structure emphasizes the eighth line of each strophe as the last line before this final couplet. These points of emphasis are indicated by italics in the brief paraphrase of the song's contents which follows.

1.   The season is one of joy for those who can be joyful. Now I must mourn *forever*, for I have lost a man (vassal? husband?) *dearer than all the rest*. I cared for him and he caused me joy—now may God take him in His loving care.

2.   No one can appreciate what I have lost who fails to recognize the worthiness of him *who has been taken from me so suddenly*. I'll never get over his loss *without suffering love-sick sorrow*. Let a woman who has experienced a happier fate show it in her gestures.

3.   That woman is fortunate who has been spared both love's joy and love's sorrow. She has a joyful season while *the happy days are full of woe for me* (lines 4 and 5 echo the first line of the first strophe). And she may in her contentment not believe that *I was filled with joy by love*—which will be balanced a thousand times by sorrow if I live long enough.

Even if one rejects the notion that certain lines could have been emphasized by the interaction of strophic and melodic form or makes the reasonable objection that there is insufficient evidence to support the suggestion that lines 5 and 8 of each strophe were thus emphasized in this song, one cannot deny that the song derives its poignancy from the contrast between the joy of a fortunate woman who (as the audience is gradually told) eschews love's delights and sorrows, and the sorrow of the persona who has loved and lost her beloved. If the performance emphasized certain lines as suggested—and, to a lesser extent, even if it did not—the persona states her preference for love despite its sorrow.

The function of the song is much the same for the courtly audience whether the song is a widow's or a sweetheart's. The persona's preference for love over the ascetic life could be condemned in certain circles in either case, since love in marriage was scarcely less suspect than love outside it. Hartmann's concern with the social and moral implications of love and marriage, as well as of the secular versus the ascetic life, pervades his works, as, for example, in "Ob man mit lügen die sêle nert":

    1 If one saves one's soul with lies
        then I know a man who is holy,
      who repeatedly swears false oaths to me.

> I succumbed to his clever cunning
>> and chose him as my lover.
>>> With him I thought to find constancy.
>> My own good sense deserted me there
>>> as I proclaim to the world:
>> he is as devoid of falsity
>>> as the ocean is of waves.

2 Why should I seek the advice of others
> since my own heart deceived me
by leading me astray to him
> who has never been of use to me nor to any other
>> good woman?
>> It is a paltry praise by a man
>>> which he inflicts on women.
>> He is so skilled with sweet words
>>> that one could write them down.
>> I followed them out onto thin ice:
>>> the damage must remain with me.

3 If I should come to hate all men
> I'd do it because of my hate for him alone.
How guilty would they be of it?
> After all, many a one will reward him better.
>> She has, in her fine good sense,
>>> made a happy choice of a companion.
>> She smiles whenever I am sad—
>>> we grow old at different rates.
>> My undertaking began in pain;
>>> may God the Powerful assuage it.

Here the first two strophes and the *Aufgesang* of the third contain the lady's lament that she has fallen in love with a false and deceitful knight. Then, in the *Abgesang*, in the final six lines of the third and last strophe, the lady attacks a rival. The rival and the lover's inconstancy are subtly linked by the lady, and a unity of what might seem disparate parts is created. Even in the first strophe, where there is no mention of a rival, Hartmann's audience can assume, upon hearing a female persona lament her lover's deceit, inconstancy, and falsity, that she is also thinking about her rival. The shift from an exposition of the relationship between lover and lady to a comparison of the lady's lot with that of her rival may surprise us, but it need not have surprised Hartmann's audience.

Her words dripping with sarcasm, the lady announces to the court that her lover, who gained and retained her love with lies, has been inconstant. After closing this topic with a spectacular negative image at the end of the first strophe, she shifts to a self-accusation in the *Aufgesang* of the second strophe, introducing at the same time a hint that she plans to concern herself with her rival. Though self-accusation also rounds off the strophe, the predominant topic of the *Abgesang* is ironic praise of her lover's sweet words (through which she hints he is a singer—whom the audience can, if it wishes, identify with the poet/performer). The *Aufgesang* of the third strophe is equally reflective, and there is another hint that the lady is not just concerned with society's image of her lover and her relationship to him, but also with her rival, whose joy is portrayed in the *Abgesang* as being so different from the lady's sorrow. Experienced as a total-ity, the song is an effective lament, a perfect counterpart to the lover's laments as sung by a male persona. As presented by a male poet/performer, the lady's lament becomes not just a sort of dramatic monologue, but also a poignant apology for the singer's lack of constancy.

Richard Kienast and Ekkehard Blattmann have followed the lead of innumerable scholars of *Minnesang* in viewing these songs as something other than individual songs, namely as parts of an elaborate song cycle.[9] The more successful such interpretations be-come, the more they provide their own refutation. Thus Blattmann skillfully destroys Kienast's theory that the songs contained only in manuscript *C* (the Large Heidelberg Song Codex) represent a cycle planned and arranged by the author, but his ingenious substitute is far less credible. We are asked to believe that the extant songs attributed to Hartmann, with the exception of "Dir hât enboten, vrowe guot" were originally ordered by him in an elaborate cycle of seventeen songs interlinked in a fixed sequence by rhyme echoes and a narrative line more coherent and psychologically true to life than any found in the romances of the day, but that none of the manu-scripts containing these songs reflects this cycle. None of the songs of the cycle, however, was lost after it was broken up in trans-mission, and Hartmann never wrote a song which was not a part of the cycle (though scribes erroneously assigned him one of Walther's), or if he did so, such songs are lost. Even if we were to concede that by some miracle every strophe Hartmann wrote is preserved in the manuscripts we have, despite their being so far from the songs' origin that they completely distort the original arrangement, there is no way to get around the fact that "Ich sprach, ich wolte ir iemer leben" is not one song, but two. Not only is Blattmann's version of this poem (and that of the editors of *Des Minnesangs Frühling*) an editorial construct, but the versions in *B* (the Weingarten Song Codex) and *C* are demonstrably also scribal contaminations of a version from their common source which had strophes 3, 1, 2. No version which could have stemmed from Hartmann can be assumed

to have had all six strophes unless we assume that the contamina-
tion in *C* miraculously re-created Hartmann's original (in a strangely garbled sequence of strophes).[10]

The recurrent concern with cycles, however, though it has led
able and perceptive scholars astray, does remind us that these songs
were not sung in isolation, and as soon as we accept the fact that
several were probably sung during most performances, we have to
admit that no reading of a song in isolation completely represents
the way that song was perceived by its original audience. Despite the
remarkable attempts by such scholars as Kurt Herbert Halbach to
reconstruct *Vortragsgruppen*, there is no way for us to know what
songs created a horizon of expectation for any individual song.[11]
The crucial preparatory song or strophe may well no longer be
extant, and it is most likely in any case that the context within which
a song was heard and understood varied from performance to
performance (and within each performance from auditor to
auditor). Nevertheless, such contexts must have existed, and if we
assume that some performances of "Ob man mit lügen die sêle nert"
or "Diz waeren wunneclîche tage" followed a performance of "Swes
vröide hin ze den bluomen stât" (understood as a sweetheart's
lament), then the song may have been understood quite differently
from the manner I have suggested.

The choices the lady has or discusses in "Swes vröide" and "Diz
waeren" are between a life of love and a life of withdrawal. The
"other woman" in these songs is not a rival, but rather an ascetic. If
this dichotomy had been established for Hartmann's audience, it
might well have understood the *Abgesang* of the third strophe of
"Ob man" to constitute the jilted lady's admission that the ascetic
"has, in her fine good sense, / made a happy choice of a companion"
(i.e., Christ). As the persona in "Diz waeren" commands, the ascetic
"lets it be seen in her expression"—that is, "she smiles whenever I
am sad." And the God whom the lady in "Ob man" calls on to sooth
her pain is not the courtly God of lovers, but the bridegroom of the
nun the lady suddenly yearns to become. The ironic condemnation
of the false lover at the beginning of the song is doubled and intensi-
fied. The love which one should follow is not that of man, but that
of God: "when will you poor (minnesingers) love such a love as I?"
Hartmann's male persona asks in his crusading song (XVII, 3, 8).

Such diverse songs as "Iam dulcis venite" and Jaufré Rudel's
"Quan lo rossinhols el folhos" exist in multiple versions, which may
arguably be viewed as "religious" and "secular" ones.[12] It may well
be that even songs such as Hartmann's "Ob man mit lügen," for
which we have only one version extant, were conceived by their
author to have similarly contrary senses, depending on the context
of performance. The "secular" sense has been remarked on—with an

emphasis dependent on whatever fictitious or actual biographical situation is assumed—by a number of scholars such as Anton Schönbach, Kienast, and Blattmann.[13] The "religious" sense presupposes that the allusions to a woman refraining from love have reference to the religious vow of chastity, a vow frequently taken in Hartmann's times by widows and, one may assume, abandoned sweethearts. This sense for "Ob man" is unlikely if the song is heard in isolation, and it is not necessary even in the possible context suggested. But some portion of Hartmann's audience may have understood him to mean—and have been intended to understand him to mean—that the lady's final words ("may God the Powerful assuage it!") signal a *revocatio*, a conversion to the attitude of the other woman.

Hartmann's three woman's songs, and the *Wechsel* which may also be his, confront us with at least four attitudes toward love, at least four different positions in the courtly entertainment entitled *Minnesang*. From them we learn something about medieval notions of the female psyche, something about medieval thoughts concerning love, and much about how Hartmann juggled themes, forms, attitudes, and audience. The technique of these songs is essentially identical to the technique of his other songs. What then is the function of the woman's voice?

In part, of course, woman's song and woman's strophes are a part of the tradition within which Hartmann is creating. A statistical survey of strophes with a female persona in twelfth- and very early thirteenth-century *Minnesang* demonstrates that such strophes were quite common among the earliest songs, less common or even absent among the first wave of singers strongly influenced by Provençal and French models, and somewhat more common again in the songs of Albrecht von Johansdorf, Heinrich von Rugge, Reinmar der Alte, Hartmann, Wolfram von Eschenbach, and Walther von der Vogelweide.

Anonymous Love Songs	7	58.3%
Der von Kürenberg	8½	56.7%
Meinloh von Sevelingen	3	25%
Burggraf von Regensburg	3	75%
Burggraf von Rietenburg	1	14.3%
Dietmar von Eist	15½	37.8%
Kaiser Heinrich	2	25%
Friedrich von Hausen	6	10.9%
Heinrich von Veldeke	7 (12)	13.5% (19.7%)[14]
Ulrich von Gutenburg	0	
Rudolf von Fenis	0	
Albrecht von Johansdorf	4 [7½]	11.4% [17.9%][15]

Heinrich von Rugge	6	12.5%
Bernger von Horheim	0	
Hartwig von Rute	0	
Bligger von Steinach	0	
Heinrich von Morungen	6	5.2%
Engelhart von Adelnburg	0	
Reinmar der Alte	44 (48½)	16.9% (17.4%)
Hartmann von Aue	11	17.7%
Gottfried von Strassburg	0	
Wolfram von Eschenbach	4½	13.2%
Walther von der Vogelweide	25 (30)	9.3% (9.1%)[16]

Hartmann, who was (next to Heinrich von Rugge) a key model for Reinmar, shares with this master of languishing love songs a clear predilection for the woman's voice. In all probability the reason is the same for both. Reinmar and Hartmann seem fascinated with the psychological intricacies of love in a social framework. Their lyrics are relatively poor in imagery, though there are some striking exceptions. Rather, they are characterized by a preponderance of rationalistic musing, by a sophisticated employment of the arsenal of learned rhetoric and school wisdom. Both poets delight in teasing their audience, in keeping their audience in suspense as to which way a given argument will turn. In fact, Reinmar may have given the same basic song a number of different turns to keep his audience's interest alive, a tendency which is sparingly attested in the songs of Hartmann. The rather rarified songs of these two poets are substantially enlivened by interaction with the audience and by the use of roles. The woman's voice may have been employed to provide variety only, or (and this is my belief) its use may reflect an interest in exploring and exploiting the problems encountered by a woman as the result of the grand game of seduction and desire at court.

   *Notes*

[1] Peter Bründl, "*Unde bringe den wehsel, als ich waen, durch ir liebe ze grabe.* Eine Studie zur Rolle des Sängers im Minnesang von Kaiser Heinrich bis Neidhart von Reuenthal," *DVLG*, 44 (1970), 409–32; Frederick Goldin, *Lyrics of the Troubadours and Trouvères: An Anthology and a History* (Garden City, N.Y.: Doubleday, 1973), pp. 6–19, 108–22, 443–53. and *German and Italian Lyrics of the Middle Ages: An Anthology and a History* (Garden City, N.Y.: Doubleday, 1973), pp. 36–41, 71–83; Hubert Heinen, "Observations on the Role in *Minnesang*," *JEGP*, 75 (1976), 198–208. Derk Ohlenroth has denied that the early woman's songs in German were role songs: *Sprechsituation und Sprecheridentität. Eine*

Untersuchung zum Verhältnis von Sprache und Realität im frühen deutschen Minnesang, GAG, 96 (Göppingen: Kümmerle, 1974).

[2] See the studies by Jeanroy, Frings, and Dronke listed in Helmut Tervooren, *Bibliographie zum Minnesang und zu den Dichtern aus "Des Minnesangs Frühling"* (Berlin: Erich Schmidt, 1969). Other studies of the woman's voice by Mihail Isbăşescu, Gerhard Pomassl, Ernst Lesser, Adolar Angermann, Heinz Fischer, Erika Mergell, Peter F. Ganz, and Rolf Grimminger are also listed in Tervooren. In addition, see Peter Dronke, *The Medieval Lyric,* 2nd ed. (London and New York: Cambridge Univ. Press, 1977), and Peter Wapnewski, *Waz ist minne. Studien zur mittelhochdeutschen Lyrik* (Munich: Beck, 1975).

[3] This and the subsequent translations and references are based on the texts in Hugo Moser and Helmut Tervooren, eds., *Des Minnesangs Frühling* (Stuttgart: S. Hirzel, 1977).

[4] See Hugo Kuhn, "Minnesang als Aufführungsform," rpt. in *Hartmann von Aue,* ed. Hugo Kuhn and Christoph Cormeau (Darmstadt: Wissenschaftliche Buchgesellschaft, 1973), pp. 478–90; in English translation as "*Minnesang* and the Form of Performance," *Formal Aspects of Medieval German Poetry: A Symposium,* ed. Stanley N. Werbow (Austin: Univ. of Texas Press, 1969), pp. 27–41.

[5] See Hubert Heinen, "*Mit gemache lân:* A Crux in Hartmann's 'Maniger grüezet mich alsô' (*MF* 216,29)," *Studies in Medieval Culture,* 12 (1978), 85–90.

[6] See Carl von Kraus, *Des Minnesangs Frühling. Untersuchungen* (Leipzig: S. Hirzel, 1939), pp. 423–29.

[7] Stolte, "Hartmanns sogenannte Witwenklage und sein drittes Kreuzlied," *DVLG,* 25 (1951), 184–98; (rpt. in *Hartmann von Aue,* ed. Kuhn and Cormeau, pp. 49–67); see also Richard Kienast, *Das Hartmann-Liederbuch C²,* Sitzungsberichte der deutschen Akademie der Wissenschaften zu Berlin, Klasse für Sprachen, Literatur und Kunst, I (Berlin: Akademie, 1963), pp. 47–61; Ekkehard Blattmann, *Die Lieder Hartmanns von Aue, PSuQ,* 44 (Berlin: Erich Schmidt, 1968), pp. 13–55; Salmon, "The Underrated Lyrics of Hartmann von Aue," *MLR,* 66 (1971), 810–25, esp. 820–21.

[8] Cf. Hubert Heinen, "Walthers Mailied (L 51,13): Vortragsbedingter Aufbau und gesellschaftlicher Rahmen," *ABäG,* 6 (1974), 167–82; Peter Frenzel, "*Minnesang:* Sung Performance and Strophic Order," *Studies in Medieval Culture,* 6/7 (1976), 83–94.

[9] Blattmann, pp. 13–55; Kienast, pp. 47–61.

[10] I am preparing a study on the significance of multiple versions of songs by Friedrich von Hausen, Hartmann von Aue, Reinmar der Alte, and Walther von der Vogelweide. A part of this study is an investigation of the contaminations in *C.* See Moser and Tervooren, II, pp. 15–16, for a discussion of multiple versions with bibliography.

[11] See, for example, Halbach's "Die Weingartner Liederhandschrift als Sammlung poetischer Texte," *Die Weingartner Liederhandschrift* (Stuttgart: Müller und Schindler, 1969), pp. 29–132, esp. 78–88, 100–02.

[12] See Karl Strecker, ed., *Die Cambridger Lieder*, 2nd ed. (Berlin: Weidmann, 1955), pp. 69–73; Rupert T. Pickens, ed., *The Songs of Jaufré Rudel* (Toronto: Pontifical Institute, 1978), pp. 61–87, and for a discussion of *mouvance* (= multiple versions), pp. 22–39.

[13] Anton E. Schönbach, *Über Hartmann von Aue. Drei Bücher Untersuchungen* (Graz: Leuschner und Lubensky, 1894), pp. 369–70; Kienast, pp. 24–28; Blattmann, pp. 192–94.

[14] Moser and Tervooren consider some of the strophes to be spurious (the numbers in parentheses).

[15] The numbers in brackets refer to a dialog which is different in character from the other songs.

[16] According to Friedrich Maurer, ed., *Die Lieder Walthers von der Vogelweide*, Vol. II: *Die Liebeslieder*, Altdeutsche Textbibliothek, 47 (Tübingen: Max Niemeyer, 1956).

Ruth P. M. Lehmann

Woman's Songs in Irish,
800–1500

Irish stories were told with sequences of prose interspersed with verse. Verse-speeches also occur independently of the tales, and scribes often assign them, then, to an appropriate character. The tales may gather other poems, some independent ones that scribes have interpolated, perhaps without much authority, and others that the scribes themselves, charmed by the story, have composed.[1] The simplest way of introducing such poems was to precede them with an ascription or a sentence relating them to a well-known story. Of course any famous person may be assigned poems; those accredited to Colum Cille, for example, cover fully six hundred years from his death in 593 A.D.

    Since women are prominent figures in many of the tales, and since we hear of women satirists, poets, and prophets, woman's songs are not unusual in the corpus of Irish lyric poetry. Additionally, poems are sometimes given in lives of female Irish saints, or put in the mouths of women of the Bible—e.g., Eve. These poems will not be duscussed here, since they seem to belong to a different genre. The woman's songs under discussion here are a way of vivifying a story and intensifying its emotional appeal. The same is also true, to be sure, of verses attributed to men. Perhaps this manner of telling a story in both prose and verse influenced the Norse sagas, though beyond that very general resemblance little in the sagas can be confidently derived from Irish stories—surely not the passionate laments or songs of personal delight.

Before discussing Irish woman's songs, a word is necessary on the translations given. These imitate the Irish meters as closely as possible in syllabic count (usually seven syllables to the line), in rhythm of line endings, rime scheme—including internal rime (between two words in the interior of adjacent lines) and linking rime (between the last word of one line and a word in the interior of the next)—assonance, consonance, and alliteration. The hope is that, besides the imagery, something of the intricate music of Irish verse can be appreciated from the translations. Such imitations are possible because, like modern English, early Irish had lost most of the original endings and had substituted internal changes, resulting in many more monosyllables than are found in other early languages; furthermore, most of the verse is very free in the distribution of stressed syllables.

To a limited extent I have also availed myself of riming consonants by class, rather than by identity, thus treating *ripple/little/ fickle*, *sob/odd/bog*, and *turf/worth* as perfect rimes. Except for nasals such as *rim/thin/sing*, I have only sparingly used different resonants and voiced fricatives as equivalents. Since Irish has but one sibilant (and that is in a class by itself) but English has several, I have occasionally treated any sibilant as the equivalent of any other. Clusters I have treated, for the most part, freely, as the Irish do, but perhaps not as rigidly, since they take only the final consonant as significant. To my ear *man* is a better rime for *band* than *lad*. The Irish might rime any of the following: *sought/haunt/court/fault/ soft*.

The most unusual verse form for English ears is called *deibide*, one of the most popular in Irish. This is a quatrain of riming couplets, but the usual form has the second and fourth lines end in words one or two syllables longer than the first and third lines, so that a stressed word rimes with an unstressed syllable. In Irish the length of the unstressed syllable does not need to match that of the stressed syllable. Since English no longer distinguishes vocalic length, I have availed myself of similar confusion among reduced vowels. Further, I sometimes treat adjective plus noun as if it formed a compound in order to get the rocking stress necessary for the second or fourth lines of *deibide*.

To illustrate the verse, I cite here the Irish and its literal translation for some of the stanzas of the "Old Woman of Beare," a poem which contains many verse forms. Thus *deibide* of several varieties and other common forms can be compared with the imitative translation given below. In describing forms other than the *deibide* it is customary to raise or lower the figure giving the number of syllables at the end of lines. The number in normal position indicates the number of syllables in the line.

2. Is mé caillech Bérri, Buí;   *deibide*
   no meilinn léini mbithnuí;
     indíu táthum, dom šéimi,
     ná melainn cid aithléini.

3. It moíni   *deibide* with
   cartar lib, nídat doíni;   rhythmic rimes
     sinni, ind inbaid marsaimme and shortened
     batar doíni carsaimme.   first line.

4. Batar inmaini doíni; $7_2 7_2 7_1 7_2$
    ata maige 'ma-ríadam;   rime 2/4
  ba maith no-mmeilmis leo,
    ba becc no-mmoítis íaram.

5. Indíu trá caín-timgairid, $7_3 7_2 7_3 7_2$
    ocus ní mór nond-oídid;   rime 1/3 2/4
   ciasu becc don-indnaigid,
    is mór a mét no-mmoídid.

6. Carpait lúaith $3_1 7_1 7_1 7_1$ first line
   ocus eich no beirtis búaid, assonates with
     ro boí, denus, tuile díb: rime 2/4, linking
   bennacht for Ríg roda-úaid! rime 3/4

7. Tocair mo chorp co n-aichri $7_2 7_2 7_1 7_2$ rime 1/2/4;
   dochum adba dían aithgni;   linking rime 3/4
     tan bas mithig la Mac nDé
   do-té do brith a aithni.[2]

(2. I am Bui, the Old woman of Beare (or the Nun); I used to wear ever-new linen; today I have become so thin, I could not wear out even a worn shirt.

3. They are riches that are loved by you, they are not people; as for us, while we lived, there were people that we loved.

4. Dear were the people whose plains we rode across; it was well we enjoyed ourselves among them; it was little they promised afterwards.

5. Today they make fine claims, and it is not much

that they lent; though they give little, great was the amount that they promised.

6. Swift chariots and horses that won the prize, a while there was a flood of them: bless the King who gave them!

7. My body bitterly makes its way toward the mansions where it is known: when it seems timely to the Son of God let Him come to receive his loan.)

Another rather common form with linking rime between 1/2 and 3/4, with rime 2/4 is exemplified in the quatrain Grainne speaks on first seeing Diarmait:

Fil duine $3_27_27_27_2$ rime 1/3
   frismad buide lemm díuterc,   2/4; linking rime
dia tibrinn in mbith mbuide,   1/2 3/4
   huile, huile, cid díupert.[3]

(There is someone whom I would thank at sight [of him]; to whom I would give the fertile earth, all, all, though it were a poor bargain.)

Double linking rime as in Grainne's speech is frequent also in "Creide's Lament for Cael," a poem largely from the Finn Cycle, but not as early in language, with one stanza from the *Acallam na Senorach*, much of which is a retelling by Oisin to St. Patrick of some of the adventures of Finn and his men. In this "Lament" rime between the ends of 1/2 is often substituted for linking rime.

One note that seems to me characteristic of woman's songs in Irish is the number that dwell more on past joys than on present miseries—so unlike the few woman's songs that have come down to us from Old English. One such poem, in language from the ninth century, is the lament of Liadain who loses her lover at his banishment when they fail the test of "consortium," that peculiarly Irish test in which a nun and a monk sleep together with a young boy present to witness whether or not they keep their vows. This poem occurs with difficult prose that tries to make a story of it—that Liadain took the veil against Curithir's wishes, and now regrets it. But we may also have here an association of poems originally written in different contexts.[4]

1. No pleasure
       in deed done to loving-one;
    tormenting without measure.

2. What madness
     not to give him happiness,
   though fear of God feed sadness.

3. No ruin,
     his affair desirable
   through pain heaven pursuing.

4. Cause slender
     through me troubled Cuirithir,
   though I was gentle, tender.

5. I'm Liadain;
     it is I loved Cuirithir
   truly, though said by heathen.

6. Brief hour
     together with Cuirithir;
   our closeness then a dower.

7. Woods singing
     to me beside Cuirithir
   with somber sea-sounds dinning.

8. I wonder
     it would trouble Cuirithir
   any deal made asunder.

9. No hiding:
     he was my heart's true-lover,
   though I loved all beside him.

10. Flames flowing
     burst my heart, now desperate,
   dead without him—this knowing.

The "Old Woman of Beare," like Liadain's song, speaks as
much of delight in past pleasures as of the misery of old age. Furthermore, even her present condition seems to assure her of ultimate
salvation with no diminishing of her relish for the joys of youth:

1. Ebbing I, unlike ocean;
     old age has made me sallow;
   although for that I grieve
     glad sea-feast fills the shallow.

2. Bui am I, of Beara nun,
     once clad in stuff new woven;

today I am grown so thin
I'd not wear out old linen.

3. Not people
you love, but wealth—the cheaper;
but we, living meagerly
loved people more eagerly.

4. Beloved were the people
whose plains we rode with laughter;
good the time we spent with them,
little they promised after.

5. Today they claim merrily,
but not much have they yielded;
though small our gain verily,
a great lot they conceded.

6. Racing steeds,
prize chariots for their speeds,
once a flood of them they'd bring;
bless the King Who gave me these.

7. My body fiercely making
toward due acknowledged rating;
when it seems time to God's Son,
let Him come, loans retaking.

8. Look at my arms all scrawny,
skinny and thin and bony!
Dear was the art that graced 'em,
embracing great kings wholly.

9. Skinny and thin and bony,
look at my arms all scrawny!
unfit to raise, though humbly,
round comely boys and brawny.

10. Joyful are all the maidens
when comes the time of Mayday;
more fitting for me my moan,
old crone long past my heyday.

11. No honied words I'm saying;
no wethers for my wedding;
scant my locks, pale and graying;
a mean veil I'm not dreading.

12. No tears shed
at this white veil on my head;

scarves of all colors glinting
on my head at ale-drinking.

13. Naught old I envy but this:
old Feimen's fertile surface;
  I spent that all—naught to show—
Feimen's crop is still yellow.

14. On Feimen stands the King's Stone;
Ronan's dwelling on Bregon;
  long since storms have struck each one,
but their cheeks aren't old, shrunken.

15. The waves of the great sea stir;
storms rouse the roar of winter;
  no nobleman nor slave's son
will come here today—no one.

16. I know what they are doing:
back and forth they are rowing;
  (Ath Allen—reed and lily)
to chilly sleep they're going.

17. Many days
since I sailed on youth's seaways;
  many years with beauty gone;
spent are my days as wanton.

18. Many days
whatever come though suns blaze;
  shawl I wear where'r I go:
old age is mine—that I know.

19. I have spent youth's summertime
and autumn, that othertime;
  in winter of age men drown;
its first frost comes—my sundown.

20. Soon my youth I wasted, cropped;
  I think good the course I kept,
old would be my cloak though small
the wall over which I leapt.

21. Fair is the fine cloak greening
  hills where my God spreads it;
nobly that cloak He's cleaning:
  wool hides bare ground, He treads it.

22. I'm wretched, alas for me,
  each fair eye is darkening;

since feasts with lights a-dapple,
chapel's gloom disheartening.

23. Awhile with kings unthinking,
    mead and wine were we drinking;
    today but whey and water
    with women, withered, shrinking.

24. Be a cup of whey my ale;
    what vexes, ay be God's will.
    God, I pray in my behalf
    let not wrath my body fill.

25. Clotted cloak of age on me;
    my sense deceives me surely;
    gray the hair grows through my skin
    as on old trees the lichen.

26. My right eye taken away,
    sold for land, mine alway;
    the left eye taken surely
    to clench the claim utterly.

27. Stanza from the *Acallam*.

28. Wave flooding
    and swift ebb along the land;
    what full flood waves bring to you,
    ebb waves carry from your hand.

29. Wave flooding
    and the second wave ebbing
    have come to me, not sudden,
    I know their tangled webbing.

30. Wave flooding
    comes not to chamber studding;
    my company, though ample,
    on all a hand fell thudding.

32. Woe to all!
    Of creatures man is most small;
    his floodtide was seen flowing,
    but unseen his ebbtide's fall.

33. My flooding
    kept well my loan from spending.
    Christ helped me hoard in heaven;
    not sad am I at ebbing.

34. Happy isle in the great sea:
flood after ebb comes duly;
 I think no more will fate bring
 flood to me after ebbing.

35. Scarce a house I know today,
 hut or shelter or steading;
what was once in prime budding,
 then flooding, now all ebbing.

This poem is a good example of accretion. Stanza 27, interpolated from the *Acallam*, begins "Trí tuile" (Three floods), and, since the underlying metaphor of so much of the Old Woman's lament is the ebb and flow of youth and fortune, it was added to the poem. Similarly stanza 16 is suspect but has not been found elsewhere. The metaphor of the sea of life has again brought it into the circle of the Old Woman's lament.

Both Liadain and the Old Woman show some independence of action: Liadain by taking the veil and causing the problem, Bui by having jumped the convent wall in her youth. Bui, Gerard Murphy tells us, was "originally an immortal mythological figure, ancestress of races and builder of mountains and cairns. The Old Woman of Beare is looked on by the late-eighth- or early-ninth-century author of the poem as a very old human being who, having outlived friends and lovers, received the *caille* or nun's veil from Saint Cuimine."[5] These other-world women often show more independence than the weaker mortals whom fate afflicts without hope of achieving more than suffering. Another such woman is Fand, wife of Manannan, God of the sea, in the *Serglige Con Culainn*. First Cú Chulainn is summoned to the Otherworld, after a mysterious weakness has lingered on for a year. Cú Chulainn cautiously sends his charioteer, but after receiving his report goes to the Otherworld and falls under the spell of Fand, who had sent her subordinate to fetch him. Cú Chulainn is powerless against the earlier illness—a magic spell—and against his love for Fand. Even when Fand has released him following her farewell, Manannan must shake his cloak between them to obliterate the memory for both.

1. See the warrior son of Ler
 from plains of Eogan Inbir:
 Manannan mounts the world's hill;
 his love once my heart would fill.

2. Today my cry would be sharp;
 no love lies in heavy heart;

for love is a vain affair,
quickly fading everywhere.

3. When I and Mac Lir, my spouse,
   shared Dun Inbir's bright sunhouse,
     we thought no moment would bring
     to him and me a parting.

4. When Manannan married me,
   I, a fitting mate, surely,
     he would try to win in vain
     from me once the odd chess-game.

5. When Manannan married me,
   I, a fitting mate, surely:
     my golden bracelet he says
     paid the price of my blushes.

6. I had far across the moors
   fifty girls in bright colors;
     I gave him, too, fifty men
     besides the maidens given.

7. Four times fifty—no mistake—
   folk of one house as keepsake:
     a hundred women, fair, fit,
     hundred men, fine, fortunate.

8. O'er the sea I watch him come;
   none mad sees aught on ocean;
     horseman on heaving seas sits,
     not following on longships.

9. Until now your going past
   just fairies saw by contrast;
     large each small host to your sense,
     though far away in distance.

10. I found it fitting and just—
    for women are not to trust—
      he whom I loved beyond all
      has brought about my downfall.

11. Farewell, kind Cu, here abide;
    I go from thee in high-pride.
      Parting wish is left undone;
      good every rule till broken.

12. It is time for me to go;

one finds it hard—that I know;
great indeed the loss I fear,
O Loeg, son of Riangabir.

13. I shall go with my own mate:
he breaks not my will, my fate.
Do not say in stealth I flee:
watch if you will; let all see.[6]

Though laments are one of the commonest themes of Irish, there are some joyful quatrains. Grainne's offer to give the world for Diarmait, in the poem cited earlier for its verse form, is one such:

That fellow,
I give thanks, him regarding;
for him I'd sell earth—yellow,
mellow, all—though bad bargain.

Another comes from a treatise on Irish versification in the *Book of Ballymote*.

Heart is he,
nuts of oaks;
brisk is he,
kissed one dotes.[7]

The third example of a joyful quatrain is a marginal addition to the *Book of Leinster*:

Dear each new thing, never dull;
young folks' wishes are fickle;
fair the choices love can bring;
sweet the words of youth wooing.[8]

Less happy because of the undercurrent of impending disaster is Grainne's lullaby for Diarmait:

1. Sleep a little, a little bit;
for you no fear, not a bit,
lad for whom I loved and lived
son of O'Duibne, Diarmait.

2. Sleep here soundly, deep and long,
Duibne's grandson, Diarmait strong,
safely a while watched by me,
O'Duibne's son, the shapely.

3. Sleep a little (blessings yours)
   above Trengort Well waters,
      light foam on lakes at land's edge
      of stilled strong streams once savage.

4. Sleep as in the south afar
   good Fidach, the high scholar,
      who took Morann's girl to bed
      despite Conall of Branch-red.

5. Sleep as in the north below
   Finnchad Fair of Assaroe,
      who snatched Slaine, lucky win,
      despite Failbe Chotachinn.

6. Sleep as in the west away
   daughter of Gailian, Aine,
      who went, hair hanging, soft smile,
      with Dubthach come from Oak-isle.

7. Sleep as in the east, O lad,
   as doughty daring Dedaid,
      who stole Benn's Choinchenn apart
      despite Deichell of Dark-dart.

8. I shall remain with you to guard,
   great champion of Greece westward;
      my heart will break, not endure,
      if sight of you meets failure.

9. Parting us two among men
   is parting fellow children,
      or body from soul undone,
      O warrior of Loch Carman.

10. Cailte's course brings no foul play;
    charms we lay on your pathway;
       no grief nor death on you fall,
       leave you in sleep eternal.[9]

When Grainne has tried to soothe her lover to sleep and has wished him the sleep of other eloping lovers, he replies with a list of wild creatures that do not sleep. The poem, then, should perhaps be classified as a dialogue rather than a woman's song.

More clearly a woman's song is Deirdre's farewell to Scotland, which has the same undercurrent of approaching doom as does Grainne's lament. Two less familiar songs from the earlier version of the story of Deirdre and Naise illustrate other themes in Irish woman's songs. In the first Deirdre praises Naise and his two brothers Ainnle and Ardan.

1. Though fair you think each fierce thane
   striding from field to Emain,
      nobler strode the valiant three
      homeward, brave boys of Uisle.

2. Naise brought hazel brew bright—
   his head I washed by firelight—
      Ardan, hart or boar from glen,
      on Ainnle's back his burden.

3. Though you think sweet merry mead
   from Nessa's son strong, storied,
      once I'd dainties to prefer—
      plates piled high I found sweeter.

4. When noble Naise had dressed
   grill and fare in the forest,
      the foods Uisle's son would feed,
      sweeter than morsels honeyed.

5. Though ever sweet to you blare
   clarion call and flute fanfare,
      for me this day, I admit,
      I have heard sweeter music.

6. Conchobar, your king, thinks fair
   clarion call and flute fanfare;
      to me sweeter—heard, a thrill—
      Uisle's sons' chorus tuneful.

7. Naise's voice—surf's roar and swing,
   sweet music ever sounding;
      good was Ardan's deeper chant;
      from Ainnle's hut his descant;

8. Naise, his grave-mound is done;
   unlucky his protection;
      crowds he fostered, him I brought
      death's draught for lack of forethought.

9. Dear the cropped head, finest cloak,
   fair fellow, e'en a grandcoat,
      alas today I've no hope
      for Uisle's son but wanhope.

10. Dear his mind, firm and fair,

dear the great modest warrior;
   after crossing the wood's rim,
   dear the clasp in the morning.

11. Women loved the dear blue eye
   once flashed against foes fiercely;
     riding round the forest ring
     through the dark wood—dear singing.

12. No sleeping,
   no redd'ning my nails ever,
   no joy known but it dwindles,
     since Tindell's son comes never.

13. No sleeping
   half the night as I'm lying;
   at crowds my sense is turning,
     food spurning, smiles denying.

14. Joy for me today unknown
   in Emain's host where earls stare;
   no peace, no pleasure at all,
     no great hall nor comrade fair.

The second lament is addressed to Conchobar mac Nessa who had the sons of Uisle slain. It describes Naise and his apparel with the detail characteristic of Irish story:

1. Conchobar does trouble loom?
   You brought me weeping on gloom;
     while I live and mem'ries stir
     my thoughts of you are bitter.

2. What seemed best of all to us
   and what we thought most precious,
     you took from me—a loss deep—
     seen no more till my deathsleep.

3. As loss of Naise I sense,
   I sorrow at his absence:
     jet black curls against skin fair
     to many men well known there.

4. Pink cheeks, soft as hay in mows,
   red lips, beetle-black eyebrows,
     pearly teeth that sparkling gleam
     like new snow under sunbeam.

5. Well known were his splendid clothes

   among bands of Scots heroes:
      comely crimson cloak—match fit—
         with redgold border round it.

6. Silk tunic—a treasure's worth—
      hundred gems, of wealth no dearth;
         on its broid'ry clear it is,
            of white bronze fifty ounces.

7. Gold-hilted sword on his hip,
      two gray spears with jav'lin tip,
         yellow-gold rim on white shield,
            silver boss in central field.

8. Fergus fair made our fate worse;
      brought us across wide waters;
         for ale was his honor dulled,
            his great exploits all tumbled.

9. Though Ulster was on the heath
      with Conchobar, their lordchief,
         I'd give them all, I confess,
            for Naise's constant nearness.

10. My heart, do not break today;
      my grave gapes on my pathway;
         griefs deeper than ocean scar:
            wise are the words, Conchobar.[10]

Laments like these of Deirdre are the most common woman's songs in the Irish tales, as they are in other literatures. The poems attributed to Queen Gormfhlaith are all laments, supposedly composed after the death of her husband Niall Glundub. Gormfhlaith was the "daughter of Flann Sionna, high king of Ireland between 878 and 916. After the death of her third husband, Niall Glundub, high king of Ireland, who fell fighting against the Northmen in 919, she is said to have lived in great poverty, forsaken of all her friends and allies, and glad to be relieved by her inferiours."[11] Osborn Bergin gives eleven of Queen Gormfhlaith's songs in *Irish Bardic Poetry*. Eight of these are elegiac poems lamenting the empty halls without the king. The other three, quoted below in Irish and with Bergin's translations, are more personal and illustrate the emphasis on details already noted in other Irish woman's songs.

No. V   1. Iomdha bréid ort a cheirt si!
                ní leatsa gan bheith giobach,

óir ní lámha ban málla
do bhí dot snadhmadh go brionnach.

2. Do bhádhasa lá a tTeamhraigh,
   fa ré Nıall Eamhna úaine;
   aige séin fa mór mh'onóir,
   do-geibhinn comól a chúacha.

3. Do bhádhasa lá a Luimneach,
   fa re Níall suirgheach Oiligh;
   dob áluinn mh'earradh datha
   eidir flatha bhfear bhfoinidh.

4. Clann Néill mear meanmnach,
   re bféachtháoi seannrioth searrach,
   do ibhinn fíon dá ngúaluinn,
   as barr a mbúabhall mbeannach.

5. Seacht fichit bean ar mbannáil
   a cceartlár gacha háonaigh;
   as dúinne do churtháoi an graifne
   ar faithche í Néill tháoibhghlain.

6. Bean mé Laidhghneach Mhidheach,
   gidh eadh ní híad as andsa,
   annso go ró mór Ulaidh,
   dar mo chubhais as annsa!

7. Minic mé a láim acc dreasaibh,
   as íad ag casadh fam cheartaigh,
   ní cara damh na droidhne,
   'sas biodhbha damh an drisóg.

(There's many a patch upon thee, thou rag! well
mayest thou be ragged, for no hands of gentle ladies
have cunningly stitched thee. Once I was in Tara, beside
Niall of green Emain; he delighted to honour me; I
would drink from his own cup. Once I was in Limerick
with loving Niall of Ailech; lovely was my coloured
raiment among the chiefs of the western men.

The swift and gallant Clann Neill, who were wont to
gaze upon the ancient racing of foals, I would quaff wine
beside them out of their horn goblets. Seven score
women were our retinue in the midst of every assembly;
for us the race would be run on the green of the descendant of stainless Niall.

I am a woman of Leinster, of Meath, yet they are

not the dearest; dearer, far dearer is Ulster, by my con-
science it is dearer! Often the brambles take hold of me,
twisting about my rags; the thorn is no friend to me, and
the briar is a foe.)

No. VIII 1. Beir a mhanaigh leat an chois,
                tóccaibh anos do tháobh Néill:
             as rothrom chuireas tú an chré.
             ar an té re luighinn féain.

       2. Fada a mhanaigh atáoi thíar,
              acc cúr na críadh ar Níall nár;
           fada liom é a ccomhraidh dhuinn,
              'snach roichid a bhuinn an clár.

       3. Mac Aodha Finnléith an óil,
              ní dom dhéaon atá fa chrois;
           sín ar a leabaidh an leac,
              beir a mhanaigh leat an chois.

       4. Fa Chloinn Uisnigh dob fearr clú
              do bhí Deirdre mur tú anois,
           a croidhe ina clíaph gur att—
              beir a manaigh leat an ccois.

       5. As mé Gormlaith chumas rainn,
              deaghinghean Floinn ó Dhúin Rois;
           trúagh nach orom atá an leac—
              beir a mhanaigh leat an ccois.

(Monk, take thy foot away, lift it now from Niall's
side: too heavily thou heapest the clay upon him with
whom I was wont to lie. Long, O monk, hast thou been
yonder, heaping clay upon noble Niall; too long, me-
thinks, he has been in a dark coffin, while his feet do not
reach the board. The son of Aed Finnliath of the
banqueting, not by my good will is he under a cross. Lay
the flagstone on his bed. Monk, take thy foot away.
    Concerning Uisnech's famous children Deirdre was
as I am now, until her heart burst within her bosom.
Monk, take thy foot away. I am Gormlaith who make
verses, noble daughter of Flann from Dun Rois. Would
that the flagstone were over me! Monk, take thy foot
away.)

No. XI 1. Mithid sgur do chaoineadh Néill
   mac Aodha na n-each n-óigréidh;
   trúagh, a Dhé, an cás ionar chuir
   mé idir bhás is beathuidh.

  2. Bliaghuin is tríochad go ceart
   ó theasda an rí si go reacht,
   do-nínnsi dá chaoineadh choidhche
   seacht ccéad déar gach aonoidhche.

  3. Tar éis na híarmheirghe aréir
   is ann do ráidh rium ó Néill,
   "Sguir dhod tuirsi a Ghormflaith gheal,
   's diomdhach dhíot Rí na n-aingeal."

  4. Is ann do ráidheas re Niall,
   tré feirg mar nár ráidhis riamh,
   "Créd fá mbeith fearg Rí nimhe
   riúm is mé ag aithrige?"

  5. "An bhfidir tú, a Ghormflaith gheal,
   gurab é Dia do dhealbaidh neamh,
   's gurb é do dhealbh na daoine,
   's nach áil leis a ndéarchaoine?"

  6. Cuireas Niall, fa deaghmhac d'Aodh,
   a dhruím riúm, fá cairdeas claon,
   sgairtimsi 'ga faicsin soin,
   agus lingim iona leanmhuin.

  7. Uaithne don iobhar áluinn
   fám iomdhaigh is eadh tárruinn;
   tarla mh'ucht fan uaithne ccorr,
   gur ro scoilt mo chroidhe a ccomhthrom.

  8. Aiscead bháis iarruim anocht
   ar Mhac Dé do dhealbh gach corp;
   cidh bé ionadh a bhfuil Niall,
   go rabhar-sa is é ar énrían.

  9. Trí chéad bó [is] dá chéad each
   tug damhsa Cearbhail cloidhmheach;
   tug Cormac [i]s nír bheart ghann
   dá oiread a ttug Cearbhall.

  10. Créd fa cceilfinn ar mo rí[gh]
   a bhfuarus uadha do mhaoín?
   Oiread sin uile fa thrí
   fuarus ó Niall a n-aonmhí.

('Tis time to cease lamenting Niall, son
of Aed of the smooth steeds. Sad, O God, is
the plight to which it has brought me between
death and life. For one and thirty years, truly,
since this upright king died, every night weeping for him I used to shed seven hundred tears.
Last night after matins the descendant of Niall
said to me: "Cease thy mourning, fair
Gormlaith; the King of the angels is dis-
pleased with thee."

Then I said to Niall, angrily as I had never
said before: "Why should the anger of the
King of heaven be against me while I am
penitent?"

"Knowest thou, fair Gormlaith, that it
was God who created heaven, and that it was
He who created men, and that He desires not
their bitter weeping."

Niall, Aed's good son, turned his back
upon me—it was perverted love: I shriek at the
sight of this and spring after him. A post of
beautiful yew that supported my bed was what
I seized (?); my breast came against the
smooth post, so that it split my heart in the
middle. Tonight I pray the Son of God who
created everybody to grant me death; wherever Niall is, may he and I be on one path.
Three hundred horses Cerball of the sword
gave me; Cormac—it was no mean act—gave
twice as many as Cerball. Why should I hide
from my king the wealth I have got from him?
All that thrice over I got from Niall in one
month.) [12]

Language and meter suggested to Bergin that none of these
poems is of the same century (tenth) as Queen Gormfhlaith, and her
authorship is thus unlikely. Indeed, this last poem tells the traditional story of her death. There is, in fact, no reason to assume that
any of the Irish woman's songs were not composed by men.

An earlier quatrain, also a lament of a queen, is recorded in the
Annals of the Four Masters, after the death of Aed son of Ainmire
in 594:

Beloved were the three sides
no return for me again:

sides of Tara, of Teltown,
        of Aed—none I'll see again.[13]

The simple statement of this lament for Aed is characteristic of
earlier verse. Deirdre's more complex laments are not in the earliest
version of her tale, but another song, the lament for Dinertach,
which Murphy dates about 800, demonstrates that more elaborate
poems exist even in early sources. In the few lines of introduction to
this poem the speaker is identified as Creide, daughter of the king
Guaire, but in some versions she is Guaire's wife, lamenting her
lover.

1. These darts slay sleep, all rest gone,
    through every numb hour, nightlong;
        love pangs from num'rous nights spent
        with one from Roigne pleasant.

2. Great love for a foreign lad,
    better than any comrade,
        took my beauty, paled my cheek,
        allows me no more sound-sleep.

2. Dinertach,
    woe he was unseen ere that
        'round him danger might threaten,
        'round Guaire's son O'Nechtan.

4. Sweeter than song his speaking,
    except God's hymns, heav'n-seeking;
        fierce flame without boast or pride,
        a slender spouse with soft-side.

5. No evil tryst broke my rest
    when I was young, modest;
        grown to greater years, more free,
        my wanton ways deceive me.

6. With Guaire I find all well,
    king of cold Aidne, able,
        but my thoughts would go flying
        to Irluachair outlying.

7. They sing in old Aidne well
    around calm Colman's chapel
        of Dinertach, fierce flame stirred
        from Limerick, grave-covered.

8. Holy Christ, my heart is rent;

his murder is my torment:
these darts slay sleep, all rest gone,
through every numb hour, nightlong.[14]

A later lament, that of another Creide, exemplifies the use of
sympathetic nature. This is a Fenian poem, not earlier than the
twelfth century.

1. Cries the cove:
   moan of fierce flood Rinn Da Barc;
   the man from Loch Da Chonn drowned,
   keened by sound of wave on rock.

2. Calls the crane
   at bog Druim Da Thren she wailed;
   no help for young who'd elude
   the two-hued fox on their trails.

3. Sad the keen
   of thrushes upon Druim Chain;
   blackbirds, not less sad their song
   along Leitir Laig unseen.

4. Sad the call,
   on Druimlesh the stag stands tall;
   on Druim Silenn, dead the doe;
   in woe the strong stag will bawl.

5. Grief to me
   his death who once lay with me;
   son of one in Derry Dos,
   a cross above him I see.

6. For Cael, grief:
   beside me dead—no relief;
   the wave went o'er his white side,
   he died: beauty past belief.

7. Sad the sound
   when waves along the strand pound;
   my grief that Cael wandered there,
   since that fair fine man has drowned.

8. Sad the roar
   waves make on the northern shore
   tumult round a rugged rock
   in shock that Cael is no more.

9. Sad the strife
waves make on the southern hithe.
My time has come, all know now
my brow tholed the worst of life.

10. Music strange,
at Tulach Leis waves rage high;
gone my dear—no more to lose—
news, a bitter boast, they cry.

11. Dead the swan,
gloomy her mate and she gone;
great feeling to me was taught
by sorrow that caught the swan.

12. Since the son of Crimthann drowned
I found none dear—none have I.
By his hand great chieftains fell;
his shield gave no yell, no cry.[15]

One curious poem might be added. It is a woman's song, perhaps as late as the fifteenth century. Kuno Meyer printed it without translation, and the subject is unusual in any language. It seems to be spoken by a girl who has been deserted by her lover. That theme is common enough, but it has been suggested to her that she has been abandoned for a man. However reluctant she may be to accept this, she realizes that in any case she is alone.

1. Woe, I am away too long
from one I love, gone is he;
though it serve as fate this way,
each day seems longer to me.

2. With him I'm not without cheer,
though his smiles here briefly hang;
two stories go not with me:
be he woman, be she man.

3. I am my comrade till doom.
I'll not have room to love so;
though it were she or were he,
pity me, God, ochone, woe![16]

The very personal note of this last poem is one of the chief characteristics of Irish verse, a characteristic that appears in the philosophy of Pelagius and Duns Scotus, as well as in the hermit verse and elsewhere. Other typical features of the poems include the abundant use of nature as in Creide's "Lament for Cael," Grainne's "Lullaby for Diarmait," and other verses, and the detailed descriptions, as in Deirdre's poems. But personal notes, the abundant use of precise nature imagery, the expression of joy or of sorrow, are characteristics of Irish verse in general, and the elegiac tone of many of the woman's songs is characteristic of comparable poems in many languages. Irish woman's songs differ from woman's songs of other countries only in reflecting the spirit and the elaborate verbal play of all Irish verse.

There are aspects of man-woman relationships, commonly expressed in other European literatures, that one does not find in Irish. These include the appeals of a man to a wayward mistress, his celebration of her in verse in dawnsongs, laments at the misery and sleeplessness attendant on unrequited love, appeals for mercy, and reactions against the lady's disdain. In contrast, a man's infatuation with a woman is told in Irish through actions: he falls ill; he is attacked by her husband or father and brothers; he may be killed; but the action, not the emotion, is the subject of verse. In the thirteenth century we do find touching laments for a dead wife, but nothing of the courtships. Perhaps the Irish had too much humor to take seriously the love-loneliness of a man as they do that of the woman. The last poem cited, of the deserted woman, is the one so personal and so unusual in theme that it may actually have been written by a woman.

 *Notes*

[1] Ruth P. Lehmann, "A Study of the *Buile Shuibne*," *EC*, 5 (1955), 289–311; 6 (1956), 115–38. Probably stanza 16 and surely stanza 27 of the "Old Woman of Beare" are also in this category.

[2] Gerard Murphy, *Early Irish Lyrics* (Oxford: Oxford Univ. Press, 1956), no. 34, pp. 74 ff. Murphy's readings are accepted. The content and spirit of these poems are the concern of this paper. See also David Greene and Frank O'Connor, *Golden Treasury of Irish Poetry* (Macmillan, 1967), no. 9, pp. 48 ff.; James Carney, *Medieval Irish Lyrics* (California, 1967), no. 15, pp. 28–41. (Hereafter abbreviated as *MIL*); Kuno Meyer, *Ancient Irish Poetry*, new ed. (1959), pp. 90 ff.; the imitative translation below, Ruth P. M. Lehmann, *Poems* (Austin: Westlake Press, 1977), pp. 38–41.

[3] Murphy, *Lyrics*, no. 54, pp. 160–61; Greene and O'Connor, no. 26.6, p. 112.

[4] *Líadain and Curithir*, ed. Kuno Meyer (London: Nutt, 1902); Murphy, *Lyrics*, no. 35, pp. 82–84; Greene and O'Connor, no. 13, pp. 72 ff.; Carney, *MIL*, no. 13, pp. 24–28.

[5] Murphy, *Lyrics*, p. 206.

[6] Late eleventh century: the text is from *Seirglige Con Culaind*, ed. Myles Dillon, Medieval and Modern Irish Series, no. 14 (Dublin: Dublin Institute for Advanced Studies, 1953), pp. 27–28.

[7] Translations include Kuno Meyer, *Bruchstücke der älteren Lyrik Irlands*. Abhandlungen der Preussischen Akademie der Wissenschaften. Philosophisch-historische Klasse, no. 7. erster Teil (Berlin, 1919), no. 160, p. 69; Greene and O'Connor, no. 26.4, p. 112; Carney, *MIL*, no. 14, p. 28.

[8] Greene and O'Connor, no. 53.5, p. 203.

[9] *Duanaire Finn* I, ed. Eoin MacNeill. Irish Texts Society, no. 7 (1908), no. 33, pp. 84 ff.; Murphy, *Lyrics*, no. 55, pp. 160–64.; Greene and O'Connor, no. 48, pp. 184–88.

[10] Vernum Hull, *Longes Mac n-Uislenn: The Exile of the Sons of Uisliu*, Modern Language Assoc. of America, Monograph Series, no. 14 (New York: Modern Language Assoc. of America, 1949), pp. 48 ff., 50–51. Though much indebted to Hull, I have not always accepted his choices of interpretation, especially in his curious note on Naise as blonde, against the tradition he translates earlier in this text of Naise's raven black hair and white skin like snow. Notice especially the third stanza of the second poem.

[11] Eleanor Knott, *Irish Syllabic Poetry*, 1200–1600 (Dublin: Dublin Institute for Advanced Studies, 1957), p. 83.

[12] See Osbern Bergin, *Irish Bardic Poetry*, eds. David Greene and Fergus Kelly (Dublin: Dublin Institute for Advanced Studies, 1970), no. 5, pp. 207–08 (trans. p. 310), no. 8, pp. 209–10 (trans. pp. 311–12), no. 11, pp. 214–15 (trans. pp. 314–15).

[13] See *Annals of Ireland by the Four Masters*, ed. John O'Donovan (Dublin, 1856), where the lament is given in the year 595, and the *Chronicum Scotorum*, ed. W. M. Hennessy (London, 1866), where it is assigned to 598. See also: Myles Dillon, *Early Irish Literature* (Chicago: Univ. of Chicago Press, 1948), p. 155; Myles Dillon and Nora K. Chadwick, *Celtic Realms* (London: Weidenfeld and Nicholson, 1967), p. 230.

[14] See the article by Kuno Meyer in *Ériu*, 2 (1905), 15 ff.; Murphy, *Lyrics*, no. 36, pp. 86–88; Greene and O'Connor, no. 16, pp. 78–80. For another interpretation see James Carney, "The So-Called 'Lament of Créidhe,'" *Éigse*, 13 (1970), 227–42. For an explanation of the present rendering see my essay in *EC*, 15 (1978), 549–51.

[15] See *Irische Texte*, ed. Rudolf Thurneysen (Leipzig, 1891), 4, 24; Standish O'Grady, *Silva Gadelica* (1892), p. 113; Kuno Meyer, *Cath Finntraga* (1885), 11. 995–1034; and note especially Murphy, *Lyrics*, no. 49, pp. 148–50 and notes.

[16] See article by Kuno Meyer in *ZCP*, 13 (1921), 18. Stanza 3, ll. 1–2 have been slightly emended here for purposes of rime.

John F. Plummer

The Woman's Song in Middle English and its European Backgrounds

In light of the interest which has been shown in Old English and continental examples of woman's songs,[1] it is curious that the Middle English examples have attracted almost no critical attention.[2] One suspects that an important factor in this disinterest has been the perception of the woman's songs in Middle English as a popular form, quite unrelated to the study of the male-voiced "courtly" lyric. I would like to suggest that this perception has been mistaken, at least if it implies, as I think it does, that woman's songs and the male-voiced love lyric arose from fundamentally different social and cultural milieux. The very real differences between the two genres, I will argue, bespeak not a lack of cultural relation between them but rather a specific relation of organized contrast.

The woman's songs are largely about love and sex; they contrast with the male love lyric in being more highly narrative and in striking the reader at first glance as more realistic. The *ethos* of the woman's song, a combination of tone, event, and character, is carnal. On the Virgilian wheel of styles the woman's song is to be found within *stilus humilis*; it shares that space with such literary forms as the *fabliau*, the *pastourelle*, and the farce. Largely on the basis of such stylistic features, the woman's songs have struck their editors as being popular. Those Robbins printed he assembed in the "Popular Song" section of his *Secular Lyrics of the XIVth and XVth Centuries*,[3] and he said of a group which included eight woman's songs that "these love poems . . . are among the freshest and most charming of all early English compositions. They are genuinely popular, as is shown by their realistic content, their simple form, and their casual manner of preservation."[4] Greene said of two of the group that "because of their homeliness, their directness of speech, and their theme of the betrayed girl [they] have a strong case for consideration as authentic folk-song."[5]

The term "popular" is notoriously ambiguous, but critics' remarks on these lyrics do seem to have shared at least the idea that a radical dissimilarity in stylistic level between two works is suggestive of two different audiences for those works. But the work of Per Nykrog[6] on the *fabliaux* has thrown serious doubts on such assumptions. The *fabliau*, once believed to be bourgeois in origin and audience, was shown by Nykrog to be as aristocratic as the *roman courtois*. "This noble public," he wrote, "partial to the most refined psychological subtleties, could also be seduced by a rather elementary, even gross, humor. These enthusiasts of the adoration of the idealized Woman enjoyed the depiction of the thoroughly vicious shrew. These inventors of purely intellectual love could be transported, provoked to hilarity, by stories of sexual obscenity or simple brutality."[7] Nykrog's work has demonstrated the immense latitude of courtly taste, ranging from Chrétien's romances to the *fabliaux*, and from Chaucer's "Knight's Tale" to his "Miller's Tale." This breadth of taste seems beyond debate now, as far as concerns narrative art, but the question seems to remain open for lyric poetry, and the woman's song has yet to be admitted to court.

I believe that the male-voiced lyric deals with and in a sense locates the center of what Peter Dronke has called the courtly experience;[8] the woman's song, like the *fabliau* and certain episodes in courtly romances, deals with the boundaries of that experience, defining the court in contrast to its opposite. Erich Köhler has written of the anarchic world lying just beyond Arthur's court in the romance as being the poetic representation of what the world would be in the absence of aristocratic society.[9] That world is bestial, unordered, and violent, and the depictions of its confrontation with the Arthurian knight serve to suggest by opposition the values of dignity and order of Arthurian society. The world of the *fabliau* is also unordered and, if not bestial, at least exquisitely rude. But it is a comic rather than serious antithesis of courtly society, and its members destroy one another rather than threatening the court. Though the early history of female-voiced song in Europe remains obscure, an examination of some examples of its later development suggests that the woman's song often had much this same function of defining what courtesy was not.

There seems to be no question that popular woman's songs associated with the dance were once common in Europe, and to judge from the evidence of church councils they flourished at least as early as the sixth century.[10] The dance, and ecclesiastical grumblings over it, did not die out in the early Middle Ages. Lyrics in the *Carmina Burana* speak of the dance and its songs as a feminine activity, though in terms quite different from the strictures of the councils.[11] Impressive evidence in terms of sheer volume is the collection of female-voiced *refrains* assembled by Alfred Jeanroy during his investigation of the origins of French lyric poetry. The *refrains*, found embedded in romances and sophisticated song of the twelfth and thirteenth centuries, were originally, Jeanroy argued, refrains or burdens of popular dance songs.[12]

An excerpt from a French motet, probably of the thirteenth century, illustrates the way in which the *refrains* were incorporated into aristocratic song and also gives further evidence that caroling/ dancing was perceived as a womanly pursuit:

> C'est tot la gieus en mi les prez,
> *Vos ne sentez mie les maus d'amer:*
> Dames i vont por caroler,
> Remirez voz braz.
> *Vos ne sentez mie les maus d'amer*
> *Si com ge faz.*[13]

> (It's over there in the middle of the meadow;
> | *You never feel the pains of love;* | Ladies
> come there for caroling; | Now look to your
> arms! | *You never feel the pains of love* |
> *The way I do.*)

The woman's song was common in other French dance forms as well, as for example the *ballette*, *sons d'amour*, and *virelais* such as Deschamps' "Sui-je belle?"[14] But though the dance songs of Europe, especially in France, preserved the female voice, it is important to note that virtually none of these is popular, and many are demonstrably courtly—e.g., Deschamps' *virelai*, the *ballettes* collected by Jeanroy, and the *motets*. The *refrains* do, perhaps, reflect an older, popular lyricism (although it is not difficult to conceive of a court poet composing new examples once those he had collected had been exhausted), but that they are found embedded in such distinctly aristocratic songs bespeaks an interest in them on the part of court poets and their patrons.

The firm connection between dance and the female lyric voice probably accounts for the fact that almost all of the woman's songs in Middle English are carols. The carol both was (as dance form), and *was conceived of as being*, appropriate to the female voice.[15] The distinction between fact and the perception based upon it, between songs sung by women in their dances (those complained of by the councils), and songs which served to evoke the picture of dancing women, should be insisted upon. One calls to mind the *chansons de toile*, believed by a generation of scholars to have been sung by women as they spun and did their needlework. But these lyrics which had seemed at first to be remnants of the earliest popular French lyrics were shown on careful inspection to be archaizing, sophisticated artifice—to be, in the words of Faral, "faux ancien." Arguing that a social group does not often engage in self-depiction in its songs, and that the very care which has been taken to paint a scene makes one doubt the genuineness of that scene, he concludes that "the mode of presentation and the wit excludes the possibility that any were sung by spinning women at their work."[16]

One wonders whether a great number of the woman's dance songs which have come down to us, including the Middle English examples, were not in fact composed by poets out of a similar desire to evoke a scene and activity which, though not of the court itself, might interest a courtly audience, whose reactions might vary from self-satisfied smiles to something like a romantic fascination. One clear example of a court poet's evocation of the dance and of the world of simple and sensuous maidens is Walther von der Vogelweide's "Under der linden":

1

Under der linden
an der heide,
dâ unser sweier bette was
Dâ muget ir vinden
schône beide
gebrochen bloumen unde gras.
Vor dem walde in einem tal,
tandaradei,
schône sanc die nahtegal.

2

Ich kam gegangen
zuo der ouwe:
dô was min freidel komen ê.
Dâ wart ich empfangen,
hêre frouwe,
das ich bin saelic iemer mê.
Kuste er mich? wol tûsentstunt:
tandaradei,
seht wie rôt mir ist der munt.

3

Dô hete er gemachet
alsô riche
von bluomen eine bettestat.
Des wirt noch gelachet
înnechliche
kumt iemen an daz selbe pfat.

4

Daz er bi mir laege,
wesse ez iemen
(nû enwelle got!) sô schamte
ich mich.
Wes er mit mir pflaege,
niemer niemen

Bî den rôsen er wol mac,
tandaradei,
merken wâ mirz houbet lac.

bevinde daz, wan er und ich,
und ein kleinez vogelîn:
tandaradei,
daz mac wol getriuwe sîn.[17]

(1. Under the lime tree / on the meadow, / where our bed was / there you can find, / fair to see, / broken flowers and grass. / Near the woods in a valley / tandaradei! / Sweetly sang the nightingale. 2. I had come / to the meadow; / My friend had come there too. / There I was greeted, / lucky lady, / and I've been happy ever since. / Did he kiss me? A thousand times! / tandaradei! / Look how red my mouth is! 3. There had he made / wonderfully fine / a little bed of flowers. / If someone came by there / he'd hear laughter / within. / In the roses he could see / tandaradei! / where my head lay then. 4. That he lay with me, / if anyone knew / —God help us—I'd be ashamed. / What he did with me / no one will / know but he and I / and a little bird. / tandaradei! / And he won't tell.)

The open sensuousness here is an artistic male creation, but it is not, it seems to me, intended to evoke a smirk. Part of the success with which Walther controls the tone of the piece is to be ascribed to the way in which our attention is directed away from the speaker herself. She points to the bed, the "gebrochen bluomen unde gras," and the "bettestat" of flowers, and asks us to "merken wâ mirz houbet lac." The last detail completes a movement, begun with the opening lines, which associates, even blends together, the girl's body and the site of her tryst. The meadow becomes a metaphor for the speaker's body; both are warm, soft, and colorful ("seht wie rôt mir ist der munt"). Like so many woman's songs, "Under der linden" is a confession. The last stanza makes explicit what was quite clearly suggested in the first three stanzas: "Daz er bi mir laege . . . ." But even here a convincing innocence is preserved, not merely in that the speaker says that she would be shamed to have the event discovered, but also in that her "wesse ez iemen . . ." suggests that what we had taken to be addressed to us has in fact been overheard by chance. The girl is speaking to herself, sharing her secret consciously only with the "kleinez vogelîn," an image which echoes the nightingale of stanza 1 and reasserts the metaphorical associations between nature and the speaker.

The guileless, sensuous quality of Walther's dance song provides us, as I believe it provided his courtly audience, with just what one expects to find in the poetry of the "folk": un-self-conscious avowals of delight in love and the uninspected pursuit of simple (and thus somehow pure and fulfilling) pleasures—what E. K. Chambers called "full-blooded southern love, abandoning itself beneath the white moon and to the music of the nightingale. . . ."[18] The role of the female persona in such poetry is central. By speaking of the pleasure she has taken (and by extension given) in her sexuality, pleasure with no attendant complications or responsibilities, she embodies a fantasy which is male as well as aristocratic.

Though there is a real distance between the speaker and audience in "Under der Linden," that distance is not primarily ironic. The audience is invited to enjoy the speaker's joy more than to smile at it. Similarly, there are many woman's songs in which the speaker laments the absence of her lover, and in which, I believe, the audience's reaction would be sympathetic. Examples of this latter kind of song are most common among the German lyrics, where they dominate the *Frauenlieder*.[19] In addition to these two types, the celebration and the lament, in both of which the audience's response is non-ironic, one may distinguish two further types: laments in which the audience is distanced ironically from the speaker, and songs in which the speaker is, as in the *chanson de mal mariée*, joyful, or at least determined to love as she pleases, and in which the audience's reaction is also controlled by irony. One thus finds two axes: celebration versus lament on the speaker's part, and ironic versus non-ironic reaction on the part of the audience. The ironic pole seems to me to predominate, and I would like to point to a few examples, especially as these have the most bearing on the English songs.

In the ironic lament, although the speaker herself remains simple, her life has become complicated by the recognition that she has been hoodwinked. She is sometimes pregnant, sometimes merely seduced and abandoned. One such song is the macaronic "Ich was ein chint" from the *Carmina Burana*. In the refrain here the speaker curses the very linden Walther's Mädchen had blessed:

1	2
Ich was ein chint so wolgetan,	Ia wolde ih an die wisen gan,
virgo dum florebam	*flores adunare*,
do brist mich div werlt al,	do wolde mich ein ungetan
omnibus placebam.	*ibi deflorare.*
Refl: Hoy et oe!	*Refl: Hoy et oe . . . .*
maledicantur tilie	
ixuta viam posite!	

3

Er nam mich bi der wizen hant,
    sed non indecenter,
er wist mich div wise lanch
    valde fraudulenter.
Refl: *Hoy et oe.* . . .

4

Er graif mir an daz wize gewant
    valde indecenter,
er fürte mih bi der hant
    multum violenter.
Refl: *Hoy et oe* . . . .

7

Do er zu der linden chom,
    dixit: sedeamus,
—div minne twanch sêre
    den man—
    ludum faciamus!
Refl: *Hoy et oe* . . . .

8

Er graif mir an den wizen lip,
    non absque timore,
er sprah: ich mache dich ein
    wip,
    dulcis es cum ore!
Refl: *Hoy et oe* . . . .

9

Er warf mir uf das hemdelin,

    corpore detecta,
er rante mir in daz purgelin
    cuspide erecta.
Refl: *Hoy et oe* . . . .

10

Er nam den chocher unde den
    bogen,
    bene venabatur!
Der selbe hete mich betrogen.
    ludus compleatur!
Refl: *Hoy et oe* . . . .[20]

(1. I was a maiden so lovely / While in my virgin flower. / Then the whole world courted me; / I pleased everyone. / *Refrain:* Alas and oh! / Cursed be the linden trees / set beside the road. 2. I merely wished to walk the meadow, / to pick the flowers; / but a churl wished / to deflower me there. / Alas and oh! / 3. He took me by the white hand, / but not indecently; / He led me through the meadow, / very fraudulently. / Alas and oh! / 4. He seized me by my white dress / quite indecently; / He took me by the hand, / quite violently. / Alas and oh! / 7. When he to the linden came, / He said, "Let's sit." / Greatly love impelled the man. / "Let's play a game!" / Alas and oh! / 8. He seized my white body, / Not without fear. / He said, "I'll make you a wife; / You have a sweet face." / Alas and oh! / 9. He threw up my little shirt / Leaving my body bare; / He battered my little fort / with his erect spear. / Alas and oh! . 10. He took the quiver and the bow: / "Well hunted! / This same man had betrayed me. / "The game is done!" / Alas and oh!)

The "lament" of the maiden is of course a confession, and the confession is filled with details whose quality betrays a consciousness other than the speaker's at work. Her stance of naïveté is undercut by sexual metaphor, and the matter-of-fact tone of the most sexually explicit stanzas seems to match that of the *fabliau*. The macaronic verse—the most self-conscious of literary devices— contributes to a sense of distance between speaker and audience. She is both "ein chint" and "virgo." Both are fictions, but the speaker's macaronic shifting from German to Latin and back again increases our awareness of her being out of nature. Additionally, the shifting makes a single image of her impossible to hold, and we become increasingly aware of her language as language.

In addition to the *écart* which it establishes, its rhetorical visibility, the macaronic verse might also be said to symbolize a confrontation between maiden and seducer, between classes, and between masculine and feminine worlds. Although "Ich was ein chint" does not specify that the seducer was a cleric, the clerical seducer is often found in such ironic laments, especially the English ones, and "lettered versus unlettered" might be added to the series of confrontations which the vernacular/Latin shifts suggest. Such seems to have been the intention of the composer of the English *chanson d'aventure* "Vp y arose *in verno tempore*," in which the narrator overhears the maiden lament:

> "Now what shall y say *mei parentibus*
> Bycause y lay with *quidam clericus.*
> They wyll me bete *cum virgis ac fustibus*
> And me sore chast *coram omnibus.*"[21]

Much the same effect is wrought in the French lyric "*Langueo* d'amours, ma douce fillette," a male-voiced song which narrates a clerical seduction:

> *philomela* dit en sa chansonnette,
> "*non est clericus* qui n'a s'amyette."
> *Ero hodie* en vostre chambrette
> *vobiscum* jouer, s'il vous plaist, blondette,
> *ludendo saepe* le jeu d'amourette:
> *multum dulcis est* la chose doulcette.[22]

> (*Philomela* says in her song / "*There is no clerk* who has not a love" / *I will be today* in your little room / *with you* to play, if you please, blonde girl, / *to play often* the amorous game; / *oh so sweet is* that sweet thing.)

In total impact, all three poems are at a far remove from anything which could be called popular. In "Ich was ein chint," the combination of the clearly unsympathetic tone and the artifice—the verbal playfulness which would be accessible only to the educated—bespeaks an intended audience of some sophistication. On the basis of similarities in scenario, confessional stance, and tone, I would like to extend this argument to include a number of the woman's songs in Middle English.

Index 3594 is one of several ironic laments found among the Middle English woman's songs:

> A, dere god qwat i am fayn
> for i am madyn now gane.
>
> Þis enþer day i mete a clerke
> & he was wylly in hys werke;
> he prayd me with hym to herke
> and hys cownsell all forto lene.
>
> I trow he cowd of gramery,
> I xall now [telle] a good [s]kyll wy:
> for qwat i ha[l]de siccu[r]ly,
> to warne hys wyll had i no mayn.
>
> qwan he and me browt un us þe shete
> of al hys wyll i hym lete;
> now wyll not my gyrdyll met.
> A dere god quat xal i say.   *MS.* i xal
>
> I xall sey to man & page,
> þat i haue bene of pylgrymage.
> Now wyll i not lete for no rage
> with me a clerk for to pley.[23]

I would like to single out some of the conventional, generic, qualities of this song, beginning with the expression of regret found in the burden. Such a lament of lost maidenhood is found in a number of the English songs—e.g., "Were it vndo þat is y-do / i wolde be-war"; "alas, I go with schylde"; and "alas, ales, þe wyle, / þout y on no gyle." Also seemingly conventional is the speaker's claim to have been tricked, as was the speaker of "Ich was ein chint." The clerk was "wylly in hys werke," and "cowd of gramery," so that she had no power to deflect his "wyll." Glibness and trickery are of course proverbial attributes of the clergy in medieval anticlerical satire and in the *fabliaux*. The "gramery" of which the clerk is possessed is usually glossed as "magic," but the word has its roots in *grammatica*, the learning of clerks which makes them potentially dangerous to common folk. The speaker of *Index* 3409 also insists that she "was begyled-ay"; the woman in *Index* 1849 reflects, "þout y on no gyle"; and the speaker in *Index* 1268.5 says, "by such wanton men as youe be younge maydes are somtymes begyled." Clerks, or at least clerics, dominate the list of seducers in the English laments. Among those named are two Sir John's, a Jankyn, and a Jack. I dwell upon the prominence of the cleric in the ironic lament for two reasons. First, the fact that the seducer seems to be stereotyped is itself evidence of conventionality—a conventionality which suggests a tradition, an ongoing process of imitation and conscious artistry. Second, the clerical seducer represents yet another point of contact between the woman's song and the *fabliau*. The privileged role of the clerk in the *fabliau* is well known. He is the insatiable, irrepressible, and continuously successful lover. In contrast to his presence in woman's songs, however, the clerk is completely absent from the Middle English male love song, with the exception of the Harley lyric "My deþ y love, my lif ich hate," a dialogue between man and woman (and therefore not really an exception).

The simplest explanation for the exclusion of the clerical speaker from the male love song is perhaps that the speaker of those songs is not realized as a character; he is marked, as has often been noted, by his lack of individuality, and he is given no particularities of social status. Another explanation is of course that he is not eligible for the position. The priest and prelate were excluded by sacerdotal celibacy, and the minor orders were not taken seriously as lovers, but were found precisely in the burlesque world of the *fabliau*. Chaucer was exploiting these literary facts of life in giving Absolon in the "Miller's Tale" lines shot through with the language of *amour courtois*.[24] Absolon's duties as parish clerk, censing and taking up the offering, brought him into contact with the ladies of the parish in much the same manner suggested of Jankyn in *Index* 377: "iankyn at þe angnus beryt þe pax brede, / he twynkelid, but sayd nowt, & on myn fot he trede." So too did the author of the Harley lyric "My deþ y loue," referred to earlier, exploit the burlesque potential of the clerical lover. The scenario of the poem reminds us of Absolon's singing his song outside Alysoun's shot window. The clerk opens with two stanzas of quite ambitious courtly style, seeking the love of the *puella*. His ambition meets with the abrupt "Do wey, þou clerc, þou art a fol! Wiþ þe bydde Y noght chyde,"[25] a reply strikingly similar to that received by Absolon: "Go from the window Jakke Fool" (A 3708). Both the clerk and the girl are comic characters in the Harley poem; we laugh at his implied discomfiture as his posturing is deflated by the girl's first reply, and then again, after he has persisted for another stanza, by her second: "Be stille, þou fol, Y calle þe riht—cost þou neuer blynne?" We also enjoy the comic vigor of the girl's rebuffs in themselves.

The same comic clerical lover is to be found in the earlier *Dame Siriȝ*[26] and in the *Interludium de Clerico et Puella*[27] which seems to be derived from it. In the *Interludium* the clerk greets the girl, asks whether her mother and father are at home, and finding that they are not, says, "Wel wor suilc a man to life / Þat suilc a may mithe haue to wyfe" (ll. 5-6). The girl's response is interesting; she begins with the same words as the damsel of the Harley lyric: "Do way! By Crist and Leonard, / No wil Y lufe na clerc fayllard . . ." (ll. 7-8). Her reply seems to presuppose more than the clerk has yet suggested; this skipping over of preliminaries suggests the conventionality of the confrontation between cleric and maid, as if the cleric's presence on the scene were enough in itself to suggest his intentions. The girl is, of course, not mistaken, and in the cleric's next speech he declares his feelings in courtly diction reminiscent of both the clerk in the Harley lyric and of Absolon's song: "For þe Hy sorw nicht and day . . . wayleuay . . . Y luf þe mar þan mi lif . . . for þi luf ham Hi spilt . . . reu of me . . . Þu mend þi mode" (ll. 17-26). The girl's reply to this speech also suggests the conventionality of the tradition:

> "By Crist of heuene and Sant Ione,
> Clerc of scole ne kep I non,
> For many god wymman haf þai don scam" (ll. 27-29).

It is interesting that a particular word, "will," seems to have been used in this *fabliau* tradition to stand for the sexual aspirations of the clerk lover; the same usage is found in the woman's song. The speaker in *Index* 3594 says of her seducer, "to warne his wyll had I no mayn," and "of all hys wyll I hym lete"; she is echoed by the woman of *Index* 1330: "he seide his sawus he wolde fulfille, / þerfore y lat him haue al his wille." Similarly, the *puella* of the *Interludium* concludes her initial dismissal of the clerk with "Go forth þi way, god sire, / for her hastu loysd al þi wile" (ll. 11-12), and Willekin in *Dame Siriȝ* tells the dame that he must have Margeri or he will die: ". . . Hit mot me spille / Bote Ich gete hire to mi wille" (ll. 233-34). Nicolas in Chaucer's "Miller's Tale" uses identical words in speaking to Alisoun: "but if ich have my wille, / for derne love of thee, lemman, I spille" (A 3278-79). Dame Sirith's promise to help Willekin is couched in the same terms: "Me wolde þunche wel folen / þi wille forto fullen" (ll. 238-39). The girl in the Harley lyric uses the word to assent to the clerk's desires: "don al þi wille" (l. 36). The seducer of the betrayed maiden's lament is the same scamp who is found in the *fabliau*. The prominence of this sterotyped, burlesque clerical lover in these laments suggests strongly that such songs are meant above all else to be humorous—

specifically, humorous in the same manner as the *fabliau* and for the same audience.

A clue to the reaction of an audience to the betrayed maiden's lament can be found in a French *chanson d'aventure* in which the poet overhears a "plaisant brunette" singing that she has lost her lover, but not before she had "made a little mistake." Her refrain, "les jolis malz d'amorettes / ne puis plus celleir," and the lines "fait ai tant ke ma sainturette / ne puet a son point retorneir," reminds us of the "Now wyll not my gyrdyll met" (*Index* 3594), "tyll my gurdul aros, my wombe wax out" (*Index* 1849), and "sone my wombe began to swelle / as greth as a belle" (*Index* 225) of the English songs. In the French poem, the speaker's reaction to the overheard confession is to reveal his presence and to laugh, while the girl reddens and then pales in embarrassment:

> Et je qui volantiers l'oi
> me traix un petitet avant;
> et la belle tantost me vit,
> ce prist a mueir colour grant.
> et je li ai dit an riant
> "s'avient a mainte pucelette."
> et elle fut en pou pailette,
> de honte n'ozait plus chanter
> "les jolis malz d'amorettes
> ne puis plus celleir."[28]

(And I, who happily heard her / drew forward a little; / and as the beautiful one saw me / She began to blush. / And I said, laughing, / "Thus it happens to many girls." / And she grew a little pale; / For shame, she dared no longer sing / "The sweet pains of love / I can no longer conceal.")

Here, framed within the openly aristocratic *chanson d'aventure* form, the woman's lament shows itself for what it is, a light-hearted *grivoiserie*.

As for the maiden herself, she is not treated sympathetically, although overt moralizing is as absent from the woman's songs as from the *fabliaux*. She, like her lover, is a stereotyped character whose laments sound very much like one another. She reminds us of Malkyn, whose tenuous grasp on her maidenhood was proverbial. She is the type referred to in "A lutel soth Sermun" as "þeos prude maidens þat luuieþ Ianekin."[29] If pride does not strike one as being a central trait of the betrayed maiden, the characteristic is more prominently displayed in another group of the English woman's songs.

I spoke earlier of the two axes, of pleasure versus lament on the speaker's part, and of ironic versus non-ironic reaction on the part of the audience, which seem to characterize the woman's song. Paired with the ironic lament, then, one finds in Middle English, as in French, a number of songs in which the woman expresses satisfaction, even outright joy, with her sexual activities. These songs, e.g., *Index* 1269.5, no doubt did strike churchmen as expressions of pride. The burden of this lyric reads:

> If I be wanton I wotte well why;
> I wold fayn tary another year,
> My wanton ware
> shall walk for me.
> My prety wanton ware
> shal walk for me.
> I wyll nott spare
> to play with yow,
> He tygh, he tygh,
> he hyght he.[30]

The "ware," or *mons veneris*, is referred to with equal satisfaction by the speaker of the well-known "Silver White," which reads in part,

> "I leyde my ware, a bogeler brode,
> and euer he smote—
> —I leyde my ware, a bogeler brode,
> & euer he smote by syde.
> . . . .
> shalle ther neuer man iusty ther-at
> but yf he can hyt smyte."

The speakers in these songs may be proud of their sexual equipment, and they may take pride in their overall beauty as well. The speaker in *Index* 1269.5 is straightforward: "I am so prety [in] myne aray / and looke so nycely every day, / my wanton ware etc." In the specificity of their sexual pride these women remind us of both the Wife of Bath ("For if I wolde selle my *bele chose* / I koude walke as fressh as a rose" [D 447–48]; "I had the beste *quoniam* myghte be" [D 608]) and of the speaker in Deschamps' *virelai* "sui je belle":

> J'ay bonnes rains, ce m'est vis,
> Bon dos, bon cul de Paris,

> Cuisses et gambes bien faictes;
> Sui je, sui je, sui je belle?[31]
>
> (I have a nice belly, it seems to me / a good
> back, and nice Parisian ass, / thighs and legs
> well made; / tell me, tell me, am I fair?)

Both of these last two women are of course creations of court poets. The pride of the wanton woman of the songs is not simply that which she may take in her body; it is also the headstrong willfulness which she shares with the Wife of Bath, the speakers of the *refrains* found in courtly *motets* and *chansons d'aventure*, and the speaker in the *chansons de mal mariée*. As Jeanroy pointed out,[32] the speaker in the *mal mariée* song is often (I would even say always) a subject of satiric humor. Her complaints, and her expressions of intention, are entirely conventional. As the instance of the Wife of Bath attests, her willfullness and sexual appetite come directly from the pages of antifeminist literature, and what she proposes to do is exactly what the *fabliau* wife does.

One finds these same attitudes on the part of the speaker of *Index* 2494, one of the best of the English wanton woman's songs:

> Hey noyney, I wyll loue our ser Iohn & I loue eny.
> O lord, so swett ser Iohn dothe kys,
> at euery tyme when he wolde pley;
> Off hym-selfe so plesant he ys,
> I haue no powre to say hym nay.
>
> Ser Iohn loues me & I loue hym;
> the more I loue hym the more I maye.
> he says, 'swett hart, cum kys me trym,'
> I haue no powre to say hym nay.
>
> Ser Iohn to me Is proferyng
> ffor hys plesure ryght well to pay,
> & In my box he puttes hys offryng—
> [I haue no powre to say hym nay.]
>
> Ser Iohn ys taken In my mouse-trappe:
> ffayne wold I haue hem bothe nyght and day.
> he gropith so nyslye a-bought my lape,
> I haue no pore to say hym nay.
>
> Ser Iohn geuyth me reluys rynges,
> With praty plesure ffor to assay—
> ffurres off the ffynest with other thynges:
> [I haue no powre to say hym nay.][33]

The poem portrays a character filled with pride, lechery, and greed, three sins prominant in both the wife of the *fabliaux*[34] and in anti-feminist literature.

The Scots poem "Wa Worth Maryage"[35] is a *chanson d'aventure* which echoes these qualities of character point for point; only the question of marital status distinguishes the Scots wife from the English maid. Like the speaker of "Our Sir John" the wife has her eye on Sir John:

<blockquote>
iv
Thus am I bunden out of blis,
Onto ane churle says I am his,
That I dar nocht luik our the stair,
Scantlie to gif Schir Johne ane kis.
Wa worth maryage for evermair.
</blockquote>

Like the wanton maid, the wife knows what kind of sex life she prefers, and (were her husband dead) would be forward in satisfying her desires:

<blockquote>
vi
Thus am I thirlit onto ane schrew,
Quhilk dow nothing of chalmer glew;
Of boure-bourding bayth bask and bair.
God wayt gif I have cause to rew.
Wa worth maryage for evermair.
</blockquote>

<blockquote>
viii
Ye suld heir tell, and he war gane,
That I suld be ane wantoun ane.
To leir the law of Luffis layr
In our toun lyke me suld be nane.
Wa wroth maryage for evermair.
</blockquote>

The Scots poem is grouped by Robbins with "Later Poems Attacking Women" in *A Manual of the Writings in Middle English*,[36] and included in Utley's collection of antifeminist satire.[37] One would like to know, then, how it can be that "Wa Worth Maryage" is an antifeminist poem, while "Sir John," in all its conventionality and its parallelism with antifeminist satire, is to be taken as realistic and popular.

Is one to believe that the encapsulation of the woman's words within the male narrative ("I hard ane sweit and sich and say. . . .") identifies "Wa Worth Maryage" as satiric, while the unframed words of "Sir John" must be non-ironic? Judging simply on its contents, I find it very nearly inconceivable that a young woman could have sung this song in leading a carol on the village green, and, based on its affinities with literature of the sophistication of the *fabliau* and antifeminist satire, it seems unlikely that its author envisioned the market stall as the site of its performance. It would not be seriously argued that any of the ironic laments in English are autobiographical. There is no conceivable motivation for such self-exposure, in the fifteenth century or the twentieth; it is not merely that the speakers confess promiscuity—they confess ignorance. In any case, the songs are too much like one another not to be conventional. Given that the events of the songs are pure fiction, one might ask whether the setting, often a holiday (Yule, a well-waking, Midsummer's Eve) in a rural setting, is not also a fiction. It seems to me that the atmosphere of the popular festival is rather too well evoked in the songs to be a product of them. One has the sense, as one did with the *chansons de toile*, of being a detective in a room filled with too many clues. Does it not seem more likely that the woman's songs are a diversion for an audience more sophisticated than the characters depicted in them? If "Sir John" is a fly-leaf poem, it is after all in the Ellesmere manuscript, which may well have been in the possession of the twelfth earl of Oxford at the time the poem was entered. "If I be wanton I wotte well why" is found in the distinctly courtly setting of MS. Harley 7578 among courtly male lyrics. Another of the same type, "I can be wanton and yf I wyl," is found in MS. Ashmole 176, the Ritson manuscript. The Ritson manuscript offers further evidence that a sophisticated audience might enjoy the story of a wanton woman in that it contains a version of the *chanson d'aventure* "Up I arose, in *verno tempore*" referred to earlier, along with the *chanson d'aventure* "In wyldernes ther found I Besse," in which the poet recounts overhearing the lament of a pregnant, abandoned woman, "bygyled, / goten with child."

There is thus every evidence that sophisticated audiences in England as in Europe enjoyed and cultivated the woman's song in *sermo humilis*. The woman who speaks in this poetry enunciates a non-courtly position which, in the case of the English examples, most often involved either a headstrong carnality or a hapless sexual carelessness. Both qualities involve medieval stereotypes and are common features in the sexual jokes of all ages. Given the thematic connections between English woman's songs and antifeminist satire, it is probably not a coincidence that most of them date from the fifteenth century, a period which also saw a striking increase in the production of English and Scots antifeminist literature. But it would be overly simple to attribute their popularity to the resurgence of antifeminist writings alone. The late fourteenth century and the fifteenth century were also periods rich in class satire, spawned in part by increasing upward social mobility. Certainly the age had more than enough class tension to encourage satirical depictions of lower class mores. Neither antifeminism nor class feelings (nor the two together) "explains" the Middle English woman's song, of course, though each was no doubt a factor which contributed to the popularity of the type in England during the fifteenth century.

The Middle English woman's song must first and foremost be seen as one branch of a lyric tradition as old as European vernacular lyrics themselves; as stated above, there can be no doubt that popular songs in the female voice existed in medieval Europe, including England. I have sought not to deny the existence of these songs but rather to point to the ways in which they were assimilated by sophisticated courtly culture at an early date. The *kharjas* were woven into *muwashshahs* of Mozarabic Spain, the *refrains* into the courtly *motets* and *chansons d'aventure* of France. Similarly, the woman's voice was affected by male court poets like Walther von der Vogelweide, Deschamps, der von Kurenberg, by the composers of *chansons de mal mariée* and *chansons de toile*, and by the composers of some of the *Carmina Burana* lyrics and Cambridge Songs. Though the function the woman's song played in the courtly culture varied with time and place, the tradition nevertheless displays remarkable continuity from one language and one century to another, serving as a meaning-giving counterpoint to the male-voiced love song.

APPENDIX
A List of Woman's Songs in Middle English

Listed according to their number in Carleton Brown and Rossell Hope Robbins, *Index of Middle English Verse* (New York: Columbia Univ. Press, 1943), and *Supplement*, Robbins and John L. Cutler (Lexington: Univ. of Kentucky Press, 1965).

Index Number	*First Line*
225	Wybbe ne rele ne spynne y ne may.
377	As i went on ȝol day in oure prosessioun.
438	At the north end of seluer whit.
445	At the ston castyngs my lemman y ches.
1008	Ich am of Irlaunde.
1265	Alas, hou shold y syng.
1268.5	I can be wanton & if I will.

1269.5	If i be wanton, I wotte well why.
1330	Y loued a child.
1849	Ladd y the dance a myssomers day.
2494	O lord, so sweet sir john doth kiss.
2654	Of servyng men y wol biginne.
3174	Som men sayon þat i am blak.
3409	The last time y the wel woke.
3418	The man that I loved altherbest.
3594	Þis enþer day I met a clerk.
3897.5	Were þat þat is ydon.
3902.5	Waylaway whi ded y so.
None*	Iankyn of London.

*Printed in J. A. W. Bennett and G. V. Smithers, *Early Middle English Verse and Prose* (Oxford: Clarendon Press, 1966), p. 128.

Notes

[1] On the Old English poems see Clifford Davidson, "Erotic Woman's Songs in Anglo-Saxon England," *Neophil*, 59 (1975), 451–62, and Kemp Malone, "Two English *Fraunlieder*," *CL*, 14 (1962), 106–17. A representative sampling of major work done on the continental lyrics would include Alfred Jeanroy, *Les Origines de la poésie lyrique en France*, 3rd ed. (Paris: Champion, 1925); Theodore Frings, *Minnesinger und Troubadours*, Deutsche Akademie der Wissenchaften zu Berlin, Vorträge und Schriften, 34 (Berlin: Akademie, 1949); "Frauenstrophe und Frauenlied in der frühen deutschen Lyrik," in *Gestaltung Umgestaltung: Festschrift H. A. Korff*, ed. Joachim Müller (Leipzig: Koehler & Amelang, 1957), pp. 13–28; *Die Anfänge der europäischen Liebesdichtung im 11. und 12. Jahrhundert*, Bayerische Akademie der Wissenschaften, Philosophische-Historische Klasse, Sitzungsberichte 1960, Heft 2 (Munich: Bayerische Akademie, 1960); Leo Spitzer, "The Mozarabic Lyric and Theodor Frings' Theories," *CL*, 4 (1952), 1–22; Peter Dronke, *Medieval Latin and the Rise of European Love Lyric*, 2nd ed., 2 vols. (Oxford: Clarendon Press, 1968); Guido Saba, *Le "Chansons de Toile" o "Chansons d'histoire"* (Modena: Societa Tipografica Modenese, 1955).

[2] Cf. J. D. W. Crowther, "The Middle English lyric 'Joly Jankyn,'" *AnM*, 12 (1970), 123–25; Jane L. Curry, "Waking the Well," *ELN*, 2 (1964), 1–4; Richard L. Greene, "Troubling the Well Waters," *ELN*, 4 (1966), 4–6.

[3] Rossell Hope Robbins, *Secular Lyrics of the XIVth and XVth Centuries*, 2nd ed. (Oxford: Clarendon Press, 1955).

[4] Ibid., p. 233, note 15.

[5] Richard L. Greene, *Early English Carols* (Oxford: Clarendon Press, 1935), p. xcv; see also pp. xciii–cx.

[6] *Les Fabliaux*, 2nd ed. (Geneva: Droz, 1973).

[7] *Ibid.*, pp. 235-36.

[8] Dronke, *Medieval Latin*, I, p. 1.

[9] *Ideal und Wirklichkeit in der höfischen Epik*, Beihefte, *ZRP*, 97 (Tübingen, 1956), p. 78.

[10] See E. K. Chambers, *The Medieval Stage* (1903, rpt. Oxford: Clarendon Press, 1963), I, pp. 161-64; and Edmond Faral, *Les Jongleurs en France au moyen âge*, 2nd ed. (Paris: Champion, 1964), pp. 90-91.

[11] *Carmina Burana*, ed. Alfons Hilka and Otto Schumann (Heidelberg: Carl Winter, 1941), no. 75, iii, 7-8; iv, 3-6; no. 153, ii, 1-4; no. 167a.

[12] *Origines*, pp. 111-13.

[13] Printed in *Recueil de motets français des xiie et xiiie siècles*, ed. Gaston Raynaud (Paris: Vieweg, 1883), II, p. 131.

[14] Printed in *Oeuvres complètes de Eustache Deschamps*, ed. le Marquis de Queux de Saint Hélaire, SATF, IV (Paris: Firmin Didot, 1884), pp. 8-10.

[15] The *Cursor Mundi* contains the earliest instances of the word "carol" in English, one of which speaks of women: "To ierusalem þat heud bare þai. / þer caroled wiues be þe way. / of þair carol such was the sang, / atte þai for ioy had ham amange." See *Cursor Mundi*, ed. Richard Morris, EETS, o.s. 59 (London: Trübner, 1875), Fairfax text, ll. 7599-602. In Chaucer's *Legend of Good Women*, a crowd of women ". . . wenten i compas, / Daunsinge aboute this flour an esy pas, / And songen, as it were in carolewyse, / This balade, which that I shal you devyse" (G Text, ll. 199-202). In the *Book of the Duchess*: "I saw hir daunce so comlily, / Carole and singe so sweetly, / Laughe and pleye so womanly" (ll. 848-50). We learn of the priest in the *Canon's Yeoman's Tale* that "Nas never noon nightingale that luste bet to singe; / Ne lady lustier in carolinge" (G 1344-45). All Chaucer quotations are taken from, *The Works of Geoffrey Chaucer*, ed. F. N. Robinson, 2nd ed. (Boston: Houghton Mifflin, 1957).

[16] "Les chansons de toile ou d'histoire," *Romania*, 69 (1946-47), 462. See also Jean Beck, *La Musique des troubadours* (Paris: Laurens, [1910]), pp. 103-04, for the musical evidence.

[17] *Walther von der Vogelweide: Sprüche und Lieder Gesamtausgabe*, ed. Helmut Protze (Halle: Niemeyer, 1963), pp. 204-05.

[18] "Some Aspects of Medieval Lyric," in *Early English Lyrics*, ed. E. K. Chambers and F. Sidgwick (London: Sidgwick & Jackson, 1907), p. 269.

[19] Examples may be found in *Minnesangs Frühling*, ed. Carl von Kraus (Stuttgart: Hirzel, 1967): Anonymous 3:18; der von Kurenberg, 8:18; 8:34; 9:14; Friedrich von Hausen, 54:1; Heinrich von Veldeke, 67:17; Heinrich von Morungen, 142:26; and Reinmar, 168:6; 186:19; 192:25; 196:5.

[20] No. 185 in *Carmina Burana*. I am indebted to Anne Schotter for this translation.

[21] *Index* no. 3832.5, printed in Bernhard Fehr, "Die Lieder der Hs. Add. 5665," *Archiv*, 106 (1901), 284.

[22] Printed in Moriz Haupt, *Französische Volkslieder* (Leipzig: S. Hirzel, 1887), p. 81.

[23] St. John's College Cambridge MS. 259, fol. 2v.

[24] On this subject see E. Talbot Donaldson's "The Idiom of Popular Poetry in the *Miller's Tale*," in *Speaking of Chaucer* (New York: Norton, 1970), p. 13–29.

[25] *The Harley Lyrics*, ed. G. L. Brook, 4th ed. (Manchester: Manchester Univ. Press, 1968), No. 24.

[26] *Early Middle English Verse and Prose*, ed. J. A. W. Bennett and G. V. Smithers (Oxford: Clarendon Press, 1966), pp. 77–95.

[27] Ibid., pp. 196–200.

[28] *Altfranzösische Romanzen und Pastourellen*, ed. Karl Bartsch (Leipzig: Vogel, 1870), I, p. 44.

[29] *An Old English Miscellany*, ed. R. Morris, EETS, o.s. 49 (London: Trübner, 1872), p. 188.

[30] Bernard Fehr, "Weitere Beiträge zur englischen Lyrik," *Archiv*, 107 (1901), 58.

[31] Deschamps, *Oeuvres*, pp. 8–10.

[32] *Origines*, p. 154.

[33] As printed in Robbins, *Secular Lyrics*, pp. 20–21.

[34] Nykrog, *Les fabliaux*, pp. 193–207.

[35] Printed in *Chronicles of Scottish Poetry*, ed. James Sibbald (Edinburgh: Sibbald, 1802), III, pp. 195–96.

[36] In *A Manual of the Writings in Middle English*, ed. Albert Hartung (New Haven: Connecticut Academy of Arts and Sciences, 1975), V, p. 1459.

[37] Francis Lee Utley, *The Crooked Rib* (Columbus: Ohio State Univ. Press, 1944), No. 135.

Maureen Fries

The "Other" Voice:
Woman's Song, its Satire
and its Transcendence
in Late Medieval
British Literature

In one of the most striking passages of *The Second Sex*, Simone de Beauvoir notes that "what particularly signalizes the situation of woman ·is that she—a free and autonomous being like all human creatures—nevertheless finds herself living in a world where men compel her to assume the status of the Other," creating the "conflict between the fundamental aspirations of every subject (ego)—who always regards the self as essential—and the compulsions of a situation in which she is the inessential."[1] Such an "Otherness" is as true of woman in most of literature (largely written by men) as in life; it is especially apparent in medieval literature, as recent critics have demonstrated.[2] A specific focus for a few scholars during the last thirty years has been the woman's song, or the female-voiced love lyric. Theodor Frings defines such *Frauenleider* as characterized not only by the woman's speaking, rather than the man's, but by her position as the dominant figure, the active lover rather than the passive loved one.[3] Dominance as well as Otherness is also posited by Jonathan Saville in his discussion of the *alba*: here the Lady's role, "obsessively erotic and passionate" as it is, places her ahead of the Lover in importance—indeed he finishes third in triple-voiced *albas* which also include a Watchman. For Saville, the Lady's irra-

tional opposition to whatever may interfere with the sustained in-
dulgence of her love also places this mode in the misogynistic
tradition of the Middle Ages.[4] In spite of alleged female dominance,
Peter Dronke concludes that the real "stuff of courtoisie" and "the
universal courtly experience" both reflect "essentially a man's
conception of love"; he sees the *chanson,* or male-voiced lyric, as
taking absolute precedence over woman's song.[5] Doris Earnshaw
extends this view in her as yet uncompleted comparative study of
romance lyric. She finds "the female voice . . . a vehicle for hetero-
doxy of many kinds," and "generally non-courtly in some way,
either bourgeois, feudal" or peasantlike, with "speech . . . in a pre-
literate mode so that she defines literate courtly speech by contrast."[6]

While scholars therefore seem to agree that woman's song is
essentially Other to the orthodoxy of male-voiced love lyric, they
disagree in their understanding of the female role. What is the nature of its Otherness? Is the speaker of woman's song *really*
dominant—and, if so, in what way? Or does she rather serve merely
to reflect the male's image of himself, as Frederick Goldin has suggested the female does in the courtly lyric generally?[7] One must turn
from the critics and examine the texts themselves to find answers to
such questions. While my major topic of inquiry here is woman's
song in late medieval British literature, a brief survey of its predecessors is necessary for understanding the emergence of woman's
Otherness in European literature as a whole.

I

Like medieval lyric in general, the late medieval woman's song
owes much to the Latin religious lyric, and specifically to the
planctus of the Virgin.[8] Christ Himself was originally the mourned
and absent Lover, and the mourner His Mother; a complementary
rapturous expectation of this real and divine love appears in the
poems of Hadwijch of Brabant, Mechthild of Madgeburg, and
especially Hildegard of Bingen.[9] But the fictional and earthly lover
was an early intruder upon such pious meditation: in the middle of
the eleventh century, we find a woman speaker joyously inviting her
lover to her in a fragment on the last page of the *Cambridge
Songs.*[10] Whether secular or religious, *planctus* or joyous expectation, the Latin woman's song displays the female and sex-linked
obsession with the male lover—to the exclusion of all else—which
continues to characterize the development of the mode in the
vernacular.

Vernacular as opposed to learned tongue emerges as another,
and linguistic, indicator of Otherness, beginning with the macaronic
poetry of the *Carmina Burana.*[11] The earliest examples in a

Romance language, the female-voiced Mozarabic *kharjas* in the Spanish dialect of Moslem Spain, serve as codas to the male-voiced Arabic or Hebrew *muwashshah* they conclude. Dronke notes their "simplicity and directness" and occasional "provocative wit";[12] but the woman's reply in the colloquial to the man's intricate strophes in the learned language is also a comment upon woman's presumed ignorance. Perhaps the most striking example of such contrapuntal semiotics, however, is the dialogue of the troubadour Raimbaut de Vaquieras in which a man woos a woman in Provençal, and she refuses him in Genoese.[13] Such dichotomies are more than clever paradox or poetic conceit: they suggest that, when men and women speak of love, they may (literally) not be talking the same language. The very titles of male- as opposed to female-voiced lyric in Gallego-Portuguese confirm this signal differentiation: woman's song is called *cantiga de amigo* but the man's is labelled *cantiga de amor.*

The woman's absorption in the lover as opposed to the man's absorption in the image of himself in love suggested by this Iberian distinction is a recurrent theme of woman's song. Whether eagerly anticipating his presence as in the *cantiga de amigo*, bewailing his absence as in the secular *planctus*, or commemorating both as in the *chanson de toile*, woman's concern is always with the beloved male at the center of her world. This immersion in love is striking in the *barcarola* of Mendinho, with its vivid metaphor of a girl's waiting to the point of drowning for her tardy lover:

> I have no boatman, I cannot row—
> my beauty will die in the deep sea's flow,
>   waiting for my love,
>   waiting for my love![14]

Such literal engulfing—or threatened engulfing—by the sea, long symbolically associated with woman,[15] is an objective correlative to the female obsession with the beloved male. It suggests as well the actual powerlessness, as opposed to the rhetorical dominance, of the woman in woman's song—a distinction Frings and others have failed to make.

Factual powerlessness is further characterized by the woman's inability to control the movements of her lover. In spite of the female's constant and often bitter rejection of the masculine world of non-loving activity which takes—or threatens to take—her lover from her and impinges upon her own feminine world bounded entirely by their mutual love, men are absent far more than they are present in woman's song. However reluctant the lover may seem as he departs from his beloved's arms (or fails to arrive to fill them), the presumed power of her passion is insufficient to keep him from the world of men, which is, for him, the *real* world fully as much as the lady's bed upon which the *alba* or the Mozarabic *kharja* may be enacted is hers. This polarity of passive/active, static/mobile appears overtly in the imagery of many woman's songs, often traditional and associated with such familiar *topoi* as the *hortus conclusus*. For instance, in the fourteenth-century Provençal "En un vergier sotz fuella d'albespi," the longing of the deserted woman emerges in staple symbols of garden and wind, from the latter of which the woman can drink only "a ray of [her] beloved's breath."[16] The necessary absence of the male is epitomized in the *alba*, in which the Watchman and/or the omnipresent dawn of the masculine Day (as opposed to the feminine Night) interrupt the joyous lovemaking of Lady and Knight and cause them to enact dramatically their sex-linked roles: the Knight goes off to his world of male affairs, for him the important one, while the Lady remains behind "in anguish and longing."[17] Whether solo, duet, or trio, the *alba*— especially at its apex in the great German lyrics of Heinrich von Morungen, Walther von der Vogelweide, and Wolfram von-Eschenbach—underlines the Otherness of woman in medieval lyric by positing her ultimate desertion by her lover as well as her exclusion from the male community of action.

A seeming exception to this female exclusion, to the woman's absorption in her lover and her contrary inability to keep him with her because of masculine allegiances, may appear in the *pastourelle*. In its usual form, this dialogue voices an encounter between a male of superior rank and a girl of lesser status whom he attempts, usually unsuccessfully, to woo. Certainly the nearly two hundred examples of this type in Old French alone present the woman's voice as mostly, and at least superficially, resistant to love rather than absorbed in it. But, as Dronke has demonstrated, most of these lyrics show the female as complementing and encouraging the male's courtly image of himself.[18] In other languages, where the type is rarer, the *pastourelle* may demolish (in Dronke's term) "the male Arcadian fantasy," as in Marcabru's Provençal "L'autrier jost' una sebissa," or Walther von der Vogelweide's reversal of expected sex-roles in a woman's invitation to a man to join a countryside love-making.[19] Such dual-voiced lyrics are even capable of violating previously fixed linguistic distinctions, as in the "Contrasto" of the pre-*stilnovisto* Cielo d'Alcamo, where both male and female speakers combine "exalted and refined phrases" with "vivacious colloquialisms, sly irony with broad invective, homely and proverbial wit with elaborate double entendres."[20] Here the male assumes a potentially ridiculous pose when, in the face of his beloved's decision to drown herself rather than yield, he contemplates necrophilia.[21] These non-

French *pastourelles* nevertheless represent the exception rather than the rule.

We may preface our discussion of woman's song and its purlieu in late medieval British literature, then, by inducing a certain number of conventions from its European antecedents which might affect woman's status as Other and/or her supposed dominance in the type. First, from religious sources to its most secular variants, woman's song centers upon a particular beloved man and not, like male-voiced lyric, upon the persona's obsession with itself. Second, the female voice may be culturally distinguished from the male's by its expression in a vernacular or dialect as opposed to a learned tongue. Third, the woman speaker is absorbed in the experience of the beloved's presence in or absence from her arms, a passive experience as opposed to that world of male activity which occupies most of his life. Fourth, and correlatively, she may be rhetorically dominant but is actually powerless in her attempts to confine her man within the bounds of her feminine world, as most dramatically illustrated in the *alba*. Finally, while usually conforming to rigid linguistic as well as sex-role definitions as do its cognate forms, the *pastourelle*, at least, demonstrates an occasional capacity for satirizing the conventional mode suggested by the other types.

It is this tendency toward satire which most aptly characterizes secular woman's song in late medieval British literature, a subject to which I now turn in separate considerations of Middle English and Middle Scots examples.

II

The Middle English lyric, beginning late on account of linguistic and political conditions, presents some special problems for the literary critic, not all of which have yet been resolved. One is continuity: the two surviving woman's songs in Old English, "The Wife's Lament" and "Wulf and Eadwacer," both exhibiting in an unhappily married woman that absorption in the absent loved one and that powerlessness which place them in the continental mode, have no extant progeny in the Middle English corpus. The most abundant examples of English woman's song, indeed, are not secular at all but religious *planctus* of the Virgin; these are so numerous as almost to overwhelm the few other examples which survive.[22] An examination of their content enlightens the reader as to the direction secular woman's song of the period seems to take, for Mary's *planctus* defines by contrast the position of the seduced and abandoned lay female. As speaker, the Virgin exhorts the hearer/reader to meditate upon her role in the drama of Christ's Incarnation, Suffering and Death, upon her anguished love for her Son and her distinction from all other women as both Virgin and Mother. In emotional range these lyrics move from the restrained and dignified complaints of the fourteenth-century monologues of Mary, or dialogues between Mary and Christ—"Wy haue ȝe no reuthe on my child? / Haue reuthe on me ful of murni[n]g"—with their simple and affecting diction to the sentimentalized and bathetic fifteenth-century "Off alle women þat euer were borne," with its explicit passional details, as in the verse, "I pyke out thornys be on and on," so typical of the time.[23] All such poems portray the Virgin as prime archetype of female virtue,[24] nurturing her son, patiently suffering His loss, and simultaneously admonishing other females to a like conduct. Thus Mary emerges as Other not only to the male speaker but to all other female speakers as well. Combining the two most desirable male-defined womanly functions of chastity and motherhood, as elaborated earlier in folktale and saint's legend, and reminding other women that her further difference from them is that "Gode ... were ... my sone" (l. 52), she is the prime and omnipresent example of that rare quality in late medieval British literature, female goodness.[25]

In counterpoint to the Marian *planctus*, we have the betrayed young girls of the Middle English carols, representing a continuation (as does the vernacular Marian *planctus*) of a Latin-inspired tradition.[26] Here the emphasis lies upon the counter-type of Mary, Eve, as presented in the gullibility and weakness of the secular female speaker in contrast to the clerical cleverness of her seducer. In "Kyrie, so Kyrie," Jankin's seduction of Aleison proceeds in rhythm with the parts of the Mass; the refrain is a reminder, first, that the female speaker is praising God in a blasphemous way as she participates in a sexual liaison with His holy-water clerk, and second, that ultimately she has little reason to praise God at all, since her adventure has had the result that "Alas, I go with childe!" (l. 37). Even more, the refrain of "Alas! alas! the while"—"Thought I on no gile"—emphasizes not only the easy deceivability of women but their essential and Evian duplicity, since the stages of the affair are so explicit as to imply the female's willing cooperation: "Whan I to his chambre com, down he me sette— / From him might I nat go whan we were mette" (ll. 28-29). Her refrain, therefore, emerges as pretended and hypocritical ignorance rather than the real thing and is belied by her description of the affair's consummation as "the murghest night that ever I cam inne" (l. 34).

Woman in these carols still centers her complaint upon a particular man, and her voice in these Middle English examples, as in their Latin and Romance predecessors, is distinguished by its simplicity, directness and lack of learning; but in "Alas! alas! the while," the male voice is fully as colloquial and dialectal as the

female persona's: "Loke that thou be privey and grante that thou
thee bere / A peire whit gloves, I ha to thine were" (ll. 22-23).
Rather than expectation of her lover's return, the female must here
accustom herself to his permanent absence. And, because of her
pregnancy, her rhetorical dominance is matched to actual powerlessness even more than in her continental forebears. In addition, and
more than in non-French *pastourelles*, the tendency to satire is
overt and explicit: unlike the Virgin who achieved motherhood
while retaining her maidenhead, these females lose the latter and
their lovers as well; rather than the universal acclaim accorded
Mary, they meet societal disgrace, as epitomized in the meeting with
the "dame, copped and kene" and the womb's waxing out (ll. 42-
48). Even in brief snatches of woman's song in Middle English, such
naiveté is apparent. For instance, it appears in the comparatively
early "Now springes the spray" in the linguistic vulgarity of "The
clot him clinge!" and in the threat of revenge—"it shall him rewe /
By this day!" (ll. 8, 23-24)—as well as the woman's use of the
already ambiguous "lemman" (20) to describe the deserting lover.

A similar tendency to the antiform, as antithetical to the conventional mode as the secular *planctus* is to the religious, appears in
quite another quarter: Chaucer's handling of the continental *alba*.[27]
Wherever he acquired his knowledge, the principal Middle English
courtly poet also shows himself to be conscious of the traditions
behind the form and deliberately manipulative of them to evoke
comic sex- and/or class-role reversal. In the "Reeve's Tale," for
instance, Chaucer's addition of the morning song of Aleyn and
Malyne is a recognizable parody. The clerk's "Fare weel, Malyne,
sweete wight! / The day is come, I may no lenger byde"[28] casts him
into the ostensible role of the typical albic knight, called from his
lady's bed to the morning world of men. But he is, of course, merely
a vindictive young college student, and she the Miller's daughter by
a wife who is the bastard of the parish priest. Even her name,
Malyne, suggests the impersonal, the lower-class, and the sexually
soiled,[29] and thus makes ridiculous her lover's curtain line, "I is thyn
awen clerk, swa have I seel!" (I, 4239), with its echo of knightly
farewell. Malyne's reply to Aleyn's speech—with its use (twice) of
the ambivalent "lemman" and its *sandwiching* (R. W. Kaske's appropriate term) of her offer of the stolen meal cake between the conventional albic *congié* (or the granting of leave to the knight to
part), and the equally conventional prayer for the lover—is fully as
parodic. The abruptness and finality of Malyne's parting words, her
"almost" weeping, and her lack of expectation of a continuation of
the affair—much less the lifelong devotion Aleyn either seriously or
satirically has offered her—further widen the chasm between this
fabliau wench and the usual female persona of continental woman's

song. Indeed, Malyne's inelegant sharing of her bedroom both with parents and baby brother makes a continuation unthinkable, especially once the Miller discovers the double deception the clerks have practiced upon his wife and daughter and, thus, upon himself.

Such an interest in the possibilities of parodic *alba* in a *fabliau* setting appears briefly in the "Merchant's Tale." January, who unlike Aleyn is of the appropriate knightly class, twice voices morning songs, to neither of which his bride May responds. On the first occasion Chaucer does not even give us January's exact words; following his successful intercourse after a night of hard labor, this sixty-year-old "lover" of a bought young girl sits up in bed to sing "ful loude and cleer," as "the slakke skyn about his nekke shaketh" (IV, 1842–50). Far more effective than any reply is May's telling silence, underlined by the narrator's remark, "But God woot what that May thoughte in hir herte. . . . She preyseth nat his pleyyng worth a bene" (IV, 1851, 1854). To his second *alba*, uttered on an archetypal May morning after his significant blindness[30] in terms echoing the Song of Songs (IV 2138–41) but couched, the narrator tells us, in "olde lewed wordes" (IV, 2149), her only reply is a sign (presumably equally as *lewd*, in our sense of the word) to her young lover Damyan to initiate the deceit of the pear-tree.

But Chaucer's supreme parody upon the *alba* is not fabliauesque but courtly in setting; it occurs in Book III of *Troilus and Criseyde*, directly following the difficult and long-awaited consummation between two lovers of properly noble rank. R. W. Kaske has called the first of the two morning songs a "purposeful adaptation of his traditional poetic form" and credited Chaucer with a perception of "a latent aube-pattern" in his Boccaccian source, *Il Filostrato*.[31] Here, clever use of sex-role reversal results in Criseyde's assuming the usual male role and Troilus the usual female in the formal dictional pattern of the mode. Thus, it is Criseyde who suggests that it is time "to ryse and hennes go" (III, 1425), and Troilus who wants to linger (in a bed which is her uncle's rather than his beloved's own); and it is Troilus who assails the day—"Accursed be thi comyng into Troye" (III, 1450–52) and Criseyde the night—"Thow rakle nyght" (III, 1429 ff.). Further inversions of accepted motifs include Criseyde's regard for her own reputation rather than for secrecy (as in Boccaccio) or her lover's safety (III, 1426); her lack of desire for renewed lovemaking until the last possible moment (contrary both to Boccaccio and albic convention); Troilus' female-linked unwillingness and grief at parting (III, 1472–80); and his ardent desire not to linger in the world of men but to return to Criseyde (III, 1481–84). Criseyde, as speaker, contradicts not only Boccaccio's heroine's ardor but the conventional opposition to the sundering with the lover; like a male, she is more realistically resigned to parting, and her reference to the idea

(III, 1515–17) is "almost non-committal."[32] Troilus, on the contrary, appears even more womanly as he departs, not to resume the war, but to creep "into his bed . . ./ To slepe longe, as he was wont to doone" (III, 1535–36). As Kaske notes, Chaucer's "touch of farce," however delicate (and the delicacy seems to me to be the point), emerges in "a highly original thematic device" filled with pieces of "unconscious irony."[33] If Troilus and Criseyde were unaware of the *alba*, and therefore unconsciously ironic, Chaucer obviously was not.

A final use of woman's song in Chaucer which has no obvious precedents is also found in *Troilus and Criseyde*, in Book II, in the "Troian song" of Criseyde's niece Antigone (II, 827–75). As Sister Mary Charlotte Borthwick has demonstrated, this lyric stands as "Mirour" (which she uses here in its sense of "paragon" or "model") to Criseyde's situation, showing love both as it is and as it should be.[34] Antigone says that the song is not hers, but was made by "the goodlieste mayde . . . in al the town of Troye" (II, 880–81). Unlike previous versions of woman's song, the subject here is not the female's absorption in one beloved man, but the nature of love itself.

The song's maker loves a knight who is not only devoted to her but seems full of all aristocratic virtue (II, 834–44), and their love has made virtue grow (II, 848–54). Like "Antigone the shene" herself, the song seems to shine with praise of Love who has knit this lady and her knight together in an everlasting relationship (II, 869–73).[35] But in what Sister Borthwick distinguishes as the "dark, opaque backing" necessary to give the mirror-song its reflective quality, the female speaker reveals her awareness of the other, shadow side of love.[36] Her lover is not faultless. While "leest with harm desteyned" (II, 840) and "most . . . ententif / To serven well . . . / That ever was" (II, 838–40), his very limitations are a reminder of the double nature of love, a major theme of *Troilus and Criseyde*; for some say "that for to love is vice, / Or thralldom" in spite of the speaker's love-inspired "flemen alle manner vice and sinne" (II, 855–56, 852). Antigone's gloss on her song (II, 887–96) stresses the same doubleness:[37]

> Men musten ask at saintes if it is
> Aught fair in heven. Why? For they can telle,
> And asken feendes is it foul in hell (II, 894–96)

as do the final two lines of the song, "Al dredde I first to love him to beginne, / Now wot I well there is no peril inne" (II, 874–75). Chaucer's use of the doubleness of the *speculum* concept[38] in Antigone's song is in tune with his emphasis in the whole poem upon the double sorrow of Troilus. It also represents, as does much else in Chaucer, a unique response to conventional materials.[39] Other medieval makers of woman's songs turn only to idealization of the male beloved or to satire upon that idealization, as in the satirical *pastourelle* or in such satire upon the *alba* as Chaucer shows mastery of. With his usual talent and grace, Chaucer manages in Antigone's song not only to enunciate in little his poem's tenor but to avoid both idealization and satire by transcending woman's song's concern with human love through his own concern for the divine.[40]

Antigone's song is unusual in medieval lyric in its use of the female voice to question the nature of love in abstract rather than merely concrete terms. Troilus' *Cantus* in Book I, 400-20, is much more typical in being male-voiced. Chaucer's particular concern with satire upon the *alba* continues the tradition of English skepticism about woman's song observed earlier in the carols. His parodies show great variety. Malyne has not chosen to be absorbed in her lover, but is thrust into his arms by his precipitate assault; it is he, and not she, who is dialectally divergent, in his Northernisms.[41] Rather than seeking to hold her lover, she recognizes the necessity for his (aborted) escape and does not seek to confine him to her (uncourtly) world. May's silence, her tacit rejection of her husband/"lover," her eager welcoming of another suitor, all offer telling counterpoint to the conventions of previous woman's song, particularly the *alba*. Criseyde's assumption of the male role and diction, combined with Troilus' acceptance of the female, produces masterful parody in a courtly setting of an archetypal courtly mode, and adumbrates the reversal of values involving human love that Chaucer enunciates in his so-called "palinode" to *Troilus and Crisyde*—a statement that comes down in favor of the Divine Love which will "falsen no wight" (V, 1645).[42] In the Middle Scots "makars" who follow Chaucer, it is not the possibilities of Antigone's Song which will be fully explored, but Chaucer's other tendencies toward modal, and particularly sex-role, reversal. I want now to look at these as they emerge in the work of Robert Henryson and William Dunbar.

III

As has long been recognized, the most worthy continuers of Chaucer's tradition in the fifteenth century are the Middle Scots poets.[43] They demonstrate their "maister's" knowledge of woman's songs and his ability to satirize them in four remarkable poems: Henryson's *Fable of Chantecleer*, "Robene and Makyne," and "Complaint of Crisseid," and Dunbar's masterwork, *The Tua Mariit Wemen and the Wedo*.

In the third of Henryson's *Morall Fabillis of Esope the Phrygian*, there are four female speakers, in contradistinction to the usual one; the comments of the first of these, the familiar widow who keeps the flock of which the cock-hero is sire, frame and counterpoint those of the other three.[44] Like the analogous figure in Chaucer's "Nun's Priest's Tale" (who, however, is all but silent—her only admonition to her *meynee* is a brief exclamation [VII, 3380–81]), the widow is concerned with the theft of her property. But to the Chaucerian echo of her concern—"How, murther, hay!" (l. 485)—Henryson adds a mock-*planctus*: "Allace, now lost is gentill Chantecleir!" (l. 487). As if the adjective "gentill" had begun to enact itself in gesture, the widow then falls into a typical courtly-lady swoon—"Syne, paill of hew, half in ane extasty" (l. 490).[45] While she is thus "ffor cair in swoning" (l. 491), three of the cock's multiple mates discuss and dissect their missing lord.

The first of these is Pertok, a version of the familiar Chaucerian chief hen, Pertelote, and she speaks, at first, conventionally enough, in phrases echoing the *planctus* in general and the *alba* in particular (the cock has been stolen at dawn). "Makand sair murning, / With teris grit attour hir cheikis," she calls Chantecleir the hens' "drowrie," a word unusual as a noun and with ambivalent meanings.[46] Pertok evokes conventional imagery also in her appositives to the cock—"our days darling, / Our nichtingall" and "our Orloge bell, / Our Walkryfe watche" (ll. 498–99), and further in her intercalated lament:

> Quha sall our lemman be? quha sall us leid?
> Quhen we are sad, quha sall unto us sing?
> With his sweit Bill he wald brek us the breid,
> In all this world was their ane kynder thing? (ll. 502–05)

The mock-priestly quality of the cock's eucharistic breaking of bread for his many wives is reminiscent of the quasi-cleric of the English carols and, in view of what follows, a puffing-up of his authority which is not sustained by the views of his other wives.

Pertok's praise of the cock as a lover sets off a chain reaction in the other two hens, Sprutok and Toppok, which causes her shortly to revise her opinion. To her claim that "In paramouris he wald do us plesing" (l. 506), Sprutok replies that she should cease her sorrow: "Ye be to mad for him sic murning mais" (l. 510). By her account, he was angry, jealous and, most damning of all for a lover in a woman's song, "Off chalmerglew . . . / Waistit he wes" (ll. 516–19)—that is, no good in bed. Assessing him in *fabliau* terms as opposed to Pertok's courtly praise, she reminds her sisters of their new opportunity for freedom from their lover: she will "mak me fresch agane this Jolie may, / Syne chant this sang, 'wes never wedow sa gay!'" (ll. 514–15). Pertok answers this challenge, not by defending Chantecleir, but by one-upping Sprutok: declaring that "off sic as him ane scoir / Wald not suffice to slaik our appetyte," she promises that within a week she will acquire "ane berne suld better claw oure breik" (ll. 525–29).

Toppok, the third wife, interrupts this retraction with a further satirical speech: "lyke ane Curate . . . full crous," she declaims, "Yone wes ane verray vengeance from the hevin; / He was sa lous, and sa lecherous; / He had . . . kittokis ma than sevin" (ll. 530–33). Thus, his fate is a punishment of "rychteous God," smiting "rycht sair, thoch he be patient, / For Adulterie" (ll. 534–37). As John MacQueen has noted, this incongruous moralizing is operative on at least two levels: first, adultery is an impossibility in a cock-and-henly world; and second, Toppok is in any case one of the "kittokis" involved.[47] Additionally, Toppok assumes, like the other two hens, that the cock is dead, which, of course, he is not. And her sermon is followed/framed by a renewed courtly response from the widow.

Waking from her swoon, and also apparently from her courtly affectation, the widow calls her dogs to pursue the fox; the finale ensues, as in Chaucer and the folk analogues, with Chantecleir's saving himself. The widow's final courtly gesture—her cry to her dogs, "Reskew my Nobill Cok, or he be slane" (l. 549)—echoes ironically her earlier response in its reference to the popular medieval (and male-voiced) lyric, "I have a gentle cook [sic]," with its phallic *doubles entendres*.[48] Like the hens' speeches, the widow's framing lament seems designed as an inappropriately exaggerrated reaction to the theft of a cock by a fox; joined to the mock-courtly *planctus* of Pertok, the exchange of Pertok with Sprutok (the stereotyped and fabliau-linked oversexed widows), and the quasi-religious sententiousness of Toppok, it satirizes woman's song in its parody of accepted conventions. As in Chaucer, the barnyard setting also works toward humorous anti-convention. Henryson shows himself equally aware of the nature of woman's song and the ease with which it may be made fun of.

Equal fun is had with *pastourelle* convention in the same poet's "Robene and Makyne." At the beginning of the lyric, Robene is discovered at the task usually assigned to the shepherdess in the archetypal mode, "Kepand a flok of fe" (l. 2). Makyne, a name whose associations had already been exploited by Chaucer,[48] besieges him like the male in conventional *pastourelle*, with words describing her love-longing (ll. 4–8). This rural wench's use of the established vocabulary of amatory solicitation—"my dule in dern" and "Dowtless but dreid I de" (ll. 7–8)—adds to the humor of the unexpected role reversal; Robene's assumption of the rhetorical innocence appropriate to the shepherdess continues the comedy:

> nathing of lufe I knaw,
> Bot keipis my scheip undir yone wid.
> . . . .
> . . . quhat is lufe, or to be lude?
> Fane wald I leir that law. (ll. 9–10, 15–16)

Robene's concern for his sheep—"Lo, quahir they raik on raw!" (l. 11)—is a continuous theme throughout the first half of the poem and is his ostensible reason for refusing Makyne's advances: "And we wald play us in this plane, / They wald us bayth reproif" (ll. 30–32). But once he has assembled the sheep for the night in an ambiguous "fulfair daill,"[50] Robene repents, follows the girl, and avers that "thy harte for till haif myne / Is all my cuvating" (ll. 85–86). But now, in a further reversal of the original role reversal, Makyne refuses her would-be lover not only by proverbially reminding him of his un-gallant earlier refusal of her—"The man that will nocht quhen he may / sall haif nocht quhen he wald" (ll. 91–92)—but by seemingly turning religious (ll. 93–96). To this Robene returns an acknowledg-ment that the night is made for love, to say nothing of secrecy (ll. 97–101); but Makyne spurns him still "as thow has done, sa sall I say, / murne on, I think to mend" (ll. 109–12). Robene's final plea, couched in the courtly love argot of which he had earlier feigned ignorance, is also bluntly rejected: "Scho sang, he sichit sair" (ll. 123–24). Like the archetypal shepherdess of which he is a burlesque, Robene returns to keeping his herd "amangis the holtis hair" (l. 128), in place of the usual knightly retreat.

The parodic tone of these two poems, the first aimed at the familiar *planctus* in all its modes and perhaps especially also at the *alba*, and the second at the *pastourelle*, is at variance with Henryson's third and final experiment with woman's song, the intercalated lyric "Complaint of Crisseid" in his major narrative poem, *The Testament of Crisseid*. Read in context with Chaucer's "Antigone's Song" which might have inspired it, this woman's song appears almost as a reply to Antigone's Trojan maiden's musings upon the double nature of human love. The emphasis is upon the negative, or shadow side, of the mirror; indeed, at one point Crisseid admonishes the "ladyis fair of Troy and Grece" to "in ʒour mynd ane mirrour mak of me" (ll. 452, 457):

> As I am now, peraduenture that ʒe,
> For all ʒour micht, may cum to that same end,
> Or ellis war, gif ony war may be. (ll. 458–60)

Like Antigone's lyric, in the words of A. C. Spearing, this song "'amplifies' (though in a non-naturalistic way) Crisseid's emotions" as well as serving "to clarify the moral pattern exemplified up to that point [in the poem]."[51] Beyond this, Crisseid's *planctus* differs from previous examples of the type in its relentless blaming of Fortune and the speaker's own defects rather than the absence of the lover for present unhappiness. "Catiue Creisseid," in a logically progressive series of stanzas, first blames her fate and then laments in succession the archetypal ladies' domains of chamber (ll. 416–24) and garden (ll.

425-33), the *notatio* of reputation (ll. 434-42) and the *effictio* of appearance (ll. 443-51), and finally presents herself as an "exempill" to all other women and to the transitoriness of earthly happiness (ll. 452-69). Here Henryson shows himself supremely Chaucerian in his transcendence of the usual boundaries of woman's song and its satire to create a Boethian lyric which epitomizes, as Antigone's Song had done for *Troilus and Criseyde*, the opposition between earthly and heavenly values which pervades the whole of *The Testament of Crisseid*.

If "The Complaint of Crisseid" represents a rare female speaker's transcendence of the usual narrow scope of woman's song, William Dunbar's *The Tua Mariit Wemen and the Wedo* represents the extreme of female immanence.[52] This longest of woman's songs has, like Henryson's fable of Chantecleer, a trio of speakers who anatomize not just a single lover but a whole range of male (and female) behavior. Here, too, the comparison between male- and female-voiced lyric is heightened by linguistic contrast—in the distance between the chivalric and high style of the masculine I-narrator, and the bourgeois and low style of the feminine characters. Framed by the male's courtly diction—for example, his use of traditional *effictio* to describe the females' ladylike appearance—the coarse and apparently unlearned rhetoric of the women reeks of *fabliau*. Just as the narrator's extended eavesdropping undercuts the politeness of his speech, all three of the "eavesdroppees" display attitudes toward men diametrically opposed to those of the usual speaker of woman's song.

That the major complaint of the two wives is directed at their husbands' presence rather than at a lover's absence is a delightfully original and witty inversion of the conventional mode. So is the widow's refusal to confine herself to the stereotyped female world of the bedroom; in her ability to penetrate the masculine world, she is also able to impose her own female values upon it. All three speakers illustrate that self-absorption which is usually characteristic of the male-voiced lyric. Nor is it their desire to please or retain a single male lover; instead, they are anxious to please only themselves and to retain as many men as possible. Dunbar's woman's song, then, unlike the mode it satirizes, is female-centered and only tangentially concerned with the male beloved.

The two wives, in fact, have thus far been prevented by husbandly vigilance from acquiring such an extramarital lover. Not that any one man would long content them: to the Wedo's opening question as to whether marriage is "nocht ane blist band that bindis so fast" (l. 43), the first wife replies that it is "bair of blis, and bailfull" and that she wishes "matrimony were made to mell for ane yeir" (l. 56). But, being inescapably wed to a "waistit wolroun," she must instead sell him her favors before she lets him "my leggis ga betweene (ll. 90, 133–34). While the second wife's spouse is by contrast young, he too is a worn-out lecher: appearing "valyeand in Venus chalmer," he is actually "na war na he semys," and she would rather have "a fresch fair to fang in myn armes" (ll. 183, 200, 209). Of a practical nature, in the absence of opportunity she pretends that she loves this husband whom she despises.

The promiscuity which both wives desire is practiced by the widow, who commends it to them. Pretending to be a conventional restorer of rebellious married women to correct social values, she prays that "my prechyng may pers your perverst hertis, / And make yow mekar to men" (ll. 249–50). But her subsequent mock-sermon aims at the opposite extreme. As dissembling as the second wife, as covetous as the first, and cleverer and more experienced than either, she exhorts her pupils—in imagery the animality of which is in sharp contrast with the usual romantic and conventional diction of woman's song—to be "dragonis baith and dowis ay in double form" (l. 263). For her, the essential skill for wife as well as widow is to deceive the husband, and/or the world which survives his death, with woman's craft. Pretending to coddle her first husband, the widow had managed to keep "a lufsummar leid my lust for to slokyn," with whom she could "be secrete and sure and ay saif my honur" (ll. 284–85). She even managed to pass off her lover's bastard as her husband's child so successfully that she gained most of his property for this son. Upwardly mobile, she had taken as second husband a mighty merchant who, while her own age and even her own height, was her equal neither in sexuality nor in guile. Putting him down as a "pedder," she kept from any but the minutest exercise of the marital debt, "for never bot in a gentill hert is generit ony ruth" (ll. 315–16)—a Chaucerian echo of a Chaucerian echo, meant (as used in the Miller's, Reeve's and Merchant's tales) to mock the conventional nurturing role of woman in so-called "courtly love." The ripples of our remembrance of Chaucer's practice in this echo add enormously to the mixed courtly/*fabliau* ambiance of the poem.

The *fabliau* world is further evoked by the Wedo's detailing of the stages by which she has achieved the mastery over male movement denied to the usual speaker of woman's song. Like the Wife of Bath, long since identified as one of her models, she uses the husband (in this case her second) as "lumbart" for her money and clothes; to add insult to injury, she keeps the finery thus bought for her next lover as she makes him cuckold as well. Cherishing her own children, she makes "fulis of the fry of his first wif" (l. 403) and holds her husband's friends as her foes, while managing at the same time to fool the latter with pretended grief at his death. Unlike Chaucer's Wife, this particular widow exhibits no desire to marry again. Nor will she confine herself to the archetypal bedroom of woman's song. Venturing into the male world, she openly flirts in "kirk" and with a wide variety of men, "knychtis, and . . . clerikis, and cortly personis" alike (l. 435). False tears, meanwhile, make her appear a saint or an angel to her deceased husband's friends, a stratagem she recommends to all women.

She also recommends that the two wives acquire a secret bawd in order to hide their indiscretion and sin. Her own indifference to sin, as well as to the decorous behavior of woman's song, appears in her final *tour-de-force* revelation, in which she pictures herself at the center of a sort of Scots group grope. Her house full with "baronis and knychtis, / And othir bachilleris, blith bumyng in youth" (ll. 476-77), herself wantonly filled with wine, she kisses some, embraces others, and generally and generously tries to accomodate them all:

> For he that sittis me nixt, I nip on his finger;
> I serf him on the tohir side on the samin fassin;
> And he that behind me sittis, I hard on him lene;
> And him befor, with my fut fast on his I stramp;
> And to the bernis far but sueit blenkis I cast:
> To every man in speciall speke I sum wordis
> So wisly and so womanly, quhill warmys ther herts.
> (ll. 490-95)

Unlike the courtly heroine of *Le Roman de la rose*, who is divided into her various qualities for the lover's instruction and delight so that there is no integrity to her own person, the Wedo divides herself, and for her own delight, among the many men who woo her. She transcends not only the archetypal world of woman's song but rank and social class as well, including her own lowly rank as a woman within a patriarchal society.[53] Yet her transcendence emerges as more appearance than reality because of her inability to exist without the admiration of the men she so blithely courts.

The Wedo's careless rejection of the conventional values of woman's song is thus accompanied by an acceptance and exploitation of the sex-role reversal apparent in Chaucer and in Henryson's earlier practice—and ultimately by her own, pitiful exploitation of herself. In her rejection of male-dominant ideas about women she suggests satire upon other genres glorifying "good" women rather than woman's song alone: "This is the legand of my life, though Latyne it be nane" (l. 504), she concludes, turning her narrative into a deft parody of female saint's legend, with its apparent purpose of extolling chastity and obedience in women. Such a parody-in-retrospect is an apt conclusion to the minute and unbridled history of her own lustful and secretly disobedient life as told to encourage her audience of two wives to similar female-pleasing, male-using, but ultimately female-degrading behavior.

While Dunbar's poem is not obscene, or coarse and corrupt, or a projection of his own supposedly twisted celibacy upon the opposite sex as previous critics have variously suggested,[54] its picture of women is neither attractive nor balanced. In spite of its striking contradiction of—indeed its nay-saying to—the masculine mystique about the feminine in classic woman's song, *The Tua Mariit Wemen and the Wedo* has no positive alternative to offer. Dunbar's individual talent, bounded first by a long, "learned" tradition of pervasive misogyny and second by a long literary tradition of the female speaker as the heterodox, the Other voice to the male, cannot move beyond received "auctoritee." The only contrastive rhetoric he has available for the female voice is the coarse speech of *fabliau*. And, strangely enough, this rhetoric makes his three women fully as "obsessively erotic and passionate" as the seemingly opposite and ultra-conventional lady of the *alba*. It thus bears out Saville's contention that even this lady is irrevocably bound to the antifeminist tradition in spite of her seeming glorification, and it corroborates Sister Ritamary Bradley's demonstration that the praise and blame of women were but two different aspects of the male perception of their Otherness in the Middle Ages.[55]

Pace Francis Utley, there was no real argument about the "goodness" or the "badness" of women in medieval lyric.[56] In the Middle Scots poets even more than in the Middle English, the potential for satire and parody in conventional woman's song becomes increasingly overt. Whether hen or Wedo, the female speaker is absorbed in herself and her own interest rather than in her lover; and whether framed by mock-courtly lament, as in Henryson's fable, or mock-courtly *effictio*, as in Dunbar, she no longer inhabits by preference a male-defined world. With the Wedo, she even manages to escape into the hitherto-forbidden world of men, and with Makyne to entice or to reject with equal freedom. Both Makyne and the Wedo even abandon expected female powerlessness in a freedom of movement not shared by the barnyard-bound Pertok, Sprutok, and Toppok. Only in "The Complaint of Crisseid" do we hear the transcendent female voice first envisioned by Chaucer in the song of Antigone in place of the almost universal voice which characterizes other woman's song.

IV

We are now in a position to generalize, having looked at the most important texts, and to answer the questions raised about woman's song in the first section of this paper.

The nature of female Otherness in most woman's song is as a reflector of the male and male values, as Goldin has demonstrated is true of the courtly lyric as a whole. Unlike the male persona, obsessed with the narcissistic picture of himself, the female is obsessed with her male lover; she joys in his presence, pines in his absence, and lacks control over his movement from her world into his own. Rhetorically dominant, she is actually powerless, except in occasional satire, such as the non-French *pastourelle*, where, probably for comic effect, she has the right to say no if she chooses. Her voice often differs linguistically from the male's.

In late medieval British woman's song, however, the latent possibility for satire present in the distorted view of female life and personality emerging from the classic form is actualized in a number of unusual lyrics. From a mode overwhelmingly dominated by *planctus* of the Virgin, in Middle English emerges the contrasting voice of the "deceived" and pregnant ordinary woman, who cannot expect the return of her lover, and who has paid dearly for making him the center of her world. A similar lack of expectation characterizes Chaucer's satire of the *alba* in the *Canterbury Tales* where the woman's previous rhetorical dominance declines to practical advice, as with Malyne, or to complete silence, as with May. In *Troilus and Criseyde*, Chaucer systematically uses sex-role reversal— which had previously occurred only sporadically—to create a strikingly original *alba* which embodies a major theme of his poem. In Antigone's song in the same poem, this theme, the doubleness and limitations of human love as compared with divine, emerges in a female-voiced lyric which transcends previous concerns of woman's song.

Such transcendence in Middle Scots appears only in "The Complaint of Crisseid," like Antigone's song an archetypal utterance[57] moving beyond—indeed, standing outside of—previously rigid sex-role polarization. But the Chaucerian tendency toward satire continues in Henryson, who mocks both *alba* and *pastourelle* and exploits both sex- and class-role reversal for comic effect. Satire is pushed to its logical extreme in Dunbar's *Tua Mariit Wemen and the Wedo*, where earlier linguistic and sex-role distinctions between male and female speakers rise to an apex in their violation of earlier conventions of woman's song. The female voices here are self- rather than male-centered, mourn the presence rather than the absence of the male, gloatingly envision promiscuity rather than eternal faithfulness, and either have moved (the Wedo) or would like to move (the Tua Mariit Wemen) in the same male-dominant world rejected by the usual speaker of woman's song but frequented by putative lovers.

Unfortunately, the possibility for transcendence of both sex-

linked worlds, as briefly explored by both Chaucer and Henryson in
atypical lyrics, remains a rare and isolated phenomenon, even in the
poetic corpus of its innovators. Woman's song, whether in its original mode or in its satire, remains in late medieval British literature
largely still Other, not only to the predominant male voice which
utters the real "stuff of courtoisie" but to the pervasive male warrior
ethos from which the female persona emerged, and to which it came
to form an important and, until recently, overlooked, counterpoint.[58]

 *Notes*

[1] *The Second Sex*, trans. H. M. Parshley (New York: Bantam Books,
1961), p. xxviii.

[2] See especially Joan Ferrante, *Woman as Image in Medieval Litera-
ture: From the Twelfth Century to Dante* (New York: Columbia Univ.
Press, 1975); Marianne Shapiro *Woman Earthly and Divine in the* Comedy
of Dante (Lexington: Univ. Press of Kentucky, 1975); William E. Phipps,
Was Jesus Married? The Distortion of Sexuality in Christian Tradition
(New York: Harper and Row, 1970); Victor White, *Soul and Psyche: An
Enquiry into the Relationship of Psychotherapy and Religion* (London:
Collins and Harville, 1960), chapters on "The Missing Feminine," "The
Feminine Image in Christianity," "The Integration of Evil."

[3] *Minnesinger und Troubadours*, Deutsche Akademie der Wissenschaften zu Berlin, Vorträge und Schriften, 34 (Berlin: Akademie, 1949).

[4] *The Medieval Erotic* Alba: *Structure as Meaning* (New York: Columbia Univ. Press, 1972), esp. pp. 153–58 and passim.

[5] *Medieval Latin and the Rise of European Love-Lyric*, I (Oxford:
Clarendon Press, 1965), pp. 8–9.

[6] Personal communication on dissertation in progress at the University
of California, Berkeley.

[7] Frederick Goldin, *The Mirror of Narcissus in the Courtly Love Lyric*
(Ithaca: Cornell Univ. Press, 1967), passim.

[8] Especially in English, these are far more numerous than any other
type. See R. T. Davies, "Introduction," *Medieval Lyrics: A Critical Anthology*, (London: Faber and Faber, 1963), p. 40; and, for reasons why this
might have been so, Richard Leighton Greene, "The Carol and Popular
Religion," in *The Early English Carols* (Oxford: Clarendon Press, 1935),
pp. cxi–cxxxii.

[9] See Peter Dronke, *The Medieval Lyric* (London: Hutchinson, 1968),
pp. 75–85, 233–35. Also on Hildegard, see his *Medieval Latin*, I, pp. 66 ff.,
129, 153n, 310 ff.

[10] This item is said by Dronke to be "the oldest surviving secular Latin
dance-song" (*Medieval Lyric*, p. 190). For the text, see *Die Cambridger
Lieder* (Berlin: Weidman, 1926), no. 49.

[11] Dronke discusses this in *Medieval Latin*, I, pp. 302–04, and in *Medieval Lyric,* p. 194. For texts, see *Carmina Burana*, ed. A. Hilka and O. Schumann, I.a, *Die Liebeslieder* (1941; rpt. Heidelberg: Carl Winter, 1971).

[12] *Medieval Lyric*, Ch. 3, "'Cantigas de amigo,'" p. 86.

[13] Dronke, *Medieval Lyric*, p. 126, cites this as an example of the "numerous tours de force" of Raimbaut without noting its sex-linked significance.

[14] Trans. by Dronke, in *Medieval Lyric*, p. 102. Dronke, however, sees the sea as having "inward symbolic associations . . . [which make] the girl feel engulfed in the greatness of possible disappointment; the sea is time, is waiting with no way out; the sea is separation" p. 103.

[15] No recourse to Freud or Jung is necessary here; we have Venus/ Aphrodite rising from the waves, Ulysses' sea-bound temptresses, Circe, the Sirens, even gentle Nausicaa, the Rhine Maidens, and a plethora of other literary examples ranging down to Joyce's Anna Livia Plurabelle and Jean Rhys's *Wide Sargasso Sea.*

[16] Dronke, *Medieval Lyric*, pp. 174–76, cites this as an *alba* rather than a woman's song. The quotation is from his translation, p. 174. He sees the imagery rightly as deriving not from Arabic poetry but from the Song of Songs.

[17] Saville, p. 1.

[18] This is the gist of his argument, although he does not use my terminology. See *Medieval Lyric*, p. 200.

[19] *Medieval Lyric*, pp. 200–03. Dronke discusses both these songs and the pastourelles under the rubric "dance-songs" rather than "woman's songs."

[20] *Medieval Lyric,* p. 155.

[21] If you fling yourself in the sea, gracious and fine lady,
   I'll dive in and follow you, all the way through the ocean;
   then finally, when you are drowned, on the beach I'll find you,
       only that this one deed be consummated,
       and you and I in vice at last united!
   (Dronke's translation,)

[22] That the Virgin should be the prime female speaker is not surprising, given the religious orientation of the extant Middle English lyrics. See, for example, the large number of religious as compared with secular carols in Greene, where the former occupy pp. 3–252, and the latter only pp. 253–319. The earliest carol in English is religious: see no. 88 in *Religious Lyrics of the XIV*[th] *Century*, ed. Carleton Brown, 2nd ed., rev. G. V. Smithers (Oxford: Clarendon Press, 1957).

[23] Brown, *Religious Lyrics of the XIV*[th] *Century*, no. 56 (see also nos. 60, 67, 128); *Religious Lyrics of the XV*[th] *Century*, ed. Carleton Brown (Oxford: Clarendon Press, 1939), no. 7. The finest of these is generally considered to be "Quia Amore Langueo" (Brown, *Religious Lyrics of the XIV*[th] *Century*, no. 132), which echoes the Song of Songs. Additional examples in Brown, *XV*[th] *Century*, are nos. 6, 8, 9, 10.

24 The literature on Mariology is so voluminous as to be overwhelming. An extensive treatment of the medieval tradition in English appears in Yrjö Hirn's *The Sacred Shrine: A Study of the Poetry and Art of the Catholic Church* (1912; rpt. Boston: Beacon Press, 1957), Pt. II. For a more feminist treatment of Mary as archetype, see Maureen Fries, "The Characterization of Women in the Alliterative Tradition," in *The Alliterative Tradition of the Fourteenth Century*, ed. Bernard Levy and Paul Szarmach, Series in Medieval Literature, 3 (New York: Burt Franklin, 1979), pp. 25–45.

25 Brown, *XV*th *Century*, no. 7. For cultural influences leading to the decay of the already discredited female image in the later Middle Ages, see Friedrich Heer, *The Medieval World: Europe 1100–1350*, trans. Janet Sondheimer (New York: New American Library, 1961), chapt. 13, "Jews and Women"; for literary tendencies in the same direction, Ferrante, chapt. IV, "In the Thirteenth Century."

26 In the following two paragraphs, I quote nos. 73, 108, and 19, respectively, from Davies, *Medieval English Lyrics*. These carols do not appear in the compendious collection of Greene.

27 For much that is useful in the next three paragraphs I am indebted to the pioneering discussions of R. W. Kaske: "An Aube in the *Reeve's Tale*," *ELH* 26 (1959), 295–310; "January's 'Aube,'" *MLN* 75 (1960), 1–4; and "The Aube in Chaucer's *Troilus*," in *Chaucer Criticism: II*, ed. Richard J. Schoeck and Jerome Taylor (Notre Dame: Univ. of Notre Dame Press, 1961), pp. 167–79.

28 *The Works of Geoffrey Chaucer*, ed. F. N. Robinson, 2nd ed. (Boston: Houghton Mifflin, 1957), 4236–37. All further references to Chaucer's work are to this edition and appear in text by tale and verse reference.

29 Kaske, "*Reeve's Tale*," p. 300, cites the name as "lexically an oven-mop," "a typical lower-class familiar female name," and perhaps referential to the "familiar proverb about Malkin's lost maidenhead."

30 Blindness in literature is often connected with sexual offense. For two examples disparate in time, consider Oedipus' self-mutilation, and Mr. Rochester's blinding by the fire from which he attempts to rescue his previously-repudiated first wife in *Jane Eyre*. John Picarelli, who teaches physiology at the State University of New York College of Optometry, informs me that the major nerve which controls sight is located in the genital area.

31 Kaske, p. 170. I have discussed other Chaucerian changes in his Boccaccian material in "Boccaccio, Chaucer and the Concept of Criseyde," a paper read at the International Courtly Literature Society Program, Anual Meeting, Modern Language Association of America, San Francisco, December, 1979.

32 Kaske, p. 173.

33 Kaske, p. 176.

34 "Antigone's Song as 'Mirour' in Chaucer's *Troilus and Criseyde*," *MLQ*, 22 (1961), 227–35. I am indebted to Sister Mary Borthwick for much of the discussion in the next two paragraphs.

35 Borthwick, p. 227.

³⁶ Borthwick, pp. 227–28. As she notes, "the possibility for such a double interpretation is most noticeable in the first and fourth stanzas" (pp. 230–31).

³⁷ In her otherwise excellent analysis, Sister Mary Borthwick does not mention the echo of Antigone's song in its gloss.

³⁸ See Sister Ritamary Bradley, "Backgrounds of the title *Speculum* in Medieval Literature," *Speculum*, 29 (1954), 100–15, for discussion.

³⁹ For a similar response in the *Canterbury Tales*, see Sister Ritamary Bradley, "*The Wife of Bath's Tale* and the Mirror Tradition," *JEGP*, 55 (1956), 624–30.

⁴⁰ That Chaucer's female characters are unsatisfactory in spite of his own sympathy with them is probably due to the social and literary conventions of his time. See Arlyn Diamond, "Chaucer's Women and Women's Chaucer," in *The Authority of Experience: Essays in Feminist Criticism* (Amherst: Univ. of Massachusetts Press, 1977), pp. 60–83.

⁴¹ If Chaucer is deliberately reversing the device of female-dialect speech here, he displays a wider knowledge of woman's song conventions than even Kaske has shown he exhibits in his treatment of the *alba*.

⁴² For demonstration of how Chaucer's characterization of Criseyde works toward the same end, see Maureen Fries, "'Slydynge of Corage': Chaucer's Criseyde as Feminist and Victim," in *Authority of Experience*, pp. 45–59.

⁴³ But for a reminder that they deserve recognition in their own right, see Florence H. Ridley, "A Plea for the Middle Scots," in *The Learned and the Lewed: Studies in Chaucer and Medieval Literature* [in honor of Bartlett Jere Whiting], ed. Larry D. Benson (Cambridge: Harvard Univ. Press, 1974), pp. 175–96.

⁴⁴ All references to Henryson's poems are to *The Poems and Fables of Robert Henryson, Schoolmaster of Dunferline*, ed. H. Harvey Wood (1933; rpt. New York: Barnes and Noble, 1968).

⁴⁵ For the suggestion that this is a courtly parody I am indebted to John MacQueen, *Robert Henryson* (Oxford: Clarendon Press, 1967), p. 140.

⁴⁶ Wood, p. 230, gives "love in the abstract sense, illicit or otherwise, a love token or gift, or the marriage gift" or the "morning gift"; and G. Gregory Smith, ed., *The Poems of Robert Henryson*, Scottish Text Society (Edinburgh: William Blackwood and Sons, 1914), I, 107, "courtship" and "sweetheart."

⁴⁷ MacQueen, pp. 142–43.

⁴⁸ See *Secular Lyrics of the XIV*ᵗʰ *and XV*ᵗʰ *Centuries*, ed. Rossell Hope Robbins, 2nd. ed. (Oxford: Clarendon Press, 1955), no. 46, where the details "his comb is of reed corel, / his tayil is of get" (7–8) and especially his perching every night "in myn ladyis chaumbyr" (20) are obviously sexual puns.

⁴⁹ See n. 29 above. Smith, I, 59, cites the name as "sometimes used in the deteriorated sense of slut, or wanton."

⁵⁰ Smith, I, 103–04, defines "daill" as meaning both "dale, hollow" and

to "have intercourse, make love"—a sense in which Henryson twice uses it in this poem.

[51] *Criticism and Medieval Poetry,* 2nd ed. (New York: Barnes and Noble, 1972), p. 173. For complementary female images, see Maureen Fries, "Besides Crisseid: Henryson's Other Women," in *Acts of the Second International Congress on Scots Language and Literature, Medieval and Renaissance,* ed. Claude Graf (Strasbourg: Univ. of Strasbourg Press, 1979), pp. 250–67.

[52] All references to this poem are from *The Poems of William Dunbar,* ed. W. MacKay Mackenzie (1933; rpt. London: Faber and Faber, 1960).

[53] See Tom Scott, *Dunbar: A Critical Exposition of the Poems* (Edinburgh: Oliver and Boyd, 1966), p. 201.

[54] A comprehensive anthology of such comments over the centuries and extending into the 1960's is appended to the unpublished paper of Elizabeth Roth, "Criticism and Taste: Readings of Dunbar's *Tretis,*" read at the Annual Meeting of the Northeast Modern Language Association, Session on the Middle Scots Makars, University of Pittsburgh, April 21, 1977.

[55] "A Schema for the Study of the Characterization of Women in Medieval Literature," unpublished paper read at the Annual Meeting of the Midwest Modern Language Association, St. Louis, Missouri, October, 1972.

[56] While Utley's book *The Crooked Rib: An Analytical Index to the Argument About Women in English and Scots Literature to the End of the Year 1568* (Columbus: Ohio Univ. Press, 1944) suggests in its subtitle and introduction that praise of women was equal in quantity and quality to blame, an examination of its contents reveals that the misogynistic lyrics far outnumber the eulogistic ones, and that, besides the Virgin, only male-desired qualities are praised in women—e.g., beauty, mercy, graceful singing and dancing. The "onpreyse" of women (as it is called in Robbins, no. 34) was a regular genre as well. On the general subject of antifeminism, see Jill Mann, *Chaucer and Medieval Estates Satire* (Cambridge: Cambridge Univ. Press, 1973), pp. 121–27; Katherine M. Rogers, *The Troublesome Helpmate: A History of Misogyny in Literature* (Seattle: Univ. of Washington Press, 1966); G. R. Owst, *Literature and Pulpit in Medieval England,* 2nd ed. (New York: Barnes and Noble, 1961); Arthur Keister Moore, "Studies in a Medieval Prejudice: Antifeminism," unpublished diss. (Vanderbilt, 1945); and Samuel Marion Tucker, *Verse Satire in England Before the Renaissance* (1909: rpt. New York: AMS Press, 1966). Particular studies include, among others, Vern L. Bullough, "Medieval Medical and Scientific Views of Women," in *Marriage in the Middle Ages: A Symposium,* ed. John Leyerle, *Viator,* 4 (1973); and Robert A. Pratt, "Jankyn's Book of Wikked Wyves: Medieval Antimatrimonial Propaganda in the Universities," *AnM,* 31 (1962), 5–27. Recent historical studies are noted in Carolly Erickson and Kathleen Casey, "Women in the Middle Ages: A Working Bibliography," *MS,* 37 (1975), 340–89.

[57] Bradley, "Schema," has pointed out that archetypes may be persons, places, things, or events. Other archetypal utterances in *Troilus and*

Criseyde which do not fall under the rubric of "woman's song" include numerous speeches in Books II–V, which are well worth exploration from a feminist perspective.

[58] Between the time I wrote the original version of this paper for presentation at the Thirteenth Conference on Medieval Studies and its rewriting for the present volume, I was asked by Professor Rossell Hope Robbins to participate in a symposium on "Patroness, Paramour or Paper Doll: The Woman in Courtly Love," for his faculty-staff seminar in The Courtly Love Tradition at the State University of New York at Albany. While the paper I presented there, "*Vox Feminae*: The Female Speaker in Courtly Love," was quite different from the present one, comments from his students and colleagues, and especially from my co-symposiasts Professors Arlyn Diamond and Elizabeth Petroff of the University of Massachusetts, Amherst, and Professor Robbins himself, aided greatly in helping me refine my ideas. I am indebted to them all.

Mary   Beth   Winn

Poems by "The Lady" in *La Chasse et le départ d'Amours (1509)*

On April 14, 1509 Antoine Vérard published in Paris a prodigious volume with the title *La chasse et le depart damours faict et Compose par reverend pere en dieu messire Octovien de sainct gelaiz evesque dangoulesme et par noble homme blaise dauriol bachelier en chascun droit demourant a Thoulouze.* The sumptuous copy now in the Bibliothèque Nationale (Rés. vél. 583) is printed on vellum and magnificently decorated with hand-painted illustrations.[1]

The title of the book is in fact as misleading as the attribution of authorship is questionable. The three-hundred-page volume contains two major works—a lengthy poem about "la chasse du cerf amoureux" which is untitled and for which no author is named, and a poem preceded by the lines "la departie damours . . . par noble blaise dauriol." Each of these works, however, ends with a long series of ballades and rondeaux, more than four hundred in number, composed by various fifteenth-century authors, including, most notably, Charles d'Orléans. These poems are presented as compositions by the "Amant Parfait" and his lady with no mention of author.[2]

The poems by the lady appear in the section of the book dealing with the hunt of the "cerf amoureux," the stag bearing the heart of Venus. Hero of this hunt is the Amant Parfait who is rewarded for his valor with the love of a beautiful and noble lady. In her honor, he pronounces a fervent apology for women and finally engages in victorious battle against Faulx Semblant, the slanderers, and other detractors of women.[3] At last he retires to the house of happiness ("liesse"), but instead of enjoying the company of his lady, he departs alone to write poetry. He explains that he will compose "rondeaulx et ballades" about lovers of various types ("Des amoureux sains et mallades") and that once they are all written he will present a copy to his lady. She approves of this enterprise and decides to reciprocate with poems of her own composition:

> Mon doulx amy, amant parfait,
> Puis donc qu'avez telle entreprise
> Grandement la loue et prise,
> Car de mon coste faire vueil,
> Pour vous donner joyeulx reveil,
> Aultres ballades et rondeaulx
> Que trouverez plaisans et beaulx;
> Puis quant vous serez revenu
> En ce dommaine et revenu
> De tout je vous feray present. . . .
> (fol. 0₃v.)

> (My sweet friend, perfect lover
> Since you undertake such an enterprise
> Greatly I praise and value it,
> Because for my part I wish to compose,
> In order to give you joyous excitement,
> Other ballades and rondeaux
> Which you will find pleasing and beautiful;
> Then when you have returned
> to this domain
> I will make you a present of all.)

The stage is thus set for two series of poems, the first by the Amant Parfait which includes one hundred rondeaux, seven ballades, and a short "dit," and the second by the lady. Of the forty-two rondeaux and two ballades in this second series, eight rondeaux and one ballade are responses made by the "amy" and thus have a male persona. The other thirty-four rondeaux and one ballade have a female voice, and it is this group of poems with a female persona, supposedly composed by the lady, which forms the corpus for our study.[4]

Such collections of poems allegedly by women are not rare in sources of early sixteenth-century poetry, as Kathleen Chesney has noted in a recent article.[5] These poems, almost exclusively rondeaux, are often preceded by a heading "rondeaux de femmes," which calls attention to their female voice. In the *Chasse-Départ*, they are preceded by the following rubric: "S'ensuyvent plusieurs joyeulx rondeaulx que la dame de l'amant parfait estant loing de luy fist en la maison de lyesse de plusieurs dames amoureuses" (fol. Q₃). (There follow several joyful rondeaux which the lady of the perfect lover, being far from him, made in the house of happiness about several amorous ladies.) This rubric makes two important points: first, that the poems were composed by the lady; and, second, that they are about women in love. Now if the second point can be verified by an examination of the poems themselves, the first point, that of authorship, raises certain questions. First of all, the lady is herself a fictional character created, presumably, by Octovien de Saint-Gelais, the author named in the title of the *Chasse-Départ*. This has led at least one critic to assume that most of the lyric poems pronounced by the lady were also composed by Saint-Gelais.[6] Some of these poems, however, are found in contemporary manuscripts in which the name of the poet is cited. Such is the case for two rondeaux—"En la forest de Longue Actente" (22) by Madame d'Orléans, and "Pour le celler mon dolent dueil" (18) by Blosseville.[7] It is evident from these examples that if Saint-Gelais did compose some of these poems, he did not compose them all. Second, only one text can with any certainty be attributed to a woman; the authors of most of the poems were presumably men who simply assumed the voice of a woman.[8] What defines this group, in fact, is not the sex of the author(s), a fact which in any event eludes us, but the sex of the speaker. The female persona adopted by authors is embodied in the Lady of the *Chasse-Départ* who presents herself as author. A fictional character, she reminds us not only that author cannot always be identified with speaker, but also that the female lyric often represents the male view of women in love and that, as a genre, it serves as a counterpart to the more common male lyric.

Not all the poems by the lady have a clearly defined female persona. Some of the poems seem androgynous; no linguistic element of the poem (adjective, past participle, etc.) permits absolute identification of the sex of the speaker, and the poems could be pronounced as easily by a man as by a woman. Whoever compiled the poems in the *Chasse-Départ*, however, took care to specify that they are female lyrics. In addition to the general title indicating that these are "rondeaulx que la dame . . . fist," each poem is preceded by a short subtitle. "Rondel d'une dame a son amy" is the most common, but occasionally the lady is qualified as "ennuyee" (troubled) or "folle amoureuse" (amorous fool), or the poem is described as "joyeulx." The lover is qualified only twice—as old, and as "ung qui ne fait compte d'elle" (one who has no regard for her). Only one rondeau is directly related to the characters of the *Chasse-Départ*: "Rondel de la dame a l'amant parfait son amy" (Rondeau by the lady to the perfect lover her friend). The others must simply be considered rondeaux by any lady.

Of the thirty-five poems with a female persona, seven are known to have been set to music by some of the most renowned composers of the early Renaissance. The most famous of these is undoubtedly "D'ung aultre aymer" (10) which was first set to music by Johannes Ockeghem. His chanson, found in many musical sources, was also imitated by numerous other composers, so that this text was certainly widely known.[9] Ockeghem also composed chansons on the rondeaux "J'en ay dueil que je n'en suys morte" (8) and "La despourveue et la banye" (11). The rondeau "Le souvenir de vous my tue" (9) was set to music by the composer Robert Morton,[10] and "Vostre oeil s'est bien tost repenty" (13) attributed to Johannes Prioris."[11] An anonymous chanson on the rondeau "Nulle plus dolente que moy" is included in the well-known collection MS. Dijon 517.[12]

As the title introducing the lady's series of poems indicates, the poems are "de plusieurs dames amoureuses" (about several amorous ladies). Women's experience in love is thus the subject of all the texts, and although love is not always explicitly invoked as the cause of the lady's sentiments, it should be understood as such. The lady's universe is limited in virtually all of these poems to her lover and herself, with occasional reference made to a third party— the "mesdisans," a "coquart fol" (presumptuous fool) who has defamed the lady's love, the husband (used in a generic rather than a specific sense). Comparisons are also made to other women and men. The lady, for example, declares herself to be superior to all others—"Femme n'est vivant qui me vaille" (no woman alive equals me)—or more unhappy than others—"Nulle plus dolente que moy" (none more sorrowful than I). Her lover is declared to be so filled with honor that "aux aultres ne demeure le bruyt seul et d'autres bontez riens" (to others is left only empty reputation with no other merits). In another case, "il fait mieulx qu'un grant duc ou ung roy / Le jeu d'amours" (he plays better than a great duke or a king the game of love). All of these persons, however, are seen only in relation to the central figures of the lady and her lover.

Two distinct traditions manifest themselves in these poems. The first, that of courtly love, maintains love as an affair of the heart and spiritual being; the second, best exemplified perhaps in the *fabliaux*, emphasizes the carnal side of love. To some extent these two traditions may be seen as idealistic and cynical respectively. For the woman, however, happiness in love seems to be achieved only in the second tradition which is marked by quite explicit eroticism. In many poems of this sort there is also a reversal of sex roles, the lady being the one to invite, indeed to command, her lover to satisfy her overtly sexual desires. She is an active partner who does not hesitate to reject her suitor if he fails to satisfy her nor to proffer advice of a very pragmatic, if at times coarse, nature. The lady in the first tradition, in contrast, is the courtly lady who patiently awaits the return of her absent lover, who laments her unrequited love, who expresses constant anxiety for her reputation.

Most typical of the poems in the courtly tradition are the laments of the lady at being either abandoned or neglected by her beloved. Many poems focus on her suffering, and the subtitles in the *Chasse-Départ* underscore this sentiment. Six consecutive poems, nos. 19–24, are declared to be "d'une dame ennuyee" (by a troubled lady) and these follow three others, nos. 8, 17, 18, by the "dame desconfortee" (discomforted lady). Since most of the other subtitles in the *Chasse-Départ* lack descriptive adjectives for either the lady or the lover, these subtitles suggest that suffering was typically the woman's plight in love and reinforce what is evident in the initial line of the poems themselves: "Joye me laisse et dueil m'a espousee" (Joy leaves me and grief has wed me) [no. 17], "Pour le celler mon dolent dueil" (To disguise my woeful grief) [no. 18], "En la forest de Longue Attente" (In the forest of Long Awaiting) [nos. 20, 22], "Nulle plus dolente que moy" (None more sorrowful than I) [nos. 23]. And the sense of grief is further emphasized by the fact that this group of poems is, as a whole, the one most unified by a common vocabulary: "dueil" (grief) and "ennuy" (distress) render the lady so "dolente" that only death can bring comfort. Typical of such poems is rondeau no. 19:

> Des grans regretz et ennuiz que je porte
> Mon povre cueur doit bien estre lassé;
> Deuil et ennuy s'est sur luy amassé
> Tant q'un matin l'on me trouvera morte.
>
> (Of the great regrets and sorrows that I bear
> My poor heart must be very weary:
> Grief and sorrow have amassed themselves therein
> So much that one day you will find me dead.)

Here, as elsewhere, no specific reason is provided for her suffering; the lady simply insists, as she does in no. 23: "J'ay bien cause pourquoy" (I have good cause for it). But this "cause" is inevitably unhappy love, whether implicit or explicit in the poem.

In these poems, unhappiness results essentially from one of two situations: separation from one's beloved or unrequited love. Characteristic of laments caused by separation is a rondeau which became famous as the text for the chanson composed by Morton: "Le souvenir de vous my tue" (The remembrance of you is causing me to die) [9]. The second and third stanzas of this rondeau elaborate upon the source of lament:

> Quant vous estes loing de ma veue
> Je me plains, disant à par moy:
>   Le souvenir de vous my tue.
> Seulle demeure et despourveue;
> De ame nul confort ne recoy
> Et dueil porte sans faire effroy
> Jusques à vostre revenue.

> (When you are far from my sight
> I complain, saying to myself
>   The remembrance of you is causing me to die.
> Alone I remain and destitute;
> No comfort do I receive from anyone
> And grief I bear without dread
> Until your return.)

In another poem the lady's suffering at the separation is expressed more forcefully. She is victimized by a host of emotions:

> Desir m'apprent telz regretz à congnoistre
> Que je ne scay dont il en peult tant naistre,
> Et puis Douleur en sa chartre m'enferme,
> Courroux m'assault et me bat fort et ferme.
> Helas, vueillez ma grevance descroistre
>   Si vous povez. (37)

> (Desire teaches me to know such sorrows
> That I know not what can be born of them
> And then Suffering locks me in her prison,
> Vexation assaults me and beats me hard and fast.
> Alas, would you decrease my pain
>   If you can.)

She appeals to her lover to reduce her suffering by finding a means for her to see him soon: "Trouvez moyen que vous voy en brief terme." Others try without success to console her during his absence:

Chascun me veult faire chanter, danser;
Je n'en scauroye ung seul pas commencer
Quant ne vous voy. . . . (35)

(Everyone wants to make me sing, dance;
I could not begin a single step
When I see you not. . . .)

Unable to find relief, her only recourse is to her memory:

Lors je commence à moymesmes tanser
Et puis m'en vois ou j'ay veu advancer
Vostre plaisir. En ce lieu me transporte;
Mon pensement pres de moy vous rapporte.

(Then I begin to reproach myself
And so I go where I saw advancing
Your pleasing form. To that place I transport myself;
My thought brings you back near to me.)

Another lady writes of the moment of separation in this way:
"faschee je suis . . . quant departir me fault / D'avecques vous"
(Vexed I am when I must depart from you) [31]. She is consoled
only by the knowledge that her lover too suffers at the separation:

Mais tourmentee je seroys doublement
Si ne scavoye tout veritablement
Que vostre cueur de son plaisir en sault.

(But I would be doubly tormented
If I did not know for certain
That your heart from its pleasure leaps.)

This poem concludes with a moral lesson addressed to the lover:

Vivons toujours bien raisonnablement,
Portant noz maulx le plus paisiblement
Que nous pourrons, sans faire ung seul deffault
En nostre amour, car le premier qui fault
Fait l'autre après vivre muablement.

(Let us live always justly,
Bearing our woes the most peacefully
That we can, without a single offense
to our love, for the first to fault
Makes the other live inconstantly thereafter.)

It is noteworthy that in this poem the lady attends not only to her own suffering but also to that of her lover. Her lesson, moreover, appeals to reason rather than to emotion. It is a lesson of fidelity but also of stoicism.

Such stoicism, however, is difficult to achieve when the lady is faced not with temporary separation but with unrequited love, the source of grief in the second group of laments. "Ne suis-je pas bien abusee femme," asks the lady, "De ne povoir avoir la jouyssance / De mon amy?" (Am I not a truly abused woman, not to have the enjoyment of my friend). Her lament culminates in the exclamation: "Las, mon amy ne me fait obeissance" (Alas my friend does not obey me) [43]. When the lover's reaction is not merely unresponsiveness but veritable rejection, the lady's lament is even more intense:

> Joye me laisse et dueil m'a espousee
> Craincte et soucy me tiennent soubz leur tente
> Qui me font perdre de tout plaisir l'actente
> Pour ung regret où m'ont mise et pousee. (17)

> (Joy abandons me and grief has wed me,
> Fear and anxiety hold me in their power
> Which make me lose the anticipation of all pleasure
> For a sorrow into which they have thrust me.)

The object pronouns of this rondeau reinforce the idea of the lady as victim of negative sentiments, resulting from the loss of "celluy par qui suis repousee" (him by whom I am rejected). Calling herself "la despourveue d'un [sien] amy" (the deprived of her friend) [42] or "la despourveue et la banye" (the destitute and banished) [11], the lady usually expresses her love lament in a first-person soliloquy. But occasionally she addresses a complaint to her lover:

> Vostre oeil s'est bien tost repenty
> Du bon acueil que m'avez fait
> Si ne luy ay-je rien meffait. . . . (13)

> (Your eye has quickly repented
> Of the warm greeting you gave me
> And yet I have done nothing against it.)

Normally it is her own regret which she voices:

> Mon cueur vous a eu en pensee
> Mais j'en suis mal recompensee
> Car je voy que n'en faictes compte . . . . (12)

(My heart has kept you in thought
But I am poorly rewarded
For I see that you take no account of it . . . .)

In one instance, however, she vehemently accuses her lover of deceitfulness:

Par voz sermens tous pleins de decevance
Je prins à vous plus qu'en autre fiance
Vous pensant autre qu'à present ne vous voy . . . . (5)

(By your oaths all filled with deceit
I took faith in you more than in another
Thinking you other than I now see you. . . .)

This direct confrontation was striking enough to be noted by the editor of the *Chasse-Départ* who provided the following subtitle for the poem: "Rondel d'une dame qui blasme son amy." The poem ends, nonetheless, with the self-pity and resignation so common to the female lyric. Faced with the man's deception, all that the lady can do is curse the hour she was born:

Las! quant de vous j'euz premier congnoissance
Je vous pensoie remply en habondance
De loyaulté, verité et de foy;
Mais le contraire bien congnoistre je doy,
Dont je mauldis l'heure de ma naissance. (5)

(Alas, when I first knew you
I thought you abundantly filled
With loyalty, truth, and faith;
But I must recognize the opposite,
Whence I curse the hour of my birth.)

Self-pity, however, is not the only sentiment developed in these poems. In fact, the element which seems to dominate many of them is the lady's concern for her reputation. This element manifests itself in two ways; in recognition of how others regard her, and in self-justification with regard to her choice of a lover, which often includes a reaction to the comments of others. In one rondeau, for example, the lady insists:

Au gré du cueur et au chois de mes yeulx
J'en esliz ung, cuidant que soubz les cieulx
N'en fust ung tel ainsi que je pensoye . . . . (24)

> (With the consent of my heart and the choice of my eyes
> I elected one, believing that beneath the heavens
> There was not such a one as I thought . . . .)

She soon discovers, however, that she lacks experience in such matters: "En cest endroit je ne my congnoissoye, / Car à ceste heure trop est malicieux" (In this domain I had no insight, for at present he is too malicious). Her lover is "tant cault et falacieux" (so sly and false) that she must admit "fis follye quant tant m'advensoye" (I behaved like a fool when I advanced so far). The same problem appears in the rondeau "Mon cueur vous a eu en pensee" (My heart has held you in thought) [12], where the lady finds herself not only poorly rewarded by her lover but also strongly rebuked by others. Regretting her precipitous actions she exclaims: "Las! trop tost me suis advansee / De vous aymer . . ." (Alas, too soon did I advance to love you).

A slightly different situation is presented in a rondeau cited earlier where the lover has abandoned the lady because of a false report (11). She swears that her love was unswerving: "Mon povre cueur . . . / Oncques ne pensa villenye" (My poor heart . . . never thought villainy). Despite this, however, "on me tient par felonnye / La despourveue et la banye" (They consider me, out of treachery, the destitute and banished). One other comment in this rondeau is particularly striking: "De mes amours je suis pugnie" (For my love I am punished). It would seem from this and similar comments in other poems that the lady is condemned to suffer public censure when she assumes too great an initiative. Her role is evidently to wait and to respond, not to choose. In the two cases where she does actively select her lover (12, 24), she is criticized by the public and finally abandoned by her lover.

Disconsolate and distressed either by the lover's absence or by his rejection of her, the lady expresses her grief in solitary laments. If occasionally she voices a complaint against her lover, she is more likely to regret her own actions and the disapprobation which ensues. This concern with public opinion is reflected in other poems of the courtly tradition which are not laments but professions of fidelity. The lady vehemently objects to criticism of her love:

> A mon advis on ne me doit reprendre
> Si j'ay osé hardiement entreprendre
> Vous pour jamais entierement aymer . . . . (27)

> (In my opinion they should not rebuke me
> For having boldly dared to undertake
> To love you steadfastly forever.)

She justifies her choice of lover by extolling his virtues:

> Ou on auroit espuysee la grant mer
> Assez plus tost que voz vertus comprendre.

> (They would sooner have drained the vast ocean
> Than contain your virtues.)

Although others have tried to ensnare her heart, she would sooner die than wrong her beloved:

> J'ay veu des gens autour de mon cueur tendre
> Rethz et filez pour les cuider surprendre
> Mais ilz n'ont sceu. . . . (27)

> (I have seen people lay nets and snares
> Around my heart thinking to catch it by surprise
> But they have failed.)

The lady has sworn fidelity to one man alone, and she reacts angrily in another rondeau to an evil tongue who has blasphemed her love:

> Il n'est pas vray, de Dieu soit donc mauldit
> Le coquart fol qui a de moy mesdit
> En te comptant que m'estoye deffaicte
> De ton amour. Ce seroit chose infaicte!
> Ma voulenté oncques ne l'entendit. (33)

> (It is not true, let him be cursed by God,
> the cocky fool who slandered me
> By telling you that I had rid myself
> Of your love. That would be depraved!
> Such was never my will's intention.)

She protests that the charge of infidelity is a lie, a "mensonge parfaicte."

To remain faithful to one alone is a question not only of love but also of honor and dignity, as the following rondeau makes clear:

> D'ung aultre aymer mon cueur s'abesseroit;
> Il ne fault ja penser que je l'estrange
> Ne que jamais de ce propos je change
> Car mon honneur s'en appetisseroit. (10)

> (To love another, my heart would debase itself;
> Think not that I'd part from him

> Nor that I'd ever change my mind,
> For my honor would diminish.)

The lady assures the listener that she will be struck by death before accepting another, for her "loyaulté trop fort si forferoit" (loyalty would be too greatly forfeited). This poem, as noted above, is one of the most renowned of the rondeaux of the *Chasse-Départ*, for it was set to music by Ockeghem. The text reflects the idealistic tradition of love where honor and fidelity abide forever. But in other poems, the lady's love is marred by anxiety, for her fidelity does not assure reciprocal affection. In several poems, the lady is forced to utter pleas not to be abandoned by her lover:

> Ne me lassez, par courroux remply de ire,
> Pour rapporter, pour flater, pour mesdire,
> Car je suis vostre comme par heritaige. (25)

> (Do not leave me, in anger filled with ire
> To recount, flatter, or revile,
> For I am yours as if by inheritance.)

She has pledged him her heart and thinks that this pledge should suffice to warrant his love: "Autant ou plus il vous doit bien suffire" (As much or more it should satisfy you). But her anxiety becomes apparent later in the text:

> Mais je vous pry, soyons tous d'ung couraige
> Sans varier en vouloir ne langaige
> Car je feray ce que me vouldrez dire.

> (But I beg you, let us be of one heart
> Without varying in intent or language,
> For I will do as you wish me to.)

This last sentence calls attention to a feature found in other female poems—total submission to the man. This idea is perhaps most clearly expressed in the refrain of another rondeau:

> De plus en plus vostre esclave me tiens,
> Recongnoissant que honneur et tous les siens
> De vostre cueur ont choisy la demeure,
> Tant que je scay qu'aux autres ne demeure
> Fors le bruyt seul et d'autres bontez riens. (39)

> (More and more I deem myself your slave
> Recognizing that honor and all his company

> Have chosen your heart as their abode
> Such that I know that to others is left
> Only empty reputation and no other merits.)

The lady submits herself voluntarily to her beloved because of his virtues. Such submission may be viewed as the counterpart to that of the knight in the courtly love tradition who surrenders himself totally to the will of his lady. But in the female lyric the inequality implied in the word "esclave" is reflected later in the poem when the lady suggests that her lover's feelings do not equal hers:

> Si voz desirs fussent telz que les miens
> On ne scauroit estimer les grans biens
> Que aurions, vous et moy, à toute heure . . . .

> (If your desires were as mine
> No one would be able to evaluate the great virtues
> That we would have, you and I, at all times . . . .)

The negative implication of the "if" is realized in the final declaration: "Pour vostre amour douleur aspre soubstiens" (For your love bitter suffering I endure).

With this note of suffering and of anxiety, the poems of fidelity often rejoin those of lament, so that from this ensemble of poems in the courtly tradition certain elements emerge; professions of fidelity but fear of being abandoned, suffering at separation or at loss of love, waiting for the lover's return, concern for reputation, plaintive resignation in the hope of suffering peacefully the ills of life.

Very different from this image of women in love is that presented by the second group of poems. No longer idealized, removed from its courtly environment, here love is considered a game whose rewards are largely physical. The idea of play is reflected linguistically in wordplay, as in the rhymes of the following rondeau:

> Tant qu'il souffist j'ay fait cela;
> Il n'est ja mestier que le celle,
> Car l'on scet que ne fuz pucelle
> Passé a long temps, mais vela!

> Alors qu'on me depucella
> On le fist sans bast et sans selle
>   Tant qu'il souffist. . . .

> (As long as necessary I did that;
> There is no need to hide it.

> For you know that I have not been a virgin
> For a long time, but so it is!

> Whereas I was deflowered,
> It was done without pack or saddle[13]
>   As long as necessary. . . .)

It is quite remarkable that this poem is the first in the series of "rondeaux de femme" in the *Chasse-Départ*. For the noble lady to present this overtly erotic poem as the initial rondeau addressed to the Amant Parfait seems quite incongruous to the modern reader, but perhaps nothing so clearly demonstrates the coexistence of courtly with coarse as their joint presence here. The same aristocratic public which enjoyed both *fabliaux* and courtly lyrics must have accepted the eroticism of these poems along with the courtly allegory of the *Chasse-Départ*. This initial poem, entitled "Rondel joyeulx d'une dame," is a foretaste, moreover, of other "joyous" texts. Certain features which distinguish this group from the more courtly series are immediately noticeable; emphasis not on moral virtues but on physical prowess both for the woman and the man, insistence on love as a game which must be well played by whatever means necessary, assertiveness on the part of the woman both in her expression of desire and in her obvious control of love's activities. Let us consider, for example, the rondeau:

> Femme n'est vivant qui me vaille
> Pour combatre en ceste bataille
> Où l'on fait son mary coqu,
> Car j'ay harnoys, targe et escu
> Qui moins craint l'estoc que la taille. (14)

> (No woman alive can equal me
> In fighting in this battle
> Where one cuckolds her husband,
> For I have harness, armor, and shield
> Which fear less the point than the edge.)

The woman's boasts of sexual prowess are matched by the intensity of her desires in the following poem:

> Cher amy, or vous apprestez
> De dresser vostre court baston
> Affin que nous en esbaton
> Et pour jouer le me prestez. (15)

(Dear friend, now get ready
To erect your short stick
So that we can enjoy it;
And to play, lend it to me.)

Such eager invitations, however, are not extended to all men. The lady's reception varies, it seems, according to the man's success at satisfying her clearly sexual desires. As one rondeau presents it:

Amours ne donne pas cela pour maistrise
Mais selon l'heur et peine qu'on a mise. (6)

(Love does not give that for skill
But according to fortune and the effort one has
put into it.)

Those whose physical prowess has diminished with age are there-fore hastily dismissed::

Amy, vous estes trop vieillart
Pour plus d'amours vous entremectre

. . . .
Dormez, ne soyez point bellart
Pour moy cuider à vous submectre;
Povoir n'avez que de promectre
Combien que ayez sens et vieil art. (4)

([My] friend, you are too old
To engage in love anymore.

. . . .
Sleep, don't be a boor [belart=male sheep]
Believing I can be submitted to you,
Power you have only to promise
Whatever your sense and old art.)

It is the lady who evidently controls love's activities, and she demands both satisfaction and obedience. The lover must respond to her will even though this may require deceiving others: "Faignez à toutes pour me plaire" (Deceive them all in order to please me). Such obedience will assure the lover of her goodwill:

En ce ne povez vous meffaire
Puis que tel est le vouloir mien;
Or vous en gardez doncques bien
De jamais aller au contraire. (3)

(In this you cannot do wrong
Since such is my wish;
And so be very careful
Not to go counter to this.)

Love, in these poems, is no longer a spiritual ideal. The lady aspires to no rapturous heights: she seeks only satisfaction. This is most clearly stated in the following rondeau:

Se pis ne vient, je me doy contenter
D'ung serviteur qui me vient fort tempter
A me servir trop mieulx que je ne doy.
Je l'aime bien et aussi fait il moy;
Si besoing est je m'en puys bien vanter.

Je ne le vueil nuyt ne jour absenter
Puys que m'aymer s'est venu presenter,
Car il fait mieulx qu'ung grant duc ou ung roy
Le jeu d'amour en bon et bel arroy,
Dont, sans qu'ays cause de m'en mescontenter,
    Se pis ne vient, je m'en doy contenter. (16)

(If nothing worse comes, I must be content
With a servitor who comes strongly to tempt me
By serving me far better than I deserve;
I like him well, and he me likewise
If need be I could boast of it.

I don't want him absent night or day
Since he has come to love me,
For he plays better than a great duke or a king
The game of love in fine array
So, without having cause to be discontent,
    If nothing worse comes, I must be content.)

If the *Chasse-Départ* introduces the perfect lover and his lady, the poems presented by the lady as her own compositions portray not only a less than ideal love but also a less than perfect lover. Two traditions manifest themselves in these poems, the one insisting on a spiritual, idealistic love, the other emphasizing carnal love. The lady of the first tradition, however, exhibits a dissatisfaction and a sense of inequality both of sentiment and of position, which suggest that she is less content than the lady of the second tradition who seeks only physical satisfaction. In this "hunt" for love, to paraphrase the title of the volume, the noble lady seems destined to lament despite her professions of loyalty unless she is able, like her less courtly counterpart, to lower her sights to a lesser ideal. It is perhaps not insignificant that once she has departed to write poetry on her own, the lady of the *Chasse-Départ* never rejoins the Amant Parfait.

Appendix

Rondeaulx que la dame fist . . .

Folio	Incipit	Subtitle in the Chasse-Départ
Q₃	1. Tant qu'il souffist j'ay fait cela	Rondel joyeulx d'une dame
	2. Si vous ny estiez l'oultrepasse	Rondel d'une dame a son amy
Q₃ᵛ·	3. Sur tant que me craignez desplaire	Rondel d'une dame amoureuse a son amy
	4. Amy vous estes trop vieillart	Rondel d'une dame a son vieil amy
	5. Par voz sermens tous pleins de decevance	Rondel d'une dame qui blasme son amy
	6. Rien ou cela vous portez en devise	Rondel d'une amant (sic) a son amy
	7. Est-ce mal fait de vous aymer	Rondel d'une dame a son amy
Q₄	8. J'en ay dueil que je n'en suys morte	Rondel d'une dame desconfortee
	9. Le souvenir de vous my tue	Rondel d'ung d'une (sic) dame a son amy
	10. D'ung aultre aymer mon cueur s'abesseroit	Rondel d'une dame
	11. La despourveue et la banye	Rondel d'une dame amoureuse
	12. Mon cueur vous a eu en pensee	Rondel d'une dame a son amy
Q₄ᵛ·	13. Vostre oeil s'est bien tost repenty	Rondel d'une dame a son amy
	14. Femme n'est vivant qui me vaille	Rondel d'une folle amoureuse
	15. Chier amy or vous apprestez	Rondel d'une dame a son amy
	16. Se pis ne vient je me doy contenter	Rondel d'une dame
	17. Joye me laisse et dueil m'a espousee	Rondel d'une dame desconfortee
	18. Pour le celler mon dolent dueil	Autre rondel d'une dame desconfortee

Q₅	19. Des grans regretz et ennuiz que je porte	Rondel d'une dame ennuyee
	20. En la forest de longue actente	Rondel d'une dame ennuyee
	21. Je ne me puis veoir a mon aise	Autre rondel d'une dame ennuyee
	22. En la forest de longue actente	Autre rondel d'une dame ennuyee
	23. Nulle plus dolente que moy	Autre rondel d'une dame ennuyee
	24. Au gre du cueur et au chois de mes yeulx	Autre rondel d'une dame ennuyee
Q₅ᵛ·	25. Autant ou plus il vous doit bien suffire	Rondel de la dame a l'amant parfait son amy
	26. C'est mal cherche vostre advantaige	Rondel d'une dame a son amy
	27. A mon advis on ne me doit reprendre	Rondel d'une dame a son amy
Q₆	28. S'il ne vous plaist me donner congnoissance	Rondel d'une dame a son amy
	29. A ceste fois pour doubte de mesprendre	Response de l'amy a la dame/ Rondel
	30. En peine suis plus aspre que jamais	Rondel d'ung amoureux a sa dame
	31. Puis que faschee je suis semblablement	Response de la dame a son amy/ Rondel
Q₆ᵛ·	32. N'avoir plaisir tant que vous voye venir	Rondel d'ung amoureux a sa dame
	33. Il n'est pas vray, de Dieu soit donc mauldit	Responce de la dame a son amy/ Rondel
	34. Pour vous revoir sur ma foy je n'ay vaine	Rondel d'ung amant a sa dame
	35. Tresennuyee plus qu'on ne peult penser	Response de la dame a son amy/ Rondel
	36. On le m'a dit dont j'ay peine trefforte	Response de l'amy a sa dame / Rondel
	37. Si vous povez une fois recognoistre	Response de la dame a son amy/ Rondel
R₁	38. De vous sans fin tousjours me souviendra	Response de l'amy a sa dame/ Rondel
	39. De plus en plus vostre esclave me tiens	Response de la dame a son amy/ Rondel
	40. De joye avoir point ne me passeray	Response de l'amy a sa dame/ Rondel
	41. Bon jour, bon an, bon moys, bonne sepmaine	Rondel d'ung amy qui survient devant sa dame
R₁ᵛ·	42. Soubz l'arbre sec desgarny de verdure	Balade d'une dame amoureuse d'ung qui ne fait compte d'elle

R₂   43. Ne suis je pas bien abusee   Rondel consonnant a la
            femme   balade
      44. Je suis devenu clerc d'escolle   Ballade de l'a.b.c.

Notes

[1] Several other copies of the Vérard edition are extant: British Library (C.34.m.2), Bibliothèque de l'Arsenal (4° B.L. 2864 Rés.), Chantilly 1739, Fairfax Murray 493, Aix-en-Provence. Other editions of *La Chasse et le départ d'Amours*, much less ornate and undated although presumably printed after 1509, were published by Phelippe le Noir and by la veuve Jehan Treperel and Jehan Jehannot. For this study, I have used the Vérard edition now in the Bibliothèque Nationale (Rés. vél. 583) from which quotations have been taken, though these have been slightly modernized with regard to punctuation and accent marks. This work will henceforth be referred to as *Chasse-Départ*.

[2] On the questions of authorship in this volume, see: Arthur Piaget, "Une édition gothique de Charles d'Orléans," *Romania*, 21 (1892), 581–96; H.-J. Molinier, *Essai biographique et littéraire sur Octovien de Saint-Gelays, évêque d'Angoulême (1468–1502)* (Rodez: Carrère, 1910), esp. pp. 20–23, 191ff; Frédéric Lachèvre, *Bibliographie des Recueils collectifs de poésies du XVIᵉ siècle* (Paris: Honoré Champion, 1922), pp. 12–14; Pierre Champion, "Pièces joyeuses du XVᵉ siècle," *Revue de philologie française*, 21 (1907), 161–96; Emile Picot, "Une supercherie d'Antoine Vérard: *Les Regnars traversans* de Jehan Bouchet," followed by a note by A. Piaget, *Romania*, 22 (1893), 244–60.

[3] I have discussed this apology in a paper presented at the conference on the Early Renaissance at Binghamton, New York, in April 1978, published in *ACTA*, 5 (1978), *The Early Renaissance*, pp. 69–80, and in "'Apologie de la femme' and 'poésie de la dame' in *La Chasse et le départ d'Amours* (1509)," *Fifteenth-Century Studies*, 2 (1978), 233–40.

[4] The poems by the lady appear on fols. Q₃ to R₂ of the *Chasse-Départ*. The incipits and their subtitles as provided in the volume are listed in the Appendix to this essay. The poems are numbered according to the order in which they appear in the volume. Whenever a poem is cited in this study, its number is indicated in parentheses. Some of these texts, with occasional variations in verses, have been published in modern editions of poetry from this period: P. Champion, "Pièces," (nos. 4, 14, 15, 26, 44); Marcel Françon, *Poèmes de Transition* (Cambridge: Harvard Univ. Press, 1938), (nos. 5, 6, 16, 24, 25, 27, 32–34, 36–40); Martin Löpelmann, ed., *Die Liederhandschrift des Cardinals de Rohan* (Göttingen: Max Niemeyer, 1923) (nos. 9–11, 41); Gaston Raynaud, *Rondeaux et autres poésies du XVᵉ siècle* (1889; rpt. New York: Johnson Reprint, 1968) (nos. 18, 22); Marcel Schwob, *Le Parnasse satyrique du quinzième siècle* (1905; rpt. Genève: Slatkine, 1969) (nos. 1, 21). The first stanza of rondeau no. 8 is printed in Marcel Françon, *Albums poétiques de Marguerite d'Autriche* (Cambridge:

Harvard Univ. Press, 1934); the entire rondeau appears with its musical transcription in Martin Picker, *The Chanson Albums of Marguerite of Austria* (Berkeley and Los Angeles: Univ. of California Press, 1965). The remaining fifteen poems have not been edited by a modern editor.

[5] Kathleen Chesney, "Two collections of early 16th-century French rondeaux," *MAE* 40 (1971), 157–71.

[6] See Molinier, pp. 20–23.

[7] These rondeaux appear with the authors' names in two manuscripts of the Bibliothèque Nationale, f.fr. 9223, published by Raynaud, and n.a.fr. 15771, discussed by Annie Angrémy, "Un nouveau recueil de poésies françaises du XVe siècle: Le ms. B.N. nouv. acq. fr. 15771," *Romania*, 95 (1975), 1–53.

[8] Poets such as Jean Marot are known to have written "rondeaux de femmes." See Chesney note 5, and Giovanna Antonini-Trisolini, "Pour une bibliographie des oeuvres de Jehan Marot," *BHR* 33 (1971), 107–50.

[9] Concerning this chanson, see Howard M. Brown, *Music in the French Secular Theatre, 1400–1550* (Cambridge: Harvard Univ. Press, 1963), pp. 209–10. For no. 8, see Picker, pp. 121, 226–28.

[10] See Knud Jeppesen, ed., *Ker Kopenhagener Chansonnier* (Copenhagen and Leipzig: 1927); Brown, p. 255.

[11] Richard M. Wexler, "The Complete Works of Johannes Prioris," unpublished diss. (New York University, 1974).

[12] A facsimilie edition of this chansonnier has been published with an introduction by Dragan Plamenac, Publications of Medieval Musical Manuscripts, 12 (Brooklyn: Institute of Medieval Music, n.d.).

[13] The reference to saddles, harnesses, etc., is entirely part of the erotic metaphor of riding or mounting ("chevaucher").

Bibliography

The bibliography is grouped by nationalities arranged alphabetically. Old and Middle English are listed separately, under *English*. The order of elements within each group is 1. Manuscripts (where these are relevant), 2. Editions, and 3. Studies. The exception to this arrangement is the bibliography on *Irish*, which of necessity is handled differently.

The study of woman's songs is tangent to many fields. In order to prevent a sprawl in this bibliography which might have rendered it nearly useless, I have attempted to exclude works whose primary focus is not woman's song. Two further specific exclusions should be noted: texts and studies of known women poets, whose work is largely not at issue here, and is catalogued elsewhere; and editions and studies of the pastourelle, which has obvious and close connections to woman's song, but which is more profitably handled separately. A brief bibliographical notice on the pastourelle is found under *French*.

I would like to express my appreciation to the authors of the essays, who helped so much in the compilation of this bibliography, with special thanks to Kathleen Ashley for her help with the Portuguese section, and to Ruth P.M. Lehmann, who wrote the Irish bibliography in its entirety. (JP)

 General

Dronke, Peter. *Medieval Latin and the Rise of European Love-Lyric*. 2 vols. 2nd ed. Oxford: Clarendon Press, 1968.

_____. *The Medieval Lyric*. London: Hutchinson, 1968. See esp. Ch. 3, "Cantigas de amigo," Ch. 5, "The Alba," and Ch. 6, "Dance-songs."

Ferrante, Joan. *Woman as Image in Medieval Literature from the 12th Century to Dante*. New York: Columbia Univ. Press. 1975.

Frings, Theodor. "Altspanische Mädchenlieder aus des Minnesangs

Frühling. Anlässlich eines Aufsatzes von Dámso Alonso."
BGDSL, 73 (1951), 176–96.

_____ . *Die Anfänge der europäischen Liebesdichtung im 11.
und 12. Jahrhundert.* BAWS, 1960, Heft 2. Munich:
Bayerische Akademie, 1960

_____ . *Minnesinger und Troubadours.* Deutsche Akademie
der Wissenschaften zu Berlin, Vorträge und Schriften, 34.
Berlin: Akademie, 1949; rpt. in *Der deutsche Minnesang.*
Ed. Hans Fromm. Darmstadt: Wissenschaftliche Buchgesellschaft, 1963.

Hatto, A.T. *Eos: An Enquiry into the Theme of Lovers' Meetings
and Partings at Dawn in Poetry.* The Hague: Mouton,
1965.

Spitzer, Leo. "The Mozarabic Lyric and Theodor Frings' Theories."
CL, 4 (1952), 1–22.

English

Old English

A helpful recent bibliography of OE Studies is Fred C. Robinson's
Old English Literature: A Select Bibliography. Toronto: Univ. of
Toronto Press, 1970.

MANUSCRIPTS

The Exeter Book (Exeter Cathedral Library). Ed. George P. Krapp
    and Elliott V.K.Dobbie. New York: Columbia Univ. Press,
    1936.
The Exeter Book of Old English Poetry. Introductory Chapters
    by Raymond W. Chambers, Max Förster, and Robin
    Flower. London: Humphries, 1933. [A facsimile.]

STUDIES

Adams, J.F. "'Wulf and Eadwacer': An Interpretation." *MLN*, 73
    (1958), 1–5.
Bouman, A.C. *Patterns in Old English and Old Icelandic Literature.*
    Leidse Germanistische en Anglistische Reeks, Deel 1. Leiden:
    Universitaire Pers, 1962.

Bambas, Rudolph C. "Another View of the Old English 'Wife's Lament.'" *JEGP*, 62 (1963), 303–09.

Davidson, Clifford, "Erotic 'Women's Songs' in Anglo-Saxon England." *Neophil*, 59 (1975), 451–62.

Davis, Thomas M. "Another View of 'The Wife's Lament.'" *PLL*, 1 (1965), 291–305.

Doane, A.N. "Heathen Form and Christian Function in 'The Wife's Lament.'" *MS*, 28 (1966), 77–91.

Frye, Donald K. "*Wulf and Eadwacer*: A Wen Charm." *ChauR*, 5 (1970), 247–63.

Greenfield, Stanley B. "The Old English Elegies." In *Continuations and Beginnings: Studies in Old English Literature*. Ed. Eric G. Stanley. London: Nelson, 1966, pp. 142–75.

_____. "*The Wife's Lament* Reconsidered." *PMLA*, 68 (1953), 907–12.

Issacs, N.D. *Structural Principles in Old English Poetry*. Knoxville: Univ. of Tennessee Press, 1968.

Lehmann, Ruth P.M. "The Metrics and Structure of *Wulf and Eadwacer*." *PQ*, 48 (1969), 151–65.

Lench, Elinor. "*The Wife's Lament*: A Poem of the Living Dead." *Comitatus*, 1 (1970), 3–23.

Lucas, Angela. "The Narrator of the Wife's Lament." *NM*, 70 (1969), 282–97.

Malone, Kemp. "Two English *Frauenlieder*." *CL*, 14 (1962), 106–17.

Renoir, Alain. "A Reading Context for *The Wife's Lament*." In *Anglo-Saxon Poetry: Essays in Appreciation*. Ed. Dolores W. Frese and Lewis E. Nicholson. Notre Dame: Univ of Notre Dame Press, 1975, pp. 224–41.

_____. "A Reading of *The Wife's Lament*." *ES*, 58 (1977), 4–19.

_____. "*Wulf and Eadwacer*: A Non-interpretation." In *Franciplegius: . . . Studies in Honor of Francis Peabody Magoun, Jr*. Ed. Jess B. Bessinger and Robert P. Creed. New York: New York Univ. Press, 1965, pp. 147–63.

Rissanen, Matti. "The Theme of 'Exile' in *The Wife's Lament*." *NM*, 70 (1969), 90–104.

Short, Douglas D. "The Old English *Wife's Lament*." *NM*, 71 (1970), 585–603.

Swanton, M.J. "*The Wife's Lament* and *The Husband's Message*: a Reconsideration." *Anglia*, 82 (1964), 269–90.

Middle English

MANUSCRIPTS

For information on manuscripts and printed editions, see Carleton Brown and Rossell Hope Robbins, *Index of Middle English Verse.* New York: Columbia Univ. Press, 1943; and the *Supplement*, ed. R.H. Robbins and John L. Cutler. Lexington: Univ. of Kentucky Press, 1965. For a listing of woman's songs in Middle English according to *Index* number, see, in this volume, Plummer, "The Woman's Song in Middle English," Appendix.

EDITIONS

Brown, Carleton. *Religious Lyrics of the XIVth Century.* 2nd ed. rev. by G.V. Smithers. 1924; rpt. Oxford: Clarendon Press, 1957.

_____. *Religious Lyrics of the XVth Century.* Oxford: Clarendon Press, 1939.

Greene, Richard L. *The Early English Carols.* Oxford: Clarendon Press, 1935.

Robbins, Rossell Hope. *Secular Lyrics of the XIVth and XVth Centuries.* 2nd ed. 1952; rpt. Oxford: Clarendon Press, 1955.

Robinson, F.N. *The Works of Geoffrey Chaucer.* 2nd ed. Boston: Houghton Mifflin, 1957.

STUDIES

Borthwick, Sister Mary Charlotte. "Antigone's Song as 'Mirour' in Chaucer's *Troilus and Criseyde*." *MLQ*, 22 (1961), 227–35.

Crowther, J.D.W. "The Middle English Lyric 'Joly Jankyn.'" *AnM*, 12 (1970), 123–25.

Curry, Jane L. "Waking the Well." *ELN*, 2 (1964), 1–4.

Daly, Saralyn R. "Criseyde's Blasphemous Aube." *N&Q*, 208 (1963), 442–44.

Dronke, Peter. *The Medieval Lyric.* See under *General.*

Greene, Richard L. "Troubling the Well Waters." *ELN*, 4 (1966), 4–6.

Kaske, Robert W. "The Aube in Chaucer's *Troilus*." In *Chaucer Criticism.* Vol. II. Ed. Richard J. Schoeck and Jerome Taylor. Notre Dame: Univ. of Notre Dame Press, 1961, pp. 167–79.

_____. "An Aube in the *Reeve's Tale.*" *ELH*, 26 (1959), 295–310.

_____. "January's 'Aube.'" *MLN*, 75 (1960), 1–4.

Kittredge, George L. "Antigone's Song of Love." *MLN*, 25 (1910), 158.

Kossick, Shirley G. "Troilus and Criseyde: The Aubades." *UES*, 9 (1971), 11–13.

Utley, Francis. *The Crooked Rib: An Analytical Index to the Argument About Women in English and Scots Literature to the End of the Year 1568.* Columbus: Ohio State Univ. Press, 1944.

 French

Note: Although works on the pastourelle have been excluded from this listing, good current bibliographies of work in this field are to be found in two recent works:

Rivière, Jean-Claude. *Pastourelles: Introduction à l'étude formelle des pastourelles anonymes françaises.* 3 vols. Geneva: Droz, 1974–76. [Bibliography in vol. I.]

Zink, Michel. *La pastourelle.* Paris: Bordas, 1972.

EDITIONS

Bartsch, Karl. *Altfranzösische Romanzen und Pastourellen.* Leipzig: Vogel, 1870.

Bec, Pierre. *La lyrique française au moyen-âge.* 2 vols. Paris: Picard, 1977. [Vol. I, studies; vol. II, texts.]

Buffum, Douglas Labarée. *Le Roman de la Violette.* Paris: Champion, 1928.

Cullmann, Arthur. *Die Lieder und Romanzen des Audefroi le Bastard: Kritische Ausgabe.* Halle: Niemeyer, 1914.

Delbouille, Maurice. *Le lai d'Aristote.* Paris: Les Belles Lettres, 1951.

Lecoy, Felix. *Le Roman de la rose ou de Guillaume de Dol.* Paris: Champion, 1962.

Metcke, Albert. *Die Lieder des altfranzösischen Lyrikers Gille le Vinier.* Halle: Kaemmerer, 1906.

Petersen Dyggve, Holger. *Moniot D'Arras: Chansons.* Helsinki: Société Néophilologique, 1938.

Ulrix, Eugène. "Les chansons inédites de Guillaume le Vinier d'Arras: Texte critique." In *Mélanges de philologie romane . . . offerts à Maurice Wilmotte.* No ed. Paris: Champion, 1910, pp. 785–814.

Varty, Kenneth. *Christine de Pisan's Ballades, Rondeaux, and Vire-*

lais: An Anthology. [Leicester]: Leicester Univ. Press, 1965. [Nos. 75–76 are *chansons de mal mariée.*]

STUDIES

Aebischer, P. "Une chanson de 'mal mariée' dans un ms. Fribourgeois du xvᵉ siècle." *Romania,* 54 (1928), 492–503.

Bartsch, Karl. "Die romanischen und deutschen Tagelieder." In his *Gesammelte Vorträge und Aufsätze.* Freiburg and Tübingen: Mohr, 1883.

Bec, Pierre. "L'aube française 'Gaite de la tor': pièce·de ballet ou poème lyrique?" *CCM,* 16 (1973), 17–33.

—————. *La lyrique française.* Vol. I, see *supra.*

Becker, P.A. "Vom geistlichen Tagelied." *Volkstum und Kultur der Romanen,* 2 (1929), 293–302.

Bédier, Joseph. *La chanson de "Bele Aeliz" par le trouvère Baude de la Quariere.* Paris: Picard, 1904.

Coirault, Patrice. "Belle Aelis et sa postérité folklorique." *RPh,* 2 (1949), 299–304.

Cremonesi, Carla. "'Chansons de geste' et 'chansons d'historie.'" *Studi Romanzi,* 30 (1943), 55–203.

Dähne, Rudolf. *Die Lieder der Maumariée seit dem Mittelalter.* Halle: Niemeyer, 1933.

Faral, Edmond. "Les chansons de toile ou chansons d'historie." *Romania,* 69 (1946–47), 433–62.

Fink, Paul. *Das Weib im französischen Volksliede.* Berlin: Mayer und Müller, 1904.

Gasparini, Eva. "A proposito delle 'chansons à toile.'" In *Studi in onore di Italo Siciliano.* No ed. Firenze: Olschki, 1966, pp. 457–66.

Godzich, Wladislav. "Le chanson de toile de Gaiete et Oriour." *Semiotexte,* 1 (1975).

Horent, J. "Altas undas que venez suz la mar." *Mélanges de philologie roman dédiés à . . . Jean Boutière.* Ed. Irenée Cluzel and François Pirot. Liège: Soledi, [1971], pp. 305–16.

Jeanroy, Alfred. *Les Origines de la poésie lyrique en France au moyen âge.* 4th ed. Paris: Champion, 1969.

Jenkins, T.A. "La chanson de Bele Doe dans *Guillaume de Dole.*" *Romania,* 40 (1911), 452–54.

Joly, R. "Les chansons d'histoire." *RJ,* 12 (1961), 51–66.

Jonin, Pierre. "Les types féminin dans les chansons de toile." *Romania,* 91 (1970), 433–66.

_____. "Le refrain dans les chanson de toile." *Romania*, 96 (1975), 209–44.

Jordan, H.S. "The Old Franch 'Chanson d'histoire' as a Possible Origin of the English Popular Ballad." *RLC*, 16 (1936), 367–78.

Lefèvre, Yves. "La Femme au Moyen Age en France dans la vie littéraire et spirituelle." In *Histoire mondiale de la femme*. Ed. Pierre Grimal. Paris: Nouvelle Libr. de France, 1966, pp. 79–134.

Le Gentil, Pierre. "La Strophe zadjalesque, les khardjas et le problème des origines du lyrisme roman." *Romania*, 84 (1963), 1–27, 209–50, 409–11.

Lewis, C.B. "The Origin of the Weaving Songs and the Theme of the Girl at the Fountain." *PMLA*, 37 (1922), 141–81.

Parducci, Amos. "La canzone di 'mal maritata' in Francia nei secoli xv–xvi." *Romania*, 38 (1909), 286–325.

Paris, Gaston. "Les origines de la poésie lyrique en France au moyen âge." *JS* (1891), 674–88, 729–42; (1892), 155–67, 407–29. Rpt. in his *Mélanges de littérature française du moyen âge*. Paris: Champion, 1912.

Planche, Alice. "Gaiete, Orior et le copiste distrait." *CCM*, 20 (1977), 49–52.

Poulaille, H., and R. Pernoud. *Chansons de toile*. Paris: Rogers, 1946.

Restori, A. "'La Gaite de la Tor.'" In *Festschrift Petraglioso Serrano*. Messina, 1904, pp. 4–22.

Riquer, Martin de. "Alba trovadoresca de autor catalán." *RFE*, 34 (1950), 151–65.

Saba, Guido. *La "chansons de toile" o "chansons d'histoire."* Modena: Societa Tipografica Modenese, 1955.

Saville, Jonathon. *The Medieval Erotic Alba*. New York: Columbia Univ. Press, 1972.

Scharff, Arthur B. "*Chanson de toile* or *chanson d'histoire*." *RomN*, 15 (1974), 509–12.

_____. "The Old French 'Chansons de toile.'" Diss. Ohio State, 1969.

Schläger, Georg. *Studien über das Tagelied*. Jena, 1895.

Schossig, Alfred. *Der Ursprung der altfranzösischen Lyrik*. Halle: Niemeyer, 1957.

Servois, G. Jean Renart. *Le Roman de la Rose ou de Guillaume de Dole*. Paris: SATF, 1893. [Contains an introduction by Gaston Paris on the lyrics inserted in the text.]

Stangel, E. "Der Entwicklungsgang der provenzalischen Alba." *ZRP*, 9 (1885), 407–12.

Storost, Wolfgang. *Geschichte der altfranzösischen und altprovenzalischen Romanzenstrophe.* Halle: Niemeyer, 1930.

Verrier, P. "Bele Aiglentine et Petite Christine." *Romania*, 63 (1937), 354–76.

Woods, W.S. "The 'aube' in 'Aucassin et Nicolette.'" In *Medieval Studies in Honor of Urban Tigner Holmes, Jr.* Ed. John Mahoney and John E. Keller. Chapel Hill: Univ. of North Carolina Press, [1965], pp. 209–15.

Zink, Michel. *Belle: Essai sur les chanson de toile.* Paris: Champion, 1978.

Zumthor, Paul. "La Chanson de Bele Aiglentine." *TLL*, 8 (1970), 325–37.

—————. *Essai de poétique médiévale.* Paris: du Seuil, 1972.

 *German*

BIBLIOGRAPHY

Tervooren, Helmut. *Bibliographie zum Minnesang und zu den Dichtern aus "Des Minnesangs Frühling."* Berlin: Erich Schmidt, 1969.

(See also the notes to articles by Heinen and Jackson, in this volume.)

EDITIONS

Carmina Burana and *Des Minnesangs Frühling* supply all of the anonymous woman's songs, and *Minnesangs Frühling* provides as well those assigned to known poets, with the exception of Walther von der Vogelweide. For further editions of the work of individual authors, consult Tervooren, *Bibliographie.*

Hilka, Alfons, and Otto Schumann, eds. *Carmina Burana.* Heidelberg: Winter, 1941. Vol. I, Part 2: "Die Liebeslieder." Nos. 145a, 149, 163a, 174a, 180a, 185.

Kraus, Carl von, ed. *Die Gedichte Walthers von der Vogelweide.* 12th ed. Berlin: de Gruyter, 1962.

—————. *Deutsche Liederdichter des 13. Jahrhunderts.* Tübingen: Niemeyer, 1952. [For texts after der Blütezeit.]

Moser, Hugo, and Helmut Tervooren, eds. *Des Minnesangs Frühling.* 36th ed. Stuttgart: S. Hirzel, 1977. Vol. I, texts.

STUDIES

Angermann, Adolar. *Der Wechsel in der mittelhochdeutschen Lyrik.* Diss. Marburg, 1910.

Becker, Reinhold. *Der altheimische Minnesang.* Halle: Niemeyer, 1882.

——————. "Uber Reinmar von Hagenau." *Germania*, 22 (1877), 70–93, 195–225.

Brachmann, Friedrich. "Zu den Minnesängern." *Germania*, 31 (1886), 443–86.

Bründl, Peter. *"unde bringe den wehsel, als ich waen, durch ir liebe ze grabe.* Eine Studie zur Rolle des Sängers im Minnesang von Kaiser Heinrich bis Neidhart von Reuenthal."*DVLG*, 44 (1970), 409–32.

Burdach, Konrad. *Über den Ursprung des mittelalterlichen Minnesangs, Liebesromans und Frauendienstes.* Sitzungsberichte der Berliner Akademie der Wissenschaft, Philosophische-Historische Klasse, 1918. Berlin, 1918, 994–1029 and 1072–98.

Ehrismann, Gustav. "Die Kürenberg-Literatur und die Anfänge des deutschen Minnesangs." *GRM*, 15 (1927), 328–50.

Fischer, Heinz. *Die Frauenmonologe in der deutschen höfischen Lyrik.* Diss. Marburg, 1934.

Frings, Theodor. "Frauenstrophe und Frauenlied in der frühen deutschen Lyrik." In *Gestaltung Umgestaltung: Festschrift H. A. Korff.* Ed. Joachim Müller. Leipzig: Koehler & Amelang, 1957, pp. 13–28.

——————. "Namenlose Lieder." *BGDSL* (Halle), 88 (1967), 307–28.

Ganz, Peter F. "The 'Cancionerillo Mozarabe' and the Origin of the Middle High German 'Frauenlied.'"*MLR*, 48 (1953), 301–09.

Götze, Alfred. "Gewollte Unkunst im Frauenlied." *BGDSL*, 61 (1937), 183–85.

Grimminger, Rolf. *Poetik des frühen Minnesangs.* Diss. Munich, 1966.

Grundmann, Herbert. "Die Frauen und die Literatur im Mittelalter." *AKG*, 26 (1936), 129–61.

Heinen, Hubert. "Observations on the Role in Minnesang." *JEGP*, 75 (1976), 198–208.

Ibăşescu, Mihail. *Problema "Monologul feminin" in lumina genezii Minnesangulin.* Bucharest, 1946.

Jackson, William E. "Reinmar der Alte: The Minnesänger as Dramatic Poet." In *Germanic Studies in Honor of Otto Springer.*

Ed. Stephen J. Kaplowitt. Pittsburgh: K & S Enterprises, 1978, pp. 149–58.

Kraus, Carl von. *Unsere älteste Lyrik*. Munich: Bayerische Akademie der Wissenschaften, 1930.

Lea, Elisabeth. "Die Sprache lyischer Grundgefüge. *MFr.* 11, 1–15, 17." *BGDSL* (Halle), 90 (1968), 305–79.

Lesser, Ernst. "Das Verhältnis der Frauenmonologe in den lyrischen und epischen deutschen Dichtungen des 12. und angehenden 13. Jahrhunderts." *BGDSL*, 24 (1899), 361–83.

McLintock, D.R. "Walther's Mädchenlieder." *OGS*, 3 (1968), 30–43.

Mergell, Erika. *Die Frauenrede im deutschen Minnesang*. Diss. Frankfurt, 1939. Limburg/Lahn: Limburger Vereinsdruckerei, 1940.

Ohlenroth, Derk. *Sprechsituation und Sprecheridentität: Eine Untersuchung zum Verhältnis von Sprache und Realität im frühen deutschen Minnesang*. *GAG*, 96. Göppingen: Kümmerle, 1974.

Ohly, Friedrich. "Du bist mein." In *Kritische Bewahrung. Beiträge zur deutschen Philologie. Festschrift für Werner Schröder*. Ed. Ernst-Joachim Schmidt. Berlin: Schmidt, 1974, pp. 371–415.

Pomassl, Gerhard. *Die Reaktion der Frau auf Minnesang und Minnedienst in der deutschen Lyrik des 12. und 13. Jahrhunderts*. Diss. Jena, 1958.

Pralle, Georg. *Die Frauenstrophen im ältesten deutschen Minnesang*. Diss. Halle, 1892.

Spitzer, Leo. See under *General*.

Stolte, Heinz. "Hartmanns sogenannte Witweklage und sein drittes Kreuzlied." *DVLG*, 25 (1951), 184–98.

Wapnewski, Peter. "Walthers Lied von der Traumliebe und die deutschsprachige Pastourelle." *Euphorion*, 51 (1957), 113–50.

—————. *Waz ist minne. Studien zur mittelhochdeutschen Lyrik*. Munich: Beck, 1975.

Werbow, Stanley N. *Formal Aspects of Medieval German Poetry. A Symposium*. Austin and London: Univ. of Texas Press, 1969.

 *Irish*

Woman's songs have not been studied as a genre in Irish, and therefore this is only a partial list. Below are grouped, alphabetically by the first line of Irish, the poems found in isolation that, according to context or ascription, are spoken in a woman's voice. Next are stories, or, more properly, poems ascribed to characters in stories. These are, perhaps, like taking the woman's parts from verse-plays as woman's songs; but some, by age of language and verse-form, are older than the prose romances about the characters they are ascribed to, and not a few exist apart from the prose romances we have, or the prose seems a flimsy frame for poems that were grouped at one time, we may guess, in a clearer tale now lost. These poems are listed in order of occurrence within tales and the tales more or less by age.

Where editions of the poems give careful lists of manuscripts, only the edited text is given, except where that is not generally available. The first edition will be the most important for the number of mss. examined. Publishers are given only for texts printed in the last fifty years. In referring to my own collection of translations from Old Irish, which is not yet in print, I give only the numbers of the poems. This collection will be referred to as RPML. Since many of the poems indexed here are discussed in my essay on the "Woman's Songs in Irish, 800–1500," in this volume, cross-references are made to page numbers in the text and to the note which contains full bibliographic information.

Aithbe dam cen bés mora The Old Woman of Beare
A mythological figure remembers past joys and hopes her present misery will lead ultimately to salvation.
Discussed in this volume, pp. 113–19. See also note 2, p. 133, and:
Gerard Murphy in *Proceedings of the Royal Irish Academy* (1953), 55 C 4, pp. 88–106.
Kuno Meyer. *Otia Merseiana*. (Liverpool, 1899), i. pp. 121–28.
Osborn Bergin. *Eriu*, 2 (1905), 240–41
Verse translation by Ruth P. M. Lehmann. *Poems*. (Austin: Westlake Press, 1977), RPML, no. 46, pp. 38–41.

Batar inmuine na tri toib His Queen Laments Aed son of Ainmire
For a translation of and a brief comment on this lament see, in this volume, p. 129, and note 13, p. 134. See also:
Kuno Meyer. *Bruchstücke der älteren Lyrik Irlands*. Abhandlungen der Preussischen Akademie der Wissenschaften. Philosophisch-historische Klasse, no. 7, erster Teil (Berlin, 1919), no. 89, p. 38.
James Carney. *Medieval Irish Lyrics*. California, 1967, no. 12, p. 24.
RPML, no. 93.

Cride é The Sweetheart
A happy love song to a boy, preserved as a metrical example.
Translation in this volume p. 121. See also, note 7, p. 133 and:

Rudolf Thurneysen. *Irische Texte* (Leipzig, 1891), 3. no. 177, p. 100.
RPML, no. 51.

Gel cech núa—sásad nglé! A Girl's Song
Another exuberant quatrain, this from the margin of the *Book of Leinster*, fol. 121a.
Translation in this volume p. 121. See also, note 8, p. 133 and:
RPML, no. 53.

Isucán Little Jesus
St. Ité imagines that she nurses the Christ child. The verses are appended to, or occur in, various accounts of the saint's life.
Gerard Murphy. *Early Irish Lyrics.* Oxford: Oxford Univ. Press, 1956, no. 11, p. 26.
David Greene and Frank O'Connor, eds. *Golden Treasury of Irish Poetry.* Oxford: Oxford Univ. Press, 1956, no. 23, p. 102.
Carney, *Medieval Irish Lyrics*, no. 26, p. 64.
RPML, no. 49.

It é saigte gona súain Lament for Dinertach
A poignant lament, perhaps from an unrecorded tale. The interpretation—is Crede daughter or wife of Guaire?—is disputed.
Translation in this volume p. 130. See also note 14, p. 134, and:
RPML, no. 50.

Mé Eba, ben Adaim uill Eve
Eve regrets the trouble her greed has brought to the world, including winter and storm.
Kuno Meyer. *Eriu*, 3 (1907), 148.
Murphy, *Early Irish Lyrics*, no. 21, p. 50.
Greene and O'Connor, *Golden Treasury of Irish Poetry*, no. 38, p. 157.
Carney, *Medieval Irish Lyrics*, no. 28, p. 72.
RPML, no. 48.

Och is fada ataim a-muigh
This curious poem by a deserted woman not only laments the loss of happier days but also suggests that she has been told her lover has been lured away by his boyfriend.
Translation in this volume p. 132. See also note 16, p. 134, and:
RPML, no. 53

Poems ascribed to Queen Gorm(fh)laith (d. 948). The poems are listed here in the order in which they appear in Osborn Bergin. *Irish Bardic Poetry*, ed. David Greene and Fergus Kelly. Dublin: Dublin Institute for Advanced Studies, 1970.

1. *Dubhach sin, a dhúin na riogh* (3 stanzas)

   An address to the Fort of Kings after the death of her third husband, Niall Glundubh.

   Bergin, *Irish Bardic Poetry*, text p. 204, trans. p. 308.

   Eleanor Knott. *Irish Syllabic Poetry*. Dublin: Dublin Institute for Advanced Studies, 1957, no. 1, p. 24.

2. *Gáir bháinnsi 'san tigh si amuigh* (10 stanzas)

   The celebration of a wedding reminds the Queen of her former happiness with Niall and his vows of love to her.

   Bergin, *Irish Bardic Poetry*, text pp. 204–05, trans. pp. 308–09.

3. *Ceananndas mairce damh ad-chi* (7 stanzas)

   The first line is the refrain of the following stanzas. Kells (Cenannas), Niall's burial place, is addressed. The Queen also mentions Cormac and Cerball, her first two husbands, but Niall is dearest to her.

4. *Folamh anocht Dún Chearma* (3 stanzas)

   An elegy on the empty fort after the princes are gone.

   Bergin, *Irish Bardic Poetry*, text pp. 206–07, trans. pp. 309–10.

   Knott, *Irish Syllabic Poetry*, no. 2, p. 24.

5. *Iomdha bréid ort a cheirt si!* (7 stanzas)

   A lament for rags and poverty and memories of better days. Though native to Leinster and Meath, the Queen prefers Niall's country, Ulster.

   Irish text and translation in this volume pp. 125–27. See also note 12, p. 134.

6. *Uchagán, mo ghalar féain* (3 stanzas)

   The Queen mourns Niall and Ireland empty without him.

   Bergin, *Irish Bardic Poetry*, text p. 208, trans. p. 310.

7. *Cú duine mur nach bhfionntur* (7 stanzas)

   The Queen finds herself friendless and opposed in Leinster, and she regrets that Niall, her equal in marriage, is dead.

   Bergin, *Irish Bardic Poetry*, text pp. 208–09, trans. p. 311.

8. *Beir a mhanaigh leat an chois* (5 stanzas)

   The queen asks a monk to take his foot from Niall's grave, compares herself to Deirdre after the death of the sons of Usnech, and regrets that flagstones are not over her.

   Irish text and translation in this volume p. 127. See also note 12, p. 134.

9. *Trum anocht mh'osnadh, a Dhé!* (5 Stanzas)

   All the Queen's family are dead as well as Niall and their son.

The poem lists his ancestors back to Niall of the Nine Hostages, but it is chiefly a lament for her only son.

Bergin, *Irish Bardic Poetry*, text pp. 210–12, trans. pp. 312–13.

10. *Ro charas tricha fo thri* (15 stanzas)

Recalls Niall's generosity to his Queen and hers to the wife of one of the churchmen. The gifts given to her in her poverty she finds a stingy return.

Bergin, *Irish Bardic Poetry*, text pp. 212–14, trans. pp. 313–14.

11. *Mithid sgur do chaoineadh Néill* (10 stanzas)

The Queen has wept for Niall each night for thirty-one years. Now Niall appears to her and asks her to cease. As he starts to go, she leaps after him and her breast is impaled on the bedpost. She hopes for death and reunion with him. Though her first husbands, Cormac and Cerball, had given her much, Niall gave her three times as much in one month.

Irish text and translation in this volume pp. 128–29. See also note 12, p. 134.

Liadan and Cuirithir

Two poems spoken by Liadan occur in this story—*Cen áinus* and *Carsam, nim ránic a less*. We know the story only from notes probably made by a storyteller. As preserved, the story has been Christianized, and the separation of the lovers is caused by her becoming a nun after their earlier acquaintance. They put themselves under Cumine of Clonfert and must choose between speaking to or seeing one another. They choose speech. Later, Cumine permits cohabitation with a witness present, but they fail this test and Cuirithir is exiled. Of the two laments by Liadan, one consists of ten three-line stanzas, the other of three quatrains. The longer poem is especially fine. John L. Savage in "An Old Irish Version of Laodamia and Protesilaus," *Classical and Medieval Studies in Honor of Edward Kennard Rand*, ed. Leslie Webber Jones (1938, rpt. Books for Libraries Press, 1968), pp. 265–72, links the story with Ovid's lovers but suggests that Liadan and Cuirithir were originally poets or druids.

A translation of *Cen áinius* appears in this volume pp. 114–15. See also note 4, p. 133, and:

Kuno Meyer. *Selections from Ancient Irish Poetry* (1911) translation of *Cen áinius* pp. 65–66.

Julius Pokorny. *Historical Reader of Old Irish* (1923) *Cen áinius* pp. 16–17.

RPML, no. 47.

The Sickbed of Cú Chulainn or the One Jealousy of Emer

Cú Chulainn is visited and beaten by women. It seems a dream, but he lies helpless for a year. Then Li Ban summons him to the Other World, but he sends Láeg, his charioteer. The story is confused. Cú Chulainn is, in parts of it, married to Emer, in others to Eithne, and the summons is repeated. Besides, the tale incorporates a quite unrelated interpolation. Eventually Cú Chulainn accompanies Li Ban to fight for her husband, Labraid Swift-Hand-on-Sword. In the Other World he meets Fand, wife of Manannan mac Lir, a mythical sea-god after whom the Isle of Man is named. Emer tries to have Fand killed, but Fand gives up Cú Chulainn to return to her husband.

Embedded in the story are a number of fine verses, eight of which are spoken by women. They are listed below under the section numbers assigned them in *Seirglige Con Culaind*, ed. Myles Dillon. Medieval and Modern Irish Series, no. 14 (Dublin: Dublin Institute for Advanced Studies, 1953).

17. *Fo chen Labraid Lúathlám ar claideb!*
    Li Ban addresses her husband in a formal *retoiric*.
18. *Fo chen Labraid Lúathlám ar claideb augra!*
    Two more alliterative speeches by Li Ban, very like the first.
29. *A meic Riangabra fó rir*
    Emer reproaches Laeg for not helping to cure Cú Chulainn.
30 *Erig, a gérait Ulaid!*
    Emer appeals to Cú Chulainn to rise from his sickbed.
37. *Ségda cairptech docing ró't*
    Fand describes the approach of Cú Chulainn.
38. *Fo chen Cú Chulaind*
    Li Ban welcomes Cú Chulainn in a formal *retoiric*.
44. *Messe ragas for astur*
    Fand tells Emer that she will give up Cú Chulainn to her.
45. *Fégaid mac láechraidi Lir*
    Fand's farewell to Cú Chulainn.

    A translation of this last section appears in this volume pp. 119–21. See also note 6, p. 133, and:

    Ernst Windisch. *Irische Texte* (1880), vol. i, pp. 197 ff.

    RPML, no. 63.

The Exile of the Sons of Uisliu

Deirdre elopes to Scotland with Naise and his brothers rather than marry Conchobar. After some years, they are lured back to Ireland under Fergus's protection. Conchobar than separates them from Fergus, and Eogan mac Durthacht kills the men. After a year of grieving in Conchobar's house, Deirdre is to be transferred to Eogan's, but she dashes her head against a rock.

Manuscripts differ in details. The best edition, with full bibliography and copious notes, is *Longes Mac n-Uislenn: The Exile of the Sons of Uisliu,* ed. Vernum Hull. Modern Language Association of America Monograph Series, no. 14. New York: Modern Language Association of America, 1949. Section numbers refer to this edition.

17. *Cid cáin lib ind láechrad lainn*
    Deirdre's lament for Naise.

18. *A Chonchobuir, cid no tai?*
    Deirdre praises Naise to Conchobar.
    Both of these poems are translated in this volume pp. 123–25.
    See also note 10, p. 134.

(Manuscripts later than that used by Hull as the basis for his text include two woman's songs in which Deirdre praises Scotland):

> *Gleann measach iasgach linneach*
> Thomas F. O'Rahilly, *Measgra Danta*, vol. ii, no. 43.
>
> *Ionmhain tir-úd thoir*
> Deirdre's farewell to Scotland.
> Set to music by Mrs. Kennedy-Fraser, this song was sung in Youth Hostels in the west of Scotland in the 1930's.
> O'Rahilly, *Measgra Danta*, vol. ii, no. 44.

From the Finn Cycle:

The Elopement of Diarmait and Grainne

On the night of her betrothal to Finn mac Cumhail, Grainne drugs the wine of her father, Cormac, and of Finn and all but a few Fenians. She persuades Diarmait to elope with her. The tale is late and is largely concerned with the narrow escapes of the lovers as Finn pursues them, finally lets Diarmait be killed by a wild boar, and marries Grainne.

In the form in which it has been transmitted to us, the tale contains none of Grainne's songs. There are very early references to this story, however, and scattered through the extant Irish materials are songs which clearly belong in this context even if they do not appear in the manuscript as we have it. The oldest of the poems, for example, is preserved as a gloss on rime words in a commentary on the *Amra Coluim Chille*.

Fil duine

A quatrain ascribed to Grainne in which she tells of her love of Diarmait at first sight.
Murphy, *Early Irish Lyrics*, no. 54, p. 160.

Green and O'Connor, *Golden Treasury of Irish Poetry*, no. 26.6, p. 112.

RPML, no. 72.

Cotail becán becán bec

Grainne's lullaby to Diarmait, from a collection of Fenian poems. Translated in this volume pp. 121–22. See also note 9, pp. 133–34, and:

RPML, no. 74.

The Conversation of the Old Men

Oisin and Caeilte meet St. Patrick and tell stories of the great days of Finn. The saint is not sure this is for his soul's good, yet keeps urging them to tell more. They constantly ridicule the decadent present, and there is much humor as well as beauty and pathos in the poems.

Géisid cúan

One of the finest laments from the Battle of Bantry Bay when Créide finds Cael drowned.

Translation in this volume pp. 131–32. See also note 15, p. 134, and:

RPML, no. 79.

The following songs belong to the Ulster Cycle, but I list them here because they have not been edited. They are laments for Cú Chulainn spoken by Emer and are cited by first lines in the notes to the *Aided Con Culainn* in *Compert Con Culainn*, ed. A. G. Van Hamel. Medieval and Modern Irish Series, no. 3 (Dublin Institute for Advanced Studies, 1933). The section numbers are Van Hamel's.

47. *Dursan liom, a Chú Chulainn*

52. *Uch, a chinn, gé rod mesgadh ar linn*

52. *Dun Dealgan an dún 'sa thiar*

52. *Uchán, uch ón ló*

 *Latin*

MANUSCRIPTS

Carmina Burana: Clm 4660 (Munich). Ed. Bernard Bischoff. *Carmina Burana: Facsimile Reproduction of the Manuscript Clm 4660 and Clm 4660a*. Brooklyn: Institute of Medieval Music, 1967. [Useful introduction, pp. 19–31.]

Hilka, Alfons, and Otto Schumann, eds. *Carmina Burana*. I, 2, *Die Liebeslieder*. 1941; rpt. Heidelberg: Carl Winter, 1971.

Cambridge Songs: UL Gg. v. 35, s. XI (Cambridge Univ. Library).

Ed. Karl Strecker. *Die Cambridger Lieder*. Berlin: Weidman, 1926.

See further in Peter Dronke, *Medieval Latin*, Vol. II, under *General.*

STUDIES

Allen, P. S. *Medieval Latin Lyrics*. Chicago: Univ. of Chicago Press, 1931.

Dronke, Peter. "Francesca and Heloise." *CL*, 27 (1975), 113–35.

—————. *Medieval Latin*. See under *General.*

—————. "The Rise of the Medieval Fabliau: Latin and Vernacular Evidence." *RF*, 85 (1973), 275–97.

Ferrante, Joan. See under *General.*

Herkenrath, E. "Tempus adest floridum." *ZDA*, 15 (1930), 135–40.

Jackson, W. T. H. "The Medieval Pastourelle as a Satirical Genre." *PQ*, 31 (1952), 156–70.

—————. "Der Streit zwischen Miles und Clericus." *ZDA*, 85 (1954–55), 293–303.

Northcott, Kenneth J. "Some Functions of 'Love' in the 'Carmina Burana.'" *DBGÜ*, 6 (1970), 11–25.

Paden, William D., Jr. "The Literary Background of the Pastourelle." In *Acta Conventus Neo-Latini Lovaniensis.* Ed. J. Ijsewijn and E. Kessler. Munich: Wilhelm Fink, 1973, pp. 467–73.

Raby, F. J. E. *A History of Secular Latin Poetry in the Middle Ages*. 2 vols. 2nd ed. Oxford: Clarendon Press, 1957.

Wailes, Stephen L. "Vagantes and the Fabliaux." In *The Humor of the Fabliaux: A Collection of Critical Essays*. Ed. Thomas D. Cooke and Benjamen L. Honeycutt. Columbia, Mo.: Univ. of Missouri Press, 1974, pp. 43–58.

Wimsatt, James. "Chaucer and 'The Canticle of Canticles.'" In *Chaucer the Love Poet*. Ed. Jerome Mitchell and William Provost. Athens: Univ. of Georgia Press, 1973, pp. 75–83.

 *Portuguese*

MANUSCRIPTS

Cancioneiro da Ajuda. Ajuda palace library, Lisbon. Ed. Carolina Michaëlis de Vasconcellos. 2 vols. Halle: Niemeyer, 1904.

Cancioneiro da Biblioteca Nacional (Antiguo Colocci-Brancuti). National Library, Lisbon. Ed. Elza Pacheco Machado and

Jose Pedro Machado. 8 vols. With facsimile and commentaries. Lisbon: Revista de Portugal, 1949-64.

Cancioneiro portuguez da Vaticana. Ed. Teófilo Braga. Lisbon: Imprensa Nacional, 1878.

EDITIONS

Nunes, José Joaquim, ed. *Cantigas d'Amigo dos trovadores galegoportugueses.* 3 vols. Coimbra: Imprensa da Universidade, 1926-28. [Vol. 1, introduction; Vol. 2, texts; Vol. 3, notes.]

STUDIES

Alín, José Maria. See under *Spanish.*

Asensio, Eugenio. *Poética y realidad.* See under *Spanish.*

Atkinson, Dorothy. "Parallelism in the Medieval Portuguese Lyric." *MLR*, 50 (1955), 281-87.

Bagley, C.P. "Cantigas de amigo and Cantigas de amor." *BHS*, 43 (1966), 241-52.

Bell, Aubrey F.G. *Portuguese Literature.* Oxford: Clarendon Press, 1922. Chs. I and II.

Crespo, Firmino. "A tradiçao de una lirica popular portuguesa antes e depois dos Trovadores." *Ocidente*, 71 (1965), 3-17, 98-108, 121-28, 185-204.

Deyermond, A.D. *A Literary History of Spain: The Middle Ages.* London: Ernest Benn, 1971.

Dronke, Peter. *The Medieval Lyric.* See under *General.*

Entwistle, William J. "From *Cantigas de Amigo* to *Cantigas de Amor.*" *RLC*, 18 (1938), 137-52.

Frenk Alatorre, Margit. *Las jarchas mozárabes.* See under *Spanish.*

Hatto, A.T. *Eos.* See under General. [Ch. on Iberian lyrics by Edward Wilson, and Appendix I, "Imagery and Symbolism."]

Hill, Kathleen Kulp. "Three Faces of Eve: Woman in the Medieval Galician-Portuguese Cancioneiros." *KRQ*, 16 (1969), 97-107.

Lapa, M. Rodrigues. *Das origens da poesia lírica em Portugal na Idade-Média.* Lisbon: Ed. do autor, 1929.

Monroe, James T. "Formulaic Diction and the Common Origins of Romance Lyric Traditions." *HR*, 43 (1975), 341-50.

Pope, Isabel. "Medieval Latin Background of the Thirteenth Century Galician Lyric." *Speculum*, 9 (1934), 3-25.

Reckert, Stephen. *Lyra Minima: Structure and Symbol in Iberian Traditional Verse.* London: n.p., 1970.

_____, Helder Macedo and Roman Jakobson, eds. *Do*

Cancioneiro de Amigo. Documenta Poetica 3. Lisbon: Assirio & Alvim, 1976.

Spitzer, Leo. See under *General*.

Sponsler, Lucy A. *Women in Medieval Spanish Epic and Lyric Traditions*. Lexington: Univ. Press of Kentucky, 1975.

Wardropper, Bruce W. "On the Supposed Repetitiousness of the *Cantigas d'amigo*." *RHM*, 38 (1974–75), 1–6.

 Spanish, the Jarchas, and the Question of Origins

For further bibliography on the origins of Romance lyrics, see, *infra*, Sola-Solé; Frenk Alatorre, 1975; and Heger, 1960.

MANUSCRIPTS

A convenient source of information on mss. containing *jarchas* is J.M. Sola-Solé, *Corpus*, pp. 51–52, q.v. *infra*.

EDITIONS

Borello, Rodolfo A. *Jaryas andalusies*. Bahia Blanca: Universidad Nacional del Sur, 1959.

Heger, Klaus. *Die bisher veröffentlichten Harǧas und ihre Deutungen*. Beihefte, *ZRP*, 101. Tübingen: Niemeyer, 1960.

Monroe, James T. "Two New Bilingual harǧas (Arabic and Romance) in Arabic muwaššahs." *HR*, 42 (1974), 243–64.

Sola-Solé, José Maria. *Corpus de poesia mozarabe: Las ḥarǧas andalusies*. Barcelona: Hispam, 1973.

Stern, Samuel M. *Les chansons mozarabes: Les vers finaux ("kharjas") en espagnol dans les "muwashshahs" arabes et hébreux*. Oxford: Bruno Cassirer, 1964.

—————. "Les vers finaux en espagnol dans les muwaššahs hispano-hébraïques: Une contribution à l'histoire du muwaššah et à l'étude du vieux dialecte espagnol 'mozarabe.'" *Andalus*, 13 (1948), 299–436.

STUDIES

Alín, José María. *El Cancionero español de tipo tradicional*. Madrid: Taurus, 1968.

Alonso, Dámaso. "Cancioncillas 'de amigo' mozárabes." *RFE*, 33 (1949), 297–349.

_____. *Primavera temprana de la literatura europea*. Madrid: Guadarrama, 1959.

Armistead, S.G. "On the Interpretation of ḫarǧas 57, 58, and 59." *HR*, 38 (1970), 243–50.

Asensio, Eugenio. "Los cantares paralelísticos castellanos: Tradición y originalidad." *RFE*, 37 (1952), 130–67.

_____. *Póetica y realidad en el cancionero peninsular de la Edad Media*. 2nd ed. Madrid: Gredos, 1970.

Bansani, Alex. "La tradizione arabo-islamica nella cultura europea." *HumB* (1957), 809–928.

Borello, Rodolfo A. "De nueovo sobre las jarchyas." *CI*, 1 (1965), 129–32.

Brown, Donn F. "A History of the Zéjel in Spanish, Portuguese and Catalan Literature." Diss. Washington, 1971.

Cabanelas, Darío. "Más sobre las Jarchas romances en muwaššahas árabes." *Clavileño*, 4 (1953), 55–58.

Cantarino, Vicent. "Lyrical Traditions in Andalusian Muwashshahas." *CL*, 21 (1969), 213–31.

Cantera Burgos, Francisco. *La canción mozárabe*. Santander: Sociedad General Española, 1957.

_____. "Versos españoles en las *muwaššahas* hispano-hebreas.' *Sefarad*, 9 (1949), 197–234.

Castro, Américo. "Mozarabic Poetry and Castile: A Rejoinder to Mr. Leo Spitzer." *CL*, 4 (1952), 188–89.

_____. *La realidad histórica de Espana*. México: Porrúa, 1954,

Cluzel, Irénée M. "Les jarŷas et l' 'amour courtois.'" *CN*, 20 (1960), 233–50.

_____. "Quelques reflexions à propos des origines de la poésie lyrique des troubadours." *CCM*, 4 (1961), 179–88.

Corominas, Juan. "Para la interpretación de las jarŷas recién halladas (MS G.S. Colin)." *Andalus*, 18 (1953), 140–48.

Criado De Val, M. "Sobre los origenes del iberorromance: Correspondencia verbal de las jarchas y las canciones de amigo." *BdF*, 19 (1960), 3.

Dronke, Peter. *The Medieval Lyric*. See under *General*.

Dutton, Brian. "Some New Evidence for the Romance Origins of the *Muwashshahas*." *BHS*, 42 (1965), 73–81.

Frenk Alatorre, Margit. "Jarŷas mozárabes y estribillos franceses." *NRFH*, 6 (1952), 281–84.

_____. *Las jarchas mozárabes y los comienzos de la lirica romanica*. Guanajuato: Colegio de México, 1975.

_____. "El nacimiento de la lírica española a la luz do los nuevos descubrimientos." *CA*, 12 (1953), 159–74.

Frings, Theodor. See under *General*.

Gangutia Elícegui, Elvira. "Poesía griega 'de amigo' y poesía arábigo-española." *Emerita*, 40 (1972), 329–96.

Ganz, P.F. See under *German*.

García Gómez, Emilio. "Dos nuevas jarŷas romances en muwaš-šahas árabes (MS G.S. Colin)." *Andalus*, 19 (1954), 369–91.

_____. "Las jarŷas mozárabes y los judios de Al-Andalus." *BRAE*, 37 (1957), 337–94.

_____. *Las jarchas romances de la serie árabe en su marco*. Madrid: Sociedad de Estudioes y Publicaciones, 1965.

_____. "La lírica hispano-árabe y la aparición de la lirica románica." *Andalus*, 21 (1956), 303–38.

_____. "Nuevas observaciones sobre las 'jarŷas' romances en muwaššahas hebreas." *Andalus*, 15 (1950), 157–77.

_____. Más sobre las 'jarŷas' romances en 'muwaššahas' hebreas." *Andalus*, 14 (1949), 409–17.

_____. *Poesía arábigoandaluza: breve sintesis histórica*. Madrid: Instituto Faruk I de Estudioes Islámicos, 1952.

Hilty, Gerald. "La poésie mozarabe." *TLL*, 8 (1970), 85–100.

Hitchcock, Richard. "Some Doubts About the Reconstruction of the Kharjas." *BHS*, 50 (1973), 109–19.

Lapesa, Rafael. "Sobre el texto y lenguaje de algunas 'jarchyas' mozárabes." *BRAE*, 40 (1960), 53–65.

Le Gentil, Pierre. *La poésie lyrique espagnole et portugaise à la fin du Moyen Age*. 2 vols. Rennes: Plihon, 1949–52.

_____. *La virelai et le villancico: Le problème des origines arabes*. Paris: Belles Lettres, 1954.

_____. See further under *French*.

Menéndez Pidal, Ramón. "Cantos románicos andalusíes, continuadores de una lírica latina vulgar." *BRAE*, 31 (1951), 187–270.

_____. *Los origenes de las literaturas románicas a la luz de un descubrimiento reciente*. Santander: Sociedad General Española, 1951.

_____. *Poesía árabe y poesia europea*. 4th ed. Madrid: Espasa-Calpe, 1956.

_____. *Poesía juglaresca y origenes de las literaturas románicas: problemas de historia literaria y cultural*. 6th ed. Madrid: Instituto de Estudios Politicos, 1957.

Roncaglia, Aurelio. *La lirica arabo-ispanica e il sorgere della lirica romanza fuori della peninsola iberica.* Roma, 1957.

_____. "Il mito delle 'origini popolari' e la scoperta di tradizioni medievali popolaresche." *Il Tesaur*, 4 (1952), 3–6.

_____. "Di una tradizione lirica pretrovatoresca in lingua volgare." *CN*, 9 (1949), 213–49.

Ross, Werner. "Sind die ḫarǧas Reste einer frühen romanischen Lyrik?" *Archiv*, 193 (1956), 129–38.

Spitzer, Leo. See under *General*.

Trend, J.B. "The Oldest Spanish Poetry." In *Hispanic Studies in Honour of I. González Llubera.* Ed. Francis Pierce. Oxford: Dolphin, 1959, pp. 415–28.

Zumthor, Paul. "Au berceau du lyrisme européen." *CS*, 41 (1954), 1–61.

Notes on Contributors

KATHLEEN ASHLEY is Assistant Professor of English at the University of Southern Maine. She has been a Fulbright Junior Lecturer at the University of Lisbon, and an Andrew Mellon Fellow at Duke University. She has published extensively on medieval drama, is the editor of *Acta III: The Thirteenth Century*, and, with Alicia Nitecki, of *The York Cycle*, forthcoming in the Everyman Series. She is currently at work on an anthology, with translations, of medieval Portuguese lyrics, and a book on medieval drama and fifteenth century thought.

MAUREEN FRIES is Professor of English at State University College, Fredonia. She has published more than a dozen articles on Chaucer, Malory, Arthuriana, and the image of women in medieval English literature, and is co-editor of *A Bibliography of Writings By and About British Women Authors, 1957–69*. She has been an NEH Fellow at the University of Chicago, and a Fellow of the Southeastern Institute of Medieval and Renaissance Studies at the University of North Carolina.

HUBERT HEINEN is Associate Professor of Germanic Languages at the University of Texas at Austin. He is the author of several books on German language and literature, the most recent being the forthcoming *Bertolt Brecht: Political Theory and Literary Practice*. His many articles on German lyric poetry, from medieval to modern, have often focused on prosodic questions. He has been a frequent reviewer for *Germanistik* and *Speculum*.

WILLIAM E. JACKSON has taught at Yale University and is presently with the National Endowment for the Humanities in Washington D.C. He has published several studies of Minnesang and woman's songs, including *Reinmar's Women: A Study of the Woman's Song (Frauenlied and Frauenstrophe) of Reinmar der Alte*.